The Best of
TaoSecurity Blog,
Volume 2

The Best of TaoSecurity Blog, Volume 2

Network Security Monitoring,
Technical Notes, Research, and
China and the
Advanced Persistent Threat

Richard Bejtlich

TaoSecurity Press

ISBN: 978-1-952809-02-6 Ebook
ISBN: 978-1-952809-03-3 Paperback

I dedicate this book to my family.

Judo is originally a teaching of the literary and military arts, and one must begin with 'waza' [physical technique] when embarking on the 'do' [way, pronounced "dough"] of Judo. How many people, although they make rapid progress with waza, require a great deal of training in order to reach the point at which they can appreciate the 'do.'

The only thing that remains gratifying no matter how much one indulges in its joys, the one undertaking that becomes even more deeply satisfying the more one pursues it, is education.

Professor Jigoro Kano, as quoted in *Mind Over Muscle: Writings from the Founder of Judo* (Kodansha International, 2013), p 65, and *The Legacy of Kano Jigoro: Judo and Education* (Japan Publishing Industry Foundation for Culture, 2011), p 293.

Preface

The purpose of this book is to help readers better understand security, and therefore better protect their digital assets. It is a sequel to the first installment, *The Best of TaoSecurity Blog, Volume 1: Milestones, Philosophy and Strategy, Risk, and Advice.* This volume focuses on network security monitoring (NSM), technical notes, research, and China and the advanced persistent threat (APT). The third and final installment features current events, law, wise people, history, and an assortment of appendices.

This book contains my second set of favorite posts from the TaoSecurity Blog. The time frame lasts from 2003 to mid-2020. While all of these posts are free online, without advertising, they have become increasingly difficult to individually locate. As of mid-2020, TaoSecurity Blog features over 3,050 posts, and despite being hosted by Google's Blogspot property, lacks sufficient search capability for the average visitor. When I know that I'm having trouble finding posts, then I expect readers are suffering the same limitations.

Rather than repeating the explanation for why I'm producing this compendium, I prefer interested readers consult the first volume. (Thanks to Amazon, the preface is available either as a Kindle sample or an online preview.) In brief, these are the posts that I believe are most relevant to security practitioners, despite having been written as early as 2003. I reference them to this day, and followers of my TaoSecurity Twitter account have noted their utility over the years.

I will repeat one element from the first volume's preface, however. I leave the introduction with the immortal words attributed to Steve Jobs:

"Real artists ship."

-- Attributed to Steve Jobs,
https://quoteinvestigator.com/2018/10/13/ship/

Richard Bejtlich
Northern Virginia, August 2020

Chapter 1. Network Security Monitoring

Introduction

If there is a constant technical and operational construct upon which I have built my career, it is network security monitoring (NSM). While elements of NSM appear in other volumes in this series, and in other chapters in this volume, this section contains the blog posts most closely associated with the topic. Rather than turning this introduction into another manuscript on why NSM matters or how to conduct it, I will let the blog posts take those steps. Along the way I will add commentary.

IPS vs IDS

Wednesday, April 16, 2003

Articles like *Intrusion prevention: IDS' 800-pound gorilla* make me sick. Quotes like this demonstrate the ignorance of the speaker:

> Intrusion-detection systems do a good job of telling companies whether they are being compromised or attacked. So good, in fact, that some question whether systems should go a step further and prevent incidents. It doesn't seem much of a stretch to have systems 'flip a switch instead of alerting' when an anomaly is found, said Pete Lindstrom, research director of Malvern, Pa.-based Spire Security.

Argh! Thankfully the same article shows some people still understand this issue:

> Other companies, however, see their intrusion-prevention products as usurping IDS. Martin Roesch, cofounder and CTO of Columbia, Md.-based Sourcefire, which sells the commercial version of the open-source intrusion-detection system Snort, rejects such a suggestion. "Anyone who tries to sell you an intrusion-prevention system at the expense of an intrusion-detection system doesn't understand the problem stack," he said. "Intrusion prevention is access control. Intrusion detection is monitoring."

> Sourcefire will probably play in the intrusion-prevention space at some point. "We see value in having an access control role on the network as well as a network-monitoring role, because it allows us to leverage the information to enhance monitoring and protection," Roesch said. "You can't have one without the other."

https://taosecurity.blogspot.com/2003/04/articles-like-intrusion-prevention-ids.html

Commentary

This was one of my earliest blog posts. I apologize to Pete Lindstrom for calling him ignorant. Over the years I've managed to chill out a bit, but I left the original post "as is" to show I am not trying to eradicate an ugly history.

Regarding the content, though, I agreed with Marty Roesch then and I agree with him now. Network security can either be active or passive. If it's active, it's interfering with the traffic. If it's passive, it's observing the traffic. Firewalls, intrusion prevention systems, and the like are active interference platforms. Network security monitors are passive observation platforms. Anyone responsible for a network requires both capabilities. They should not be combined on a single system.

Sguil 0.2 Released

Thursday, May 22, 2003

My friend Bamm Visscher released version 0.2 of his Snort-based network monitoring solution, called Sguil. I will be working on more comprehensive documentation when I finish my current incident response deployments! Also, check out the new project logo! From the announcement:

> Sguil (pronounced "sgweel") is a graphical interface to Snort. The actual interface and GUI server are written in Tcl/Tk. Sguil uses other open source software like Barnyard and MySQL for accessing data. The client interface provides 'hooks' to analyst tools like Ethereal, Tcpflow, and P0f. Sguil makes it easy for multiple analysts to work together in monitoring multiple sensors. Currently, Sguil only provides an analyst interface. Sensor and rule management is forthcoming.

> Sguil-0.2 includes numerous changes and bugfixes. Notable additions include event history, event comments, access to session data (Stream4 keepstats), abuse email templates, and user accountability. See http://sguil.sourceforge.net for downloads, updated screenshots, and more info.

https://taosecurity.blogspot.com/2003/05/my-friend-bamm-vissche r-released.html

19

Sguil was a revolutionary NSM interface. It was the successor to SPREG, the Snort Personal Real Time Event GUI, that Bamm built to support a managed security service provider (MSSP) operation in 2001. Using SPREG, on 13 July 2001, one of our analysts, LeRoy Crooks, detected the Code Red worm -- six days before it was publicly reported. I posted to a mailing list on 15 July 2001 describing what Mr. Crooks found.

https://web.archive.org/web/20011222210157/http://lists.insecure.org/incidents/2001/Jul/0069.html

Sguil provided the ability to right-click and pivot from one form of NSM data, such as an alert from Snort, to another form of NSM data, like transaction logs (initially from Snort's Stream4 output) or full content data.

For transaction logs, Sguil presented the data in another pane within the Sguil interface. For full content data, analysts could either view a reconstruction of the session in a Sguil pane, or leverage another tool like Ethereal (now called Wireshark). Furthermore, Sguil saved alert and session records in a database. Because Bamm built Sguil to support a MSSP, he also included features like levels of responsibility and individual analyst accountability.

Sguil is important because it provided full support for a specific investigative method and workflow. It did so while packing an incredible amount of information into its display, exhibiting so-called high "data density." Many products reproduced its design pattern.

What is Extrusion Detection?

Friday, October 24, 2003

Yesterday [while] reading a brief article by Robert Moskowitz, I noticed the term "extrusion detection":

> There's no sure way to track spying data that leaves your network. Perhaps the next big security tool will be outward-bound--extrusion-detection systems.

Searching the Web, I found Mozkowitz mentioned the term four years ago, in this 29 Nov 99 article:

> What you need is a reversed IDT (intrusion-detection tool), and perhaps an EDT (extrusion-detection tool) that will perform automatic searches for your own metatags...

However, Frank Knobbe has him beat, according to this 5 Nov 99 post, discussing SEC investigations of insider trading:

> ...his sounds more like an Extrusion Detection than Intrusion... There are packages available that scan inbound and outbound emails for certain key words/key phrases, and dump these emails in a bucket where analysts (humans) can read, evaluate, and approve or deny them. I guess this raises the question if email scanners should be considered Intrusion Detection tools...

Although much more recent, Ronald DuFresne wrote a short paper which mentions "EDS" but doesn't say a whole lot. Fidelis sells "Extrusion Prevention Systems" "for organizations with valuable digital assets that are concerned about the theft of proprietary information... Fidelis DataSafe EPS is an extrusion prevention system that detects and prevents the unauthorized network transfer of designated sensitive or valuable information."

Bamm and I used extrusion detection techniques during Code Red. It was easier to watch outbound traffic from our infected boxes than it was to monitor inbound intrusion attempts.

https://taosecurity.blogspot.com/2003/10/what-is-extrusion-detection-yesterday.html

Commentary

This post makes a subtle point, but it is likely taken for granted by almost everyone practicing security in 2020. At the time I wrote this entry in 2003, the dominant paradigm for detecting intrusions using the network involved doing byte string matches against inbound content. The security software, called a network intrusion detection system (NIDS) or simply an "IDS," was designed to watch for *inbound* attack attempts.

The "revolution" in thinking that occurred in the early 2000s involved watching activity *leaving* the network. Hence, a play on words -- extrusion vice intrusion -- instantiated this shift in thinking. It was still new enough that I was able to publish a book in late 2005 with the unusual title *Extrusion Detection*. The idea was to detect suspicious and malicious activity using outbound indicators of compromise. This change in viewpoint became critical with the rise of phishing as an attack pattern in 2003-2004.

Network Security Monitoring Saves My Bacon

Tuesday, November 18, 2003

Long-time readers of this blog know I subscribe to a security theory called network security monitoring. Two of NSM's principles are "some intruders are smarter than you" and "intruders are unpredictable." Believing these principles changes the way defenders look at watching their networks. If you assume a smart, unpredictable enemy, you have to take as many defensive actions as possible in the remote hope of catching a bad guy.

This morning I tested these principles not against an intruder, but against a piece of software that took an unexpected action. I was looking for an IRC proxy and found the Night-light IRC proxy. I installed it through the FreeBSD ports system without a problem. I then checked my sockstat output to see what was listening. I found the following unexpected entry:

```
USER      COMMAND      PID    FD PROTO  LOCAL ADDRESS     FOREIGN ADDRESS
root      getty        534    0  tcp4   censored:50396    213.145.164.10:25
```

This looks like my system just connected to 213.145.164.10 on port 25 TCP. I did an nslookup on the destination IP and got these results:

```
moog# nslookup 213.145.164.10
Server:   ns01.rtchrd01.md.comcast.net
Address:  68.48.0.5

Name:     brokenarrow.night-light.net
Address:  213.145.164.10
```

So apparently my box spoke to brokenarrow.night-light.net. I assumed this was a mail server for the night-light.net domain, but I checked this with nslookup:

```
-bash-2.05b$ nslookup
Default Server:  ns01.rtchrd01.md.comcast.net
Address:  68.48.0.5
> set type=mx
> night-light.net
Server:   ns01.rtchrd01.md.comcast.net
Address:  68.48.0.5
Non-authoritative answer:
```

```
night-light.net preference = 5, mail exchanger =
brokenarrow.night-light.net
Authoritative answers can be found from:
night-light.net nameserver = brokenarrow.night-light.net
night-light.net nameserver = jonas.night-light.net
night-light.net nameserver = emptyglass.night-light.net
brokenarrow.night-light.net      internet address =
213.145.164.10
jonas.night-light.net    internet address = 217.118.34.42
emptyglass.night-light.net       internet address =
217.118.34.41
```

Note I could have connected to port 25 on
brokenarrow.night-light.net directly. However, one of the NSM
principles is to never touch the source of suspicious activity, to avoid
notifying the intruder of your investigation.

I also looked at the output of the installation and saw this:

```
Sending compilation report to
ircproxy-report@night-light.net.

The ircproxy has compiled successfully. To install it type
'make install',
if you choose the root option, remember to 'su root' first.
```

So, the question is "Now what?" The event didn't trigger any Snort
alerts. After all, this is probably just my system sending email. But
what did the email contain? Did this new application mail the
contents of my password file to the developer? Can I trust this
developer?

There's two ways to proceed. A host-based approach involves
checking the system hosting the new application for odd activity.
This includes checking the source code of the application for the
routines that created the socket with brokenarrow.night-light.net.

A network-based -- or NSM -- approach involves checking alert,
session, full content, and statistical data for clues. Luckily I had

Tcpdump data available, so I rebuilt the session and found the following:

```
moog# tcpflow -c -r snoop.lpc
220 brokenarrow.night-light.net ESMTP Sendmail
8.12.6/8.12.6;
Tue, 18 Nov 2003 16:43:36 +0100 (CET)
EHLO moog.manass01.va.comcast.net
250-brokenarrow.night-light.net
Hello censored.manass01.va.comcast.net [censored], pleased
to meet you
250-ENHANCEDSTATUSCODES
250-PIPELINING
250-EXPN
250-VERB
250-8BITMIME
250-SIZE
250-DSN
250-ETRN
250-DELIVERBY
250 HELP
MAIL From: SIZE=11475
553 5.1.8 ...
Domain of sender address
richard@moog.manass01.va.comcast.net
does not exist
QUIT
221 2.0.0 brokenarrow.night-light.net closing connection
```

The email was never sent. brokenarrow.night-light.net rejected the attempt because it didn't recognize the sender. While this doesn't tell me exactly what the email would have contained, I know I did not leak any data as a result of this incident.

https://taosecurity.blogspot.com/2003/11/network-security-monito ring-saves-my.html

Commentary

In July 2020 I wrote a post for the Corelight blog titled Network Security Monitoring data: Types I, II, and III.

https://corelight.blog/2020/07/08/network-security-monitoring-data-types-i-ii-and-iii/

To recap:

Type I NSM, properly implemented and conducted, helps a CIRT identify systems within its constituency that exhibit suspicious or malicious behavior... [A]n NSM operation can help identify the handful of potentially compromised systems, among the thousands, or millions, for which a CIRT is responsible. Type I NSM is usually accomplished via some sort of alert or notice mechanism, whether driven by software or manual ("hunting") solutions.

Type II NSM can describe the general patterns of activity conducted by an actor against the potentially compromised asset. For example, the CIRT can identify 1) when the system was active; 2) how active the system was; 3) the general nature of that activity; and 4) the internal and external systems that communicated with the potentially compromised asset. This information can reveal other assets which may be compromised, or shed light on the intruder and his or her goals. Type II NSM is usually accomplished via a policy-neutral transaction logging approach, where the NSM platform records what it sees for use by investigators.

Type III NSM can possibly describe the specific nature of the activity conducted by an actor interacting with a potentially compromised asset. Having a record of the specific activity requires that the actor use protocols that are not encrypted and that are understood by the CIRT and its tools. This information tells the analyst exactly what happened, in addition to answering the questions posed in type two above. Type III NSM builds on the data available in Type II operations, and may add packet captures or extracted file content for extra levels of detail.

This 2003 blog post is an example of pivoting from endpoint data (via Sockstat output) to type III NSM data, depicted as a packet capture called "snoop.lpc." (In 2003 there was no "standard" for naming packet capture files. These days everyone uses ".pcap" or ".pcapng". Back then I used ".lpc" for "LibPCap" but others used .bin, or no suffix at all.)

Because Simple Mail Transport Protocol (SMTP, the protocol I expected to be in use when I saw my system connecting to port 25 TCP) is unencrypted, and because I was *logging everything to and from my network in Libpcap format*, I could generate a full transcript of the suspicious activity. If I had been running the software then-called Bro, now called Zeek, I would have had similar details in a compact smtp.log entry.

Without this data, I would not have known what my system was doing. Because of the data I had collected, *independent of any alert or other trigger*, I could be sure that no sensitive data had left my system.

Using Session Data to Look for Worm Activity

Tuesday, February 10, 2004

Currently a slew of worms are scanning port 3127 TCP, looking for systems infected by MyDoom.A. They include MyDoom.B, Doomjuice, and Vesser.

I collect session data using a variety of means, including Argus. I have the Argus daemon write what it sees into a directory. The elaborate date in the file name is a result of calling the date command like so:

```
DATE=`/bin/date "+%Y%m%d-%H%M%S"`
```

When the process is running, it looks like this:

```
/usr/local/src/argus-2.0.6/bin/argus_bpf -c -d -i ngeth0 -w
/nsm/argus/20040206-085201.bourque.taosecurity.com.ngeth0.arg - ip
```

This process stores Argus data in the /nsm/argus directory. To quickly search the directory, I use the following at the command line:

```
-bash-2.05b$ for i in `ls`; do ra -n -r $i - dst port 3127 |
grep -v stream >> /tmp/3127.ra; done
```

This yields results like the following:

28 Jan 04 16:47:32	tcp	80.181.182.157.2391	->	myIP.3127	RST
28 Jan 04 16:47:33	tcp	80.181.182.157.2391	->	myIP.3127	RST
28 Jan 04 16:47:34	tcp	80.181.182.157.2391	->	myIP.3127	RST
03 Feb 04 00:31:04	tcp	63.208.193.241.3127	->	myIP.3127	RST
03 Feb 04 17:32:55	tcp	24.168.219.7.3127	->	myIP.3127	RST
03 Feb 04 21:42:12	tcp	212.58.12.98.3723	->	myIP.3127	RST
03 Feb 04 21:42:13	tcp	212.58.12.98.3723	->	myIP.3127	RST
03 Feb 04 21:42:14	tcp	212.58.12.98.3723	->	myIP.3127	RST
04 Feb 04 03:55:59	tcp	129.1.61.23.3228	->	myIP.3127	RST
04 Feb 04 03:55:59	tcp	129.1.61.23.3228	->	myIP.3127	RST

...continues until today...

The RST means the connection attempt ended with a RST. From my small vantage point on the Internet, scanning for port 3127 TCP appeared 28 Jan 04, and my system did not respond.

This sort of analysis is part of Network Security Monitoring. This is how you verify your machine is not compromised with a minimum amount of effort.

https://taosecurity.blogspot.com/2004/02/using-session-data-to-loo k-for-worm.html

Commentary

"Am I compromised?" "To what degree am I compromised?" Those are the questions that *should* govern almost every aspect of an information security program. If the security team cannot answer these questions, the CIO or CEO needs a new security team.

Before I began using Zeek, I relied on session data generators like Carter Bullard's Argus. The key to using such tools and their data is that they keep track of what is happening, *regardless of whether it is good, bad, or indifferent.*

Prior to the outbreak of those worms scanning for port 3127 TCP, I did not know that I had to worry about such activity. If I waited until I knew that such activity was suspicious or malicious, I might have to write some sort of rule for an IDS like Snort (or today, Suricata). I would only gain visibility once the rule was running. Thanks to neutral session data tools like Argus or transaction logging platforms like Zeek, I can collect data continuously, and mine it later when I know what I need to find.

This methodology is the basis for so-called "hunting" methodologies that became popular in 2010-2011.

The Applicability of Corporate Fraud to Digital Security

Wednesday, March 24, 2004

I've been on the lookout for *Corporate Fraud: Case Studies in Detection and Prevention* by John D. O'Gara. I thought it might contain insights useful for intrusion detection. Looking at a sample excerpt, it seems more suited to corporate types. However, I found this statement to be fascinating:

> Effective prevention depends on the probability of detection and prosecution more than on any other single factor, because management fraud typically involves override rather than taking advantage of control weaknesses.

This ties in to my idea that prevention eventually fails, for whatever reason. I also found the emphasis on recognition of indicators to be completely in line with my ideas:

> All competent professional internal auditors should have the ability to recognize the red flags and symptoms that indicate the possible existence of management fraud, and they should also be able to perform diagnostic procedures to assess the probability of occurrence. Investigation of cases of more complex management fraud beyond determining whether fraud probably occurred normally requires specialized experience and skills. Nevertheless, we cannot overemphasize the importance of recognition. Simply put, recognition must occur before investigation can start.

> According to the Institute of Internal Auditors (IIA), "The internal auditor should have sufficient knowledge to identify the indicators of fraud but is not expected to have the expertise of a person whose primary responsibility is detecting and investigating fraud." Furthermore, the IIA maintains that "[d]etection of fraud consists of identifying indicators of fraud sufficient to warrant recommending an investigation."

That's similar to my description of Network Security Monitoring:

> NSM is the collection, analysis, and escalation of indications and warnings to detect and respond to intrusions. NSM tools are used more for network audit and specialized applications than traditional alert-centric 'intrusion detection' systems.

https://taosecurity.blogspot.com/2004/03/applicability-of-corporate-fraud-to.html

Commentary

I was never afraid to apply philosophies from the "outside world" to the information security scene. This is one example. Detecting corporate fraud is similar to security, in the sense that the adversary is an intelligent, adaptive actor. This factor means detecting fraud is more like security than other paradigms, like medicine, or weather, or engineering. Those scenarios are all driven by insentient, unswerving forces of nature.

The definition of NSM cited here was first publicly declared in a 4 December 2002 webinar hosted by myself and Bamm Visscher.

Network Security Monitoring

SearchSecurity.com webcast: 4 Dec 02

Richard Bejtlich, **Foundstone**
richard.bejtlich@foundstone.com

Robert Visscher, **Ball Corporation**
rvissche@ball.com

Figure 1. Network Security Monitoring Webinar, December 4, 2002

Detection – What is detection?

- **Detection means identifying intrusions**
- **Detection is best implemented through** network security monitoring **(NSM)**
- **NSM is the** collection, analysis, and escalation of indications and warnings **(I&W) to detect and respond to intrusions**
- **NSM is an "industry best practice" not implemented by most enterprises**
- **This material is seldom taught elsewhere**

Figure 2. Network Security Monitoring Webinar, December 4, 2002

By late 2002 I was working at Foundstone, and Bamm was still working at Ball Aerospace, where we had created a managed security service provider (MSSP).

The first time this definition of NSM appeared in print was the 2003 book *Hacking Exposed, 4th Edition*, published by my Foundstone colleagues. The following appears in a case study on page 2.

CASE STUDY: NETWORK SECURITY MONITORING

How well can intrusion-detection systems (IDSs) deal with the attacks described in this book? Vendors struggle to detect packets at ever higher wire speeds. Users complain about "false positives" and "event correlation." Encryption and polymorphic code threaten to foil signature-matching systems. Is there any light at the end of this tunnel? The answer is yes. It's called Network Security Monitoring (NSM).

NSM is the collection, analysis, and escalation of indications and warnings to detect and respond to intrusions. Inspired in name by Todd Heberlein's "Network Security Monitor," NSM is an operational model based on the Air Force's signals intelligence collection methods. NSM integrates IDS products, which generate alerts; people, who interpret indications and warning; and processes, which guide the escalation of validated events to decision makers. We'll describe Network Security Monitoring in the context of an intrusion that was detected and remediated using NSM principles.

Figure 3. *Hacking Exposed, 4th Edition* (2003), page 2

In July 2004 I published my first book on NSM, *The Tao of Network Security Monitoring: Beyond Intrusion Detection*, with Addison-Wesley.

32

Question on NSM Methodology

Tuesday, September 07, 2004

I received the following question via email today:

> I'm a huge fan of your newest book, and I read it
> cover-to-cover in a handful of evenings. However, I have a
> question about the approach you take for doing network
> monitoring.
>
> The average throughput of our Internet connection is
> around 5Mbits/sec sustained. I would love to implement
> Sguil as an interface to my IDS infrastructure (currently
> Acid and Snort on the network side), but I ran some
> numbers on the disk space required to store that much
> network traffic, and the number quickly swamped the disk
> resources I currently have available to me for this activity.
>
> Am I missing something with regards to how Snort stores
> data in this kind of scenario, or do I really need to plan for
> that much disk space?

This is a good question, and it is a common initial response to
learning about Network Security Monitoring (NSM).

Remember that NSM is defined as "the collection, analysis, and
escalation of indications and warning to detect and respond to
intrusions." There is no explicit mention of collecting every packet
that traverses the network in that definition. However, NSM analysts
find that the best way to accomplish the detection of and response to
intrusions is by interpreting alert, session, full content, and statistical
network evidence. Simply moving "beyond intrusion detection" (my

book's subtitle) -- beyond reliance on alert data alone -- moves one away from traditional "IDS" and towards NSM.

The answer for those operating in high bandwidth requirements is collect what you can. Chapter 2 of my book lists several principles of detection and security, including:

- Detection through sampling is better than no detection.
- Detection through traffic analysis is better than no detection.
- Collecting everything is ideal but problematic.

I recommend looking at Chapter 2 for more information on these principles.

Someone monitoring a data center uplink or an Internet backbone is not going to collect meaningful amounts of full content data without spending a lot of money on high-end hardware and potentially custom software. You may only be able to collect small amounts of full content data in response to specific problems like identification of a covert back door. You may have to take a cue from Internet2 and analyze NetFlow data, and hardly look at full content at all.

There is nothing wrong with either approach. The idea is to give your analysts as much supporting information as possible when they need to make a decision concerning suspicious or malicious traffic. Only giving them an alert, with no other context or non-judgement based data, makes it very unlikely the analyst will know how to make an informed validation and escalation decision.

My specific answer for the question at hand would be to try deploying Sguil with a conservative full content collection strategy. Pass BPF filters in the log_packets.sh script to limit the full content data collected on the sensor. Additionally, if you find the amount of session data logged by SANCP to be a burden, you can pass filters to SANCP as well.

If at all possible I advise not filtering SANCP and other session collection mechanisms, as these content-neutral collection measures can really save you in an incident response scenario. If SANCP and database inserts are a problem, consider the more mature code base of Argus or collecting NetFlow records from routers you control. My book also outlines how to do this.

Update: My buddy Bamm Visscher points out that a sustained 5 Mbps throughput is 2250 MB per hour or 54000 MB per day in raw traffic. However, some overhead is needed for Libpcap headers. For small packets, the header could be as large as the content, effectively doubling the disk space needed to record that packet. For large packets, the header is a smaller percentage of the overall record of the packet.

Anecdotal evidence from one of Bamm's friends says a link with sustained 10 Mbps is writing about 8 GB per hour to disk.

Speaking conservatively for the original question of 5 Mbps, a sensor like a Dell PowerEdge 750 with two 250 GB SATA drives can hold at least several days worth of Libpcap data, and potentially up to a week. That's plenty of time to retrieve useful full content data if regular monitoring is done.

https://taosecurity.blogspot.com/2004/09/question-on-nsm-metho dology-i-received.html

Commentary

This is one of the most important parts of the post:

The idea is to give your analysts as much supporting information as possible when they need to make a decision concerning suspicious or malicious traffic. Only giving them an alert, with no other context or non-judgement based data, makes it very unlikely the analyst will know how to make an informed validation and escalation decision.

Unlike too many people in information security, my approach was not "absolute." My motto was "mejor que nada," meaning "better than nothing." (That was the name of a restaurant in San Angelo, Texas popular for hosting intelligence officer school students like myself and my wife.)

If you cannot, for some reason, provide full content data to your analysts, at least be sure you are writing transaction logs to disk using software like Zeek. You should be doing that anyway, with PCAP data as a bonus. The key to the entire discussion is recognizing that an alert should be the *beginning of an investigation, not the end.*

Non-Technical Means Unearth Best Intrusions

Tuesday, December 13, 2005

Thanks again to the latest SANS NewsBites, I learned of an interesting trade secret theft case. From the CNET News story:

> John O'Neil, former CEO of Business Engine Software, pleaded guilty in a San Francisco federal court on Wednesday to conspiracy to download and steal the trade secrets of software competitor Niku over a 10-month period...

> From October 2001 until July 2002, Business Engine used the passwords to gain unauthorized access to Niku's systems more than 6,000 times and downloaded over 1,000

confidential documents containing trade secrets, the complaint alleged. The stolen documents included technical specifications, product designs, prospective customers, customer proposals, client account information and pricing.

Niku discovered the break-in after a Business Engine salesman made an unsolicited call to one of Niku's prospective clients, a Nike employee who happened to be related to Niku's chief information officer, Warren Leggett. The call raised suspicion because the Nike employee was not ordinarily responsible for software purchasing decisions, had never heard of Business Engine and had no idea how the salesman had obtained his contact information, according to a declaration by Leggett.

The incident prompted Leggett to examine his company's computer logs and files from his recent meeting with Nike. He quickly determined from a trail of Internet network addresses that someone from outside the company had been stealing files. Leggett was able to trace the intrusions back to Business Engine by using Internet domain registration information and publicly available Internet tools.

Whoa. Niku has been 0wn3d for 10 months, and accessed "more than 6,000 times," before a freak family relation caused the right gears to mesh. What kind of security did Niku have (or not have) that would let a compromise continue undetected and unimpeded for so long?

The sad fact is that many of the most interesting intrusions (i.e., not worms, or bots, or viruses) are discovered by non-technical means. Once a company is clued in to the fact they have a breach, the question becomes one of scoping the incident. For example:

- What happened/is happening?
- What systems are or may be affected?
- What information did the intruder copy, change, or destroy? (violations of confidentiality, integrity, or availability)
- When did the intruder first gain unauthorized access?
- When was the last time the intruder accessed victim systems?

Most organizations are not collecting the NSM data they need to answer these questions. Is yours?

https://taosecurity.blogspot.com/2005/12/non-technical-means-un earth-best.html

Commentary

Fifteen years ago I was more comfortable pointing the finger at organizations with less than stellar security. Eventually I performed enough incident response cases and worked in enough enterprise environments to learn that most entities do not have the resources necessary to handle many types of security events. It's baked into the incentive structure guiding most organizations.

I ended the post by asking if the reader had the NSM data necessary to answer these questions. These are the same questions I would ask today. The difference would be that I am more faithful to the original NSM definition, which does not include the word "network" at all. In other words, I would expect integration of all sorts of data, not just that which analysts derive from network traffic.

Hawke vs the Machine

Thursday, January 04, 2007

One of the better episodes of an otherwise lacklustre third season of Airwolf (one of the best TV shows of the 1980s) was called Fortune Teller. Ace helicopter pilot Hawke finds himself face-to-face with an aircraft equipped with the Fortune Teller, a machine built to out-fly the world's best. The best line in the episode follows:

> Archangel: They haven't built a machine yet that could replace a good pilot, Hawke.

> Hawke: Let's hope so.

I thought of this truth when a colleague called yesterday. He plans to bring me to his customer's security operations center. The manager of the SOC is worried that the team is not detecting and responding to intrusions properly (or at all). One of the services my company provides is assessing and evaluating detection and response teams. So, I plan to visit this SOC and see what I can do to improve the situation.

I think I already know what the problem is. My friend told me the SOC is using an IDS/IPS solution you would all recognize, coupled with a SIM/SEM you would all recognize. If that is the extent of the tools available to the SOC analysts, I pretty much know what I am going to say before I even arrive.

The vast majority of security tools -- especially prevention-oriented tools -- are alert-centric. They are created by developers who assume they can understand attacks, code them into solutions, and have a customer deploy them properly and in the expected environment. The reality is this situation fails on a majority of counts, if not all counts. For example, who would ever have expected the Adobe Acrobat JavaScript Execution Bug as explained by my friend Nitesh Dhanjani?

The problem with a purely alert-centric tool is that it cannot handle all the rich varieties of conditions that it will encounter in a production network -- ever. As soon as it's updated something new appears. The only "solutions" that truly work are those that completely eliminate classes of vulnerabilities. (I think I've written about this before, and I know others have said much more than me on that issue.)

So what does an analyst do with an alert-centric tool, like an IDS/IPS? When you only have alerts to handle, you quickly reach a dead end. This is why I know the problem at the SOC before I get there. They're using alert-centric tools. The "detection" and "response" mission becomes "process tickets" generated when the alert-centric tool blinks red. The focus is on processing tickets, not finding intrusions. What else can these analysts do? Their tools are a straightjacket.

Network Security Monitoring (NSM) is different. Generating statistical, session, full content, and alert data gives analysts some place to go when they get an alert -- or when they want to do manual analysis. All of the best intrusions I've ever found were discovered manually. Sure, I've discovered compromises solely using IDS alerts, but all of the best subsequent investigation relied on NSM data.

With NSM, an alert is the beginning of the investigation, not the end.

What does this have to do with Hawke and the Machine? An analyst using an alert-centric tool is only as good as the tool.

An analyst using NSM data can exceed the capabilities of the tool.

40

Here's a related thought. Years ago I told Snort creator Marty Roesch how I perform NSM analysis. He said "Richard, I wrote Snort so you don't have to look at packets." I replied, "Marty, I look at packets because you wrote Snort."

Why is a person better than a machine, in cases like this? The reason is a person is more creative and adaptable. A person can develop a feel for a network. A person can read about a new exploit Wednesday morning and mine NSM data for evidence of that attack faster than a vendor can issue some sort of updated detection or prevention method. Machines are good for providing hints about where to look, which is why I still use IDS'. However, I frequently do completely manual analysis with systems like Sguil, looking for interesting patterns or sessions that my IDS doesn't know.

I'll close with the note that some vendors are using what I call a "dumb is better" approach for generating alert data. For example, you can read about Tenable Security's Never Before Seen approach to identifying interesting events. This is exactly the sort of alert that is helpful, assuming I can then turn to other NSM data to learn more about it. Never Before Seen (NBS) is a great way to identify events which are new. You can apply this to many sorts of issues, which I will not address here but are mentioned by Ron Gula in his blog.

(Disclaimers: Before you argue that your system already does this, I know this approach is a lot older than the Tenable post. I know Marcus was already doing this well before he joined Tenable. The point is that I can read and learn about it thanks to the Tenable blog. I can't point my clients to vague marketing materials on other vendor's sites and expect my clients to make sense of what they're reading. Thanks to the Tenable blog I can learn about systems like Tenable written with a technical angle and real product screenshots and so on.)

To conclude, I'm not an expert in any vendor tools. I'm an expert in using the right sorts of data to detect and eject intruders. I am not going to be any better at using some popular vendor's IDS/IPS than another person who understands the interface. There might be room for differentiation based on the sorts of attacks reported or the services monitored, but not much.

At the end of the day, expertise grows from having the right forms of data available. I guarantee the SOC in this story doesn't have that data, so that will be recommendation zero.

https://taosecurity.blogspot.com/2007/01/hawke-vs-machine.html

Commentary

I wrote this when I was doing independent consulting for TaoSecurity LLC. I would not change a single word. It contains examples of how having the right data means being able to exceed the alert capabilities of a system. It also contains a record of one of my favorite exchanges with Snort and Sourcefire creator Marty Roesch:

"Years ago I told Snort creator Marty Roesch how I perform NSM analysis. He said 'Richard, I wrote Snort so you don't have to look at packets.' I replied, 'Marty, I look at packets because you wrote Snort.'"

Regarding Hawke and the machine, I have some bad news. From the 20 August 2020 Air Force Magazine article *Artificial Intelligence Easily Beats Human Fighter Pilot in DARPA Trial* by Brian W. Everstine, we read the following:

> In the battle of artificial intelligence versus a human fighter pilot, it wasn't even close.

The artificial intelligence algorithm, developed by Heron Systems, swept a human F-16 pilot in a simulated dogfight 5-0 in the Defense Advanced Research Projects Agency's AlphaDogfight Trials on Aug. 20. The company beat out seven other companies before going head to head with "Banger," a pilot from the District of Columbia Air National Guard and a recent graduate of the Air Force Weapons School's F-16 Weapons Instructor Course. The pilot, whose full name was not provided, is an operational fighter pilot with more than 2,000 hours in the F-16.

Banger and Heron Systems' AI fought in five different basic fighter maneuver scenarios with the simulated fight only using the Fighting Falcon's guns, and each time the AI was able to out maneuver and take out Banger. The algorithm operated within the limits of the F-16—meaning it did not pull Gs beyond what a real-world aircraft could do. However, Banger said after the event that the jet was not limited by the training and thinking that is engrained [sic] in an Air Force pilot.

For example, Air Force Instructions outline how an F-16 pilot performs basic fighter maneuvers and establishes some limits such as not passing within 500 feet or a limit on the angle of attack when firing the gun. The AI did not need to follow these instructions, which helped it gain an advantage. Pilots habits are built based on procedures and adhering to training rules, and the AI exploited that.

Funny enough, if I remember my Airwolf storylines properly, Hawke beat the Fortune Teller machine by executing a maneuver that was outside of what normal pilots would conduct. He flew Airwolf to the ceiling and then reversed course. When the Fortune Teller followed him, it went into a stall from which it could not recover, at least in time to survive being shot down by Hawke.

And Another Thing... More NSM Thoughts

Monday, January 08, 2007

My *Hawke vs the Machine* post elicited many comments, all of which I appreciate. I'd like to single out one set of comments for a formal reply here. These are by "DJB," which I highly doubt is Daniel J. Bernstein since the comment ends with "See you at the next ISSA meeting." (DJB lives in Illinois and I live in Virginia.)

DJB writes:

> The topic is not alert-centric vs. NSM, or even passive vs. reactive. The real issue here is Return on Investment for security and Due Care. The cost and lack of common expertise of NSM is why it has not been fully adopted. Every SOC/NOC I've ever been in (over 100) suffers the plight you have identified. Furthermore, I could hire a hundred people with your level of expertise or the same number of Gulas, Ranums and Roeschs to perform NSM. The only problem is that the problem would not go away and I would be out a significant amount of money, even if you have "the right forms of data available." The volume of traffic that we are talking about would require far too many experts.

Let me address these points in turn.

There is no ROSI (return on security investment). There is simply cost avoidance. Due care is a concept I am more likely to embrace.

NSM requires almost no cost at all. All of the software I use is open source. Most of the hardware I use is old junk. (This is one beauty of Unix.) When necessary I do buy hardware, and certainly one can spend lots of money on specialized gear. However, for the average company using an OC-3 or lower, you can get an acceptable amount of NSM data without breaking the $3000 barrier for a very fast, big-hard-drive 1U box and network tap.

What takes more expertise: interpreting cryptic output from a series of alerts (through alert-centric processes) or inspecting all of the traffic associated with an event of interest (NSM processes)? Making sense of the alerts from any leading commercial IDS/IPS can be an exercise in astrological prognostication and intestine reading. Looking at session patterns or -- unbelievably! - what commands the intruder tried to execute on the Web server and what responses came back takes very little skill. (Darn, I think I just called myself an idiot.) Furthermore, from whence does skill derive? Looking at alerts, or inspecting traffic? Q.E.D.

If every SOC/NOC (100) you've visited suffers the same problem, they need help! Contact me: I provide assessment and remediation services for exactly those sorts of broken organizations.

With NSM you don't need to hire a hundred Gulas, Ranums, and Roesches. First, they don't exist. Second, **the data helps make the expert, not the other way around.**

With or without NSM, security problems never go away. This is important: **There is no security end game. All you do is achieve an acceptable level of perceived risk.** That's my definition of security. With NSM, however, you know what is happening and can try to improve.

I think the other points have already been addressed.

One closing thought: I have never met an analyst -- a person who is actually trying to figure out what security events are occurring on a network -- who rejects NSM once exposed to its tools and techniques. In fact, when I taught at SANS CDI East last month one of my students offered one of best comments I've ever read:

Wow, practical information for network and security engineers... why isn't anyone else teaching something this useful? (Comment from student, 15 Dec 06)

Many people who are tangentially related to network security or sell products or do other services reject my ideas all the time. (Some do, not all do.) The people in the trenches see the value, and really that's all I care about. The possible exception is convincing their bosses, so the analysts get the equipment and training they need.

https://taosecurity.blogspot.com/2007/01/and-another-thing-more-nsm-thoughts.html

Commentary

This post contains two key points. The first is the following:

With NSM you don't need to hire a hundred Gulas, Ranums, and Roesches. First, they don't exist. **Second, the data helps make the expert, not the other way around.**

I have made this point repeatedly over my career and it is still true today.

The second is the following:

With or without NSM, security problems never go away. This is important: There is no security end game. All you [can?] do is **achieve an acceptable level of perceived risk**. That's my definition of security. With NSM, however, you know what is happening and can try to improve.

I imagine most people in the security world don't have a personal definition of security. Without one, how do you know if you are making a difference?

NSM and Intrusion Detection Differences

Monday, March 19, 2007

We had a good discussion this morning in the #snort-gui channel on irc.freenode.net. I was on my usual soap box complaining that no commercial tools provide all of the data I need to implement Network Security Monitoring, while developers and employees of a certain well-known intrusion detection system didn't understand why their product didn't meet my needs.

Sguil author Bamm Visscher cut through the argument with a very astute summary. He basically said that IDS developers want "Immaculate Detection" while NSM practitioners want "Immaculate Collection." Bamm is exactly right.

From my experience I know that no detection product is 100% accurate, and that even good alerts require investigation to see what is happening and what else might be happening. IDS developers are rightly trying to improve the quality of their products, but many people interpret their avoidance of NSM collection as a sign it isn't necessary. In other words, detection can be so good that you never need to investigate.

I know some IDS developers don't agree with this misplaced notion but they argue it's too expensive to collect the sorts of data I advocate. I argue that it's too expensive (in terms of damage to the enterprise) not to collect that NSM data.

I think we will see commercial solutions during the next 1-3 years that will give me the NSM data I need to detect and respond to intrusions. Already network forensic appliance vendors are publishing APIs that can be called by IDS/IPS/SIM/SEM/SIEM/etc. products for access to network traffic collected independently of any alerting mechanism. This is a great development and I can't wait to see this sort of arrangement in production.

https://taosecurity.blogspot.com/2007/03/nsm-and-intrusion-detection-differences.html

Commentary

Wow, I was optimistic about seeing commercial NSM solutions in 1-3 years from early 2007. Aside from the open source world and my current employer, we never did get commercial NSM offerings. I am glad that this situation is finally changing!

The current (2020) version of this debate revolves around "data" versus "alerts." It's the same conflict that made me emphasize NSM versus "intrusion detection." I prefer data, from which alerts can be derived, but I recognize the need for alerts. Too many in the alert camp believe alerts are all they need.

It's Only a Flesh Wound

Friday, May 18, 2007

In 2006, Gartner analyst Greg Young's 2006 presented to the Gartner IT Security Summit 2006a a talk titled *Deconfusicating Network Intrusion Prevention.* "Deconfusicating" appears to be a fake synonym for simplifying. I bet that was supposed to confuse an IDS, but not an IPS. Funny that stopping an attack requires detecting it, but never mind.

Someone recently recommended I read this presentation, so I took a look. It's basically a push for Gartner's vision of "Next Generation Firewalls" (NGFW), which I agree are do-everything boxes that will eventually collapse into security switches or Steinnon-esque "secure network fabric." The funny thing about all those IPS deployments is that I continue to hear about organizations that utilize only a fraction or none of the IPS blocking capability, and instead use them as -- wait for it -- IDS. Hmm.

That still doesn't account for the major problem with a prevention-only mindset. Let's face the facts: there are events which transpire on the network which worry you, but which you can't reliably make a policy-based allow or deny decision. When business realities rule (which they always do) you let the traffic through. Where's the IPS now? It's an IDS.

There are also events for which you have no idea how to identify them prior to nontechnical incident detection. If you care at all about security you're going to want to keep track of what's happening on the network so you can scope the incident once you know what to look for. I call that one form of Network Security Monitoring (NSM).

At about the same time I saw the 2006 Gartner slides I read *IDS in Mid-Morph*, an interview with Gene Schultz, long time security veteran. The interview states:

"Schultz says there are already signs of new life. For one thing, IDS data is being used as part of intelligence-collection for forensics, he says. 'People are gathering a wide range of data about behavior in machines, the state of memory, etc. and combining it to find patterns of attacks.

Intrusion detection is one rendition of going more toward the route of intelligence-collection. Instead of focusing on micro-details like packet dumps, [security analysts] are looking at patterns of activity through intensive system and network analysis on a global scale, to determine what the potential threats are.'

Schultz attributes this to a new breed of intrusion detection analyst, 'more like an intelligence analyst, especially in the government.'"

I wonder if Gene read any of my books or articles? For the last five years I've defined NSM as the "collection, analysis, and escalation of indications and warnings to detect and respond to intrusions."

Chapter one from *Tao* is online and must say the word intelligence a dozen times.

Incidentally, if you're near Sydney I'll be teaching my NSM course on 25 May 2007. If you're near Santa Clara I'll be teaching on 20 June 2007. Thank you.

https://taosecurity.blogspot.com/2007/05/its-only-flesh-wound.ht ml

Commentary

In 2007, "cyber threat intelligence" wasn't really a named practice yet. SANS didn't host its first Cyber Threat Intelligence Summit until March 22, 2013. You can read the keynote presented by retired Air Force Colonel Greg Rattray. He has a unique relationship with the term "advanced persistent threat":

https://web.archive.org/web/20200217054552/https://www.sans.or g/cyber-security-summit/archives/file/summit-archive-1493836738. pdf

Prior to "CTI" becoming its own discipline in the early 2010s, it was just part of the detection and response process of high-functioning

CIRTs. When I wrote my first book in 2003-2004, Marcus Ranum thought it was a bit too "militaristic" because I applied military intelligence concepts to detecting and responding to intrusions! Only a few years later, threat intelligence, driven by civilian and ex-military intelligence analysts alike, became an integral part of mature computer network defense operations.

Network Security Monitoring Case Study

Tuesday, July 10, 2007

I received the following email from a friend. He agreed to share his story in exchange for commentary from me and fellow blog readers. I've added comments inline.

> I'm now responsible for cleaning up a mid sized company perimeter defences... To be honest, at first glance the task is a daunting one, thousands of users, dozens of dis-separate systems and gigabits of network traffic plus as part of the enterprise support team, I have other projects and duties to deliver on.

> I managed to get time with the systems architect and run through a number of questions stolen from your books and other smart folks on the history and state of affairs of my new domain. My questions were answered or put into context except for one.

> "Why don't you have any monitoring tools in place on the edge and perimeter systems?"

> The answer I received wasn't what I expected. He simply stated that no-one had the time or energy to take on this massive task. He was very pro about having monitoring, but

bluntly realistic on the amount of time monitoring and response took up. The business has other priorities for the IT teams.

It's not that the company isn't security aware, they have good policies, skilled staff, hardened systems and layered defences, but no monitoring.

I was stuck with the thought "If I don't understand what's happening on the network, how can I know what's right or wrong, what's normal or abnormal?"

This is exactly right. My friend's co-workers are probably practicing management by belief instead of management by fact. If you do not know for sure what is happening inside your company, how can you make informed decisions? Failure will occur when your luck runs out because you are not spending the time and resources necessary to acquire and maintain digital situational awareness.

I gathered all the documentation, policies and firewall rules together and tried to make sense of them. I re-read Extrusion Detection on my commute to help me frame a plan of attack. I got all the basic system data of every system, check time and date stamps were all in sync and cleaned up the network maps.

Then, as silly as this seems, the obvious answer came to me on where to start: at the internal firewall internal interface.

I started to review the drop logs of the firewall for that interface, reasoning that if there is a problem on the network, it should be more apparent in those logs than anywhere else.

This is also exactly right. There is no need to start buying or building new tools if you are not leveraging your existing data sources or enabling data sources not yet activated.

Those reviews provided some startling results, fortunately for us, the problems were only mis-configured systems attempting outbound access. Mind you, they were generating considerable amounts of traffic and some over already congested WAN links.

Then I laid out the ingress and egress rule sets to find out the motives and owners of those rules in the firewalls and started to peel back those unused or unneeded rule sets, while monitoring the drop logs. All with management approval and sign off, of course!

This is another great move -- a stride towards simplification.

I'm now moving into the next stage of working with other teams to clean up their problem systems. Some are going to be harder than others as I've found VAX's, AIX, Sun systems and others bouncing off the rules. I haven't seen these types of systems in a long time and as a simple Windows administrator, I have to find time and the right people to plug these holes.

I have a very long way to go, only focused on a very small section of the entire network and no certain path forward on how to apply a reasonable monitoring system - yet :-)

It's a challenge I'm looking forward to and one I'm sure I'll learn from.

The only comment haunting me is not having any real time allotted to doing monitoring work. I'm going to talk with management and a surprisingly security literate CIO on if this can be addressed.

I know that the conversations have to be based on preventing/mitigating business risk, but believe it's going to be a hard sell with the very long list of other projects being pushed on the team as priority.

If you have any words of advice or useful pointers on convincing them the time is well spent, I'd be grateful.

So this is the major question. How do you convince management or other functional areas that monitoring is important? It sounds to me like my friend has already scored some wins by freeing bandwidth used by misconfigured systems, simplifying firewall rules, and examining individual problematic hosts.

It's important to remember that there is no return on security investment. Security is a cost center that exists to prevent or reduce loss. It is not financially correct to believe you are "earning" a "return" by spending time and money to avoid a loss.

If I need to spend $1000 to hire a guard to protect my $10000 taxi, I am not earning a return on my investment -- I am preventing the theft of my taxi. If I invest that $1000 in a ticketing and GPS system that makes me more productive ferrying passengers (perhaps increasing my dollars per hour worked), then I have enjoyed a ROI once my $1000 expense is covered.

This is not to say that money should not be spent on security. Rather, time and money should be balanced against the perceived risk. The same taxi driver will spend money on insurance, and may indeed need to spend $1000 on a guard if the protection delivered is seen to be necessary. However, the guard does not make the taxi driver more productive. Security is a "business enabler" here but it does not deliver "ROSI."

I'm not a big fan of FUD but something may be happening to executive perception of digital security. I am starting to hear questions like "How do I know that asset X is safe?" or "How do I know that asset Y is not being attacked?" (Answers: "safe" is relative, and Y is being attacked if it's accessible to anyone.)

I don't have any quick answers for my friend, which is why I'm posting this story. What are you doing to convince management that monitoring is necessary? I personally plan to do exactly what my friend did, namely starting with existing assets and showing quick wins to build momentum for more extensive visibility initiatives. You?

https://taosecurity.blogspot.com/2007/07/network-security-monito ring-case-study.html

Commentary

Occasionally in the history of TaoSecurity Blog I shared stories from friends and readers. This was a good one and could apply today. I remain a fan of demonstrating potential through "proofs of value." I've never seen an organization sign a check for a massive new security monitoring program without having a successful pilot.

Enterprise Visibility Architect

Tuesday, July 24, 2007

Last month in my post *Security Application Instrumentation* I wrote:

> Right now you [developers] are being taught (hopefully) "secure coding." I would like to see the next innovation be

security application instrumentation, where you devise your application to report not only performance and fault logging, but also security and compliance logging.

This is a forward-looking plea. In the meantime, we are stuck with numerous platforms, operating systems, applications, and data (POAD) for which we have zero visibility.

I suggest that enterprises consider hiring or assigning a new role -- Enterprise Visibility Architect. The role of the EVA is to identify visibility deficiencies in existing and future POAD and design solutions to instrument these resources.

What does this mean in real life? Here is an example.

Let's say a company operates a FTP proxy for business use. Consider various stakeholders involved with that server and the sorts of visibility they might want:

Data center managers want physical accountability for the server. They also want to know how much power is consumed and how much heat is output.

- Network administrators want to know how much bandwidth the server uses for OS and application updates. They also want to know how much bandwidth is used by data transfers and backup processes.
- System administrators want to know if the asset is performing properly.
- Users and asset owners want to know how much data is transferred (in the vent they are billed for this service).
- Human resources administrators and the legal department want to know what files are transferred, potentially to identify fraud, waste, and abuse.

- Auditors want to validate and assess secure configurations.
- Security analysts want to resist, detect, and respond to incidents.
- Forensic investigators want to know the state of the asset and the files transferred to investigate incidents.

These are all requirements that should be included in the design of the server before it is deployed. However, no one does all of this, and only a few organizations accomplish a few of these items. The role of the EVA is to ensure all of these requirements are built into the design.

When these requirements are not built into the design (as is the case with 95+% of all infrastructure, I would wager) it's the job of the EVA to work with concerned parties to introduce visibility through instrumentation. For example, how could the investigators' concern be met?

If the proxy supports logging, enable it. (This is usually not done because of "performance concerns." If the resource were appropriately sized prior to deployment to account for visibility, this would not be a problem.)

Add a passive device to monitor traffic to and from the proxy server. Application-aware monitoring tools like Bro's FTP Analyzer can record FTP control channel activities. (The resistance to this technique involves not wanting to configure a SPAN port, or lack of a SPAN port. I prefer taps, but inserting the tap requires scheduling downtime -- another sticking point.)

If the investigator only wants IP addresses for the endpoints, then NetFlow could be enabled on a router through which traffic to the FTP server passes. Note that NetFlow cannot be configured to only provide flow data for a specific port (like 21 TCP) so filtering would have to happen on the NetFlow collector. Using NetFlow effectively requires building a NetFlow collector. (Other concerns include loading the router, which could have been accounted for when the design for this business system was created.)

If the investigator only wants IP addresses for the endpoints, then a logging ACL could be enabled on a router through which traffic to the FTP server passes. Hits on this ACL could be exported via Syslog. Using Syslog requires building a Syslog server. (This option will also add load to the router.)

Depending on the architecture, intervening firewalls could also be configured to log connection details in the same manner that NetFlow or router ACLs do.

I believe that logging integrated into the application (i.e., the FTP process) is the best option when one is designing a new resource. When visibility is introduced after the asset is deployed, instrumenting it becomes more difficult.

If you hadn't guessed, I am becoming the de facto EVA in my job as director of incident response because I need data to detect and respond to incidents. However, all of the stakeholders are natural allies because they want to know more about various assets.

https://taosecurity.blogspot.com/2007/07/enterprise-visibility-archi
tect.html

Commentary

While we have seen progress towards integrating testing into code pipelines, I do not really see engineers building visibility into new networks. Instrumentation continues to be an afterthought, even for new deployments. Just consider how long it took the major cloud providers to offer native virtual tap features!

Pervasive Security Monitoring

Wednesday, August 08, 2007

After Black Hat I've been thinking of how to address gaining insight into the security state of the enterprise. My first book addressed how to detect and respond to intrusions using traffic sources in the form of network security monitoring. I've talked about gaining pervasive network awareness several times as well. Recently I've talked about security application instrumentation and several times over the years I've discussed why I am not "anti-log."

I am beginning to formulate my thoughts on what I'm calling *Pervasive Security Monitoring*. I don't have a formal definition yet, but the concept will extend past NSM data sources (traffic) into reports on the state of platforms, OS, applications, and data. The dictionary definition, to *become spread throughout all parts of*, captures the concept fairly well at this stage.

I noticed Cisco and a few others used the term pervasive security awareness, but it's used as a way to encourage employees to become security conscious. That's not what I mean. I see pervasive security monitoring as a way to achieve pervasive security awareness, in the form of collecting data to inform the decision-making process.

I considered using the term "enterprise security monitoring," but I don't think that term as previously used covers everything I have in mind. As I develop these thoughts I will discuss them here.

https://taosecurity.blogspot.com/2007/08/pervasive-security-monit oring.html

Marketing is not my strong suit. While I do well breaking down complex topics into digestible pieces, my attempts at naming processes or methodologies fall flat. In the years since this post, some practitioners have adopted the "enterprise security monitoring" term, while others have segmented a "market" into "network detection and response" (NDR) and "endpoint detection and response" (EDR). I'm not a big fan of either, because the network and the endpoint are only two of the four sources of information that feeds the detection and response process. The other two are human sources (law enforcement, intelligence agencies, constituents, peers, and the like) and software or infrastructure, such as logs from applications, devices, cloud services, and so on. Still, because NSM has the word "network" in it, it's natural to concentrate on that data source. In this post I was trying to encourage looking beyond network data. Within a few years the first viable endpoint agents that looked beyond anti-virus started to appear, which was a beneficial development.

NSM at the Endpoint

Wednesday, February 06, 2008

For many years I've advocated Network Security Monitoring (NSM) as a powerful way to improve digital situational awareness in an independent, self-reliant, and cost-effective manner. NSM relies on watching network traffic to identify suspicious and malicious activity, which prompts incident response and remediation activities. An underlying assumption is that the asset of interest is using a network you own and have adequately instrumented.

What do you do if you do not own the network?

Consider the following situation. First, a company laptop is connected via wired Ethernet to the company LAN. Here, traffic from the laptop out to the Internet can be assumed to traverse a link monitored by a NSM sensor. No problem.

Second, the user moves the laptop outdoors, and the link switches to using a company WLAN. Here, the traffic from the laptop out to the Internet eventually reaches the same wired link used in the first scenario, and hence is monitored by the same NSM sensor. Again, no problem.

In the third case, the user moves outside the reach of the company WLAN. Her laptop transitions to using an EVDO card or other metropolitan wireless network not operated by the company. Suddenly the network traffic generated by the laptop is invisible to the NSM sensor.

In a fourth case, the user moves home and uses her home network connection to access the Internet. This is the same problem as case number 3. If you think that using a VPN client that prevents split tunnels will solve this problem, what do you do when the laptop is connected to the home LAN but not yet connected to the company via VPN?

Clearly a large and definitely growing amount of network time is outside the reach of network-based sensors. I would personally still find network traffic generated by a compromised host to be extremely useful, regardless of how that host connects to any network. One option I pitched to NetWitness yesterday was to deploy a software agent to a suspected compromised system for purposes of collecting and storing network traffic to the victim hard drive.

In this model, once an asset has been identified as requiring additional monitoring, an agent is either pushed or activated that begins collection and retention. Periodically the agent reports summaries (probably session data) to a central server, and an analyst can decide what traffic should be fully retrieved for analysis. This approach has the benefit (some would say drawback, but whatever) of intercepting encrypted traffic as well. Remember, this is for an intrusion investigation. I am not a fraud/waste/abuse (FWA) investigator or privacy violator!

Of course you cannot really trust anything an endpoint does or reports once it has been compromised, but I am looking for an improvement over the current situation. The current situation is complete blindness in cases where instrumentation is lacking.

I believe at some point we will see malware that detects the various network access technologies available to a victim, and makes a choice as directed by the intruder. In other words, if the corporate LAN is too difficult for extrusion purposes, switch to a lesser controlled network -- like an EVDO connection.

If anyone knows of a product which offers the capability to remotely capture network traffic via pushing an agent, please let me know via comment. Incidentally, I am aware of Rpcap and similar technologies. Thank you.

https://taosecurity.blogspot.com/2008/02/nsm-at-endpoint.html

Commentary

I wrote "I believe at some point we will see malware that detects the various network access technologies available to a victim, and makes a choice as directed by the intruder." This happened, although I believe the malware chose to steal data when connected to Wifi. Apparently exfiltrating data when connected to the cellular network drained the battery too quickly.

Network Security Monitoring for Fraud, Waste, and Abuse

Saturday, March 08, 2008

Recently a blog reader asked the following:

> You frequently mention "fraud, waste, and abuse" in your writing (for example), most often to say that NSM is not intended to address FWA. One thing I've been wondering though--why is fraud in there? I can see waste (employee burning time/resources on ESPN.com or Google Video) or abuse (pornography, etc), but Fraud seems to be in a different class. If someone is using the network to commit a crime, why shouldn't that be in scope? Indeed, preventing loss (monetary, reputational, of intellectual property) is really the bottom line for a strong security program, correct?

My stance on this question dates back to my days in the AFCERT. Let me explain by starting with some definitions from AFI90-301:

> Fraud: Any intentional deception designed to unlawfully deprive the Air Force of something of value or to secure from the Air Force for an individual a benefit, privilege, allowance, or consideration to which he or she is not entitled. Such practices include, but are not limited to:

> The offer, payment, acceptance of bribes or gratuities, or evading or corrupting inspectors of other officials.

> Making false statements, submitting false claims or using false weights or measures.

Deceit, either by suppressing the truth or misrepresenting material facts, or to deprive the Air Force of something of value.

Adulterating or substituting materials, falsifying records and books of accounts.

Conspiring to carry out any of the above actions.

The term also includes conflict of interest cases, criminal irregularities, and the unauthorized disclosure of official information relating to procurement and disposal matters.

For purposes of this instruction, the definition can include any theft or diversion of resources for personal or commercial gain.

Waste: The extravagant, careless, or needless expenditure of Air Force funds or the consumption of Air Force property that results from deficient practices, systems controls, or decisions. The term also includes improper practices not involving prosecutable fraud.

Abuse: Intentional wrongful or improper use of Air Force resources. Examples include misuse of rank, position, or authority that causes the loss or misuse of resources such as tools, vehicles, computers, or copy machines.

Given these definitions, the first reason I do not think counter-FWA is an appropriate NSM mission is the identification of these actions. Security analysts perform NSM. Security analysts are not human resources, legal, privacy, financial audit, or police personnel. Trying to identify FWA (aside from the obvious, like wasting bandwidth or visiting pornography sites) is outside the scope of the security analyst's profession. If any of the aforementioned parties want to use some content inspection method to identify FWA, that's their job. Security analysts are generally tasked with identifying violations of confidentiality, integrity, and availability.

Second, in many organizations the inclusion of FWA would crowd out other security tasks. I have heard of some monitoring shops who do nothing but FWA because the volume of inappropriate activity seems to dwarf traditional security concerns. I think that is a poor allocation of resources.

Third, I think NSM for FWA is shaky on privacy grounds. Employees really have no expectation of privacy in the workplace, but the degree of monitoring required to identify non-obvious FWA is very invasive. Security analysts avoid reading email and reconstructing Web pages, but FWA investigations essentially rely on that very task. FWA is seldom easily detected using alert-based mechanisms, so identifying real FWA can turn into a fishing expedition where all content is analyzed in the "hope" of finding something bad. I think this is a waste of resources as well.

Having said that, in some cases NSM data can be used to support FWA tasks. However, I do not think FWA investigation should be a routine part of NSM operations.

What do you think?

https://taosecurity.blogspot.com/2008/03/network-security-monito ring-for-fraud.html

Commentary

I have never advocated using NSM capabilities to counter fraud, waste, and abuse. In the extremely rare instance where this is necessary, I have required the legal and human resources departments to direct analysts, in writing, to conduct the operation under strict guidelines. For this reason, I've also despised the "I read your email" T-shirts popular with some "hackers." That attitude breeds contempt for security personnel and demonstrates a violation of trust.

NSM vs Encrypted Traffic, Plus Virtualization

Friday, May 23, 2008

A blog reader sent me the following question, and prequalified me to post it anonymously.

> For reasons of security and compliance, more and more network connections are becoming encrypted. SSL and SSH traffic are on the rise inside our network. As we pat ourselves on the back for this, the elephant in the room stares at me...how are we going to monitor this traffic? It made me wonder if the future of security monitoring will shift to the host. It appears that the host, provided some centrally managed IDS is installed, would inspect the unencrypted traffic and report back to a HSM (host security monitoring) console. Of course, that requires software (ie an agent) on all of our hosts and jeopardizes the trust we have in our NSMs, because "the network doesn't lie".

This is an excellent, common, and difficult question. I believe the answer lies in defining trust boundaries. I've been thinking about this in relation to virtualization. As many of you have probably considered, really nothing about virtualization is new. Once upon a time computers could only run one program at a time for one user. Then programmers added the ability to run multiple programs at one time, fooling each application into thinking that it had individual use of the computer. Soon we had the ability to log multiple users into one computer, fooling each user into thinking he or she had individual use. Now with virtualization, we're convincing applications or even entire operating systems that they have the attention of the computer.

What does this have to do with NSM? This is where trust boundaries are important. On a single user, multi-application computer, should each app trust the other? On a multi-user, multi-app computer, should each user trust each other? On a multi-OS computer, should each OS trust each other?

If you answer no to these questions, you assume the need for protection mechanisms. Since prevention eventually fails, you now need mechanisms to monitor for exploitation. The decision where to apply trust boundaries dictates where you place those mechanisms. Do you monitor system calls? Inter-process communication? Traffic between virtual machines on the same physical box? What about traffic in a cluster of systems, or distributed computing in general?

Coming back to the encryption question, you can consider those channels to be like those at any of the earlier levels. If you draw your trust boundary tight enough, you do need a way to monitor encrypted traffic between internal hosts. Your trust boundary has been drawn at the individual host level, perhaps.

If you loosen your trust boundary, maybe you monitor at the perimeter. If you permit encrypted traffic out of the perimeter, you need to man-in-the-middle the traffic with a SSL accelerator. If you trust the endpoints outside the perimeter, you don't need to. People who don't monitor anything implicitly trust everyone, and as a result get and stay owned.

I do think it is important to instrument whatever you can, and that includes the host. However, I don't think the host should be the final word on assessing its own integrity. An outside check is required, and the network can be a place to do that.

By the way, this is the best method to get an answer from me if you send a question by email. I do not answer questions of a "consulting" nature privately -- I either post the answer here or not at all. Thanks for the good question JS.

https://taosecurity.blogspot.com/2008/05/nsm-vs-encrypted-traffic-plus.html

Commentary

Questions on how to handle encrypted network traffic have been asked for many years! In addition to this answer, don't forget the "type I, II, and III" NSM analysis explained earlier.

NSM vs Encrypted Traffic Revisited

Wednesday, June 04, 2008

My last post *What Would Galileo Think* was originally the first part of this post, but I decided to let it stand on its own. This post is now a follow on to *NSM vs Encrypted Traffic, Plus Virtualization and Snort Report 16 Posted*. I received several questions, which I thought deserved a new post. I'm going to answer the first with Galileo in mind.

LonerVamp asked:

"So can I infer that you would prefer to MITM [man-in-the-middle] encrypted channels where you can, to inspect that traffic on the wire? :)"

On a related note, Ivan Ristic asked:

"Richard, how come you are not mentioning passive SSL decryption as an option?"

I thought I had answered those questions when I said:

"If you loosen your trust boundary, maybe you monitor at the perimeter. If you permit encrypted traffic out of the perimeter, you need to man-in-the-middle the traffic with a SSL accelerator. If you trust the endpoints outside the perimeter, you don't need to."

Let's reconsider that statement with Galileo in mind. Originally I proposed that those who terminate their trust boundary at their perimeter must find a way to penetrate encrypted traffic traversing that trust boundary. Another way to approach that problem is to perform measurements to try to determine what cost and benefit can be gained by terminating SSL at the perimeter, inspecting clear text, and re-encrypting traffic as it leaves the enterprise.

Does that process actually result in identifying and/or limiting intrusions? If yes, use the results to justify the action. If not, abandon the plan or decide to conduct a second round of measurements if conditions are deemed to change at a later date. Don't just argue that "I need to see through SSL" because it's a philosophical standpoint.

Marcin asked:

"So what do you say and do when your NSM Sensor/SSL Load Balancer/SSL Proxy gets compromised, exposing your most sensitive data (by nature, because it is being encrypted)?

Am I supposed to rely on my IDS' and my own ability to detect 0day attacks against hardened hosts?"

To answer the first question, I would say check out my *TaoSecurity Enterprise Trust Pyramid*. The same factors which make data from sensors more reliable also make those sensors more resilient. However, no sensor is immune from compromise, and I recommend taking steps to monitor and contain the sensor itself in a manner appropriate for the level of traffic it inspects. Keep in mind a sensor is not a SSL proxy. The SSL proxy might only log URLs; it might not provide clear text to a separate sensor.

Answering the second question could take a whole book. Identifying "0day attacks," what I call *first order detection*, is increasingly difficult.

Performing *second order detection*, meaning identifying reinforcement, consolidation, and pillage is often more plausible, especially using extrusion detection methods.

Performing *third order detection*, meaning discovering indications of your hosts in someone's botnet or similar unauthorized control, is another technique.

Finally, *fourth order detection*, or seeing your intellectual property in places where it should not be, is a means to discover intrusions.

Vivek Rajan asked:

"Daemonlogger is cool, but what do you think about more sophisticated approaches like the Time Machine ? (http://www.net.t-labs.tu-berlin.de/research/tm/)

Is there some value in retaining full content of long running (possibly encrypted) sessions?"

I don't consider Time Machine "more sophisticated." It's just a question of trade-offs. Where possible I prefer to log everything, because you can never really be sure before an incident just what might be important later. Regarding encryption, what if you disable collecting traffic on port 443 TCP outbound because it's supposed to be SSL, when you later learn that an intruder is using some weak obfuscation method or no encryption at all?

To summarize, implement whatever system you select based on the demonstrable improvement it brings to your security posture, not because you think it is helpful. I am particularly critical when it comes to defensive measures. For measures that improve visibility, my objective is to gather additional data with a benefit that outweighs the costs of collection.

https://taosecurity.blogspot.com/2008/06/nsm-vs-encrypted-traffic-revisited.html

Commentary

There's a lot packed into this post. I had forgotten about my different "orders" of detection. I found an article I wrote for the May 2008 *CSO Magazine* (composed on March 23, 2008) which included the following:

> First order detection is the traditional way to apply methods to identify intrusions. **First order detection concentrates on discovering attacks during the reconnaissance (if any) and exploitation phases of compromise.** Reconnaissance is the process by which an intruder learns enough about the target to effect intrusion. Exploitation is the process of abusing, subverting, or breaching a target, thereby imposing the intruder's will upon the asset. Almost all security products that seek to detect and/or "prevent" attacks monitor activity during these stages of the compromise lifecycle.
>
> **Second order detection moves beyond reconnaissance and exploitation to the final three stages of compromise: reinforcement, consolidation, and pillage.** Reinforcement is the process by which an intruder leverages the unauthorized access gained during exploitation in order

to build a more stable platform for repeated re-entry. Downloading and installing a remote access Trojan program is a classic reinforcement activity. Consolidate is the act of controlling a compromised asset using the means installed during reinforcement. Pillage is the execution of the intruder's ultimate plan, which could be pivoting on the target to attack another system, exfiltrating sensitive information, or any other nefarious plan the intruder may wish to execute. Second order detection focuses on identifying any of these final three phases of compromise, which can be highly variable and operate at the discretion of the intruder.

Third order detection occurs outside the realm of the five phases of compromise by concentrating on post-pillage activities. Whereas first- and second-order detection is done at the enterprise, either by watching hosts, network traffic, logs, or possibly even sensitive data, third order detection takes place outside the enterprise. Third order detection seeks to discover indications that preventative and detection mechanisms have failed by finding the consequences of an intrusion. Looking for these sorts of signs could take the form of searching for, and finding, private company documents on peer-to-peer networks, or intruder-operated botnet servers, or a competitor's release of a product uncannily similar to your company's own.

[Note: for the blog post, I appear to have separated "application of stolen intellectual property," like seeing your engine design on a competitor's jet, as different from seeing your data on a criminal's computer. The former would be **"fourth order detection,"** while the latter is "third order detection.]

Each of these events indicate a breach or policy violation occurred, yet none may have been detected by conventional means. Third order detection is a powerful way to determine if the formal detection mechanisms operated by an organization's security team make any difference in the real world.

This article also includes some of my thoughts on maturity levels for CIRTs:

A complementary way to think about detection takes the form of **six maturity levels.** Using the ideas below, you can determine how advanced your detection initiative may be.

Level 0. No primary detection method exists. No formal data sources are used. No actions are taken, since this "blissful ignorance" hides the fact that the enterprise could be (and probably is) severely compromised.

Level 1. Customers, peer organizations, and users are the primary detection methods. No data sources beyond those provided by the aforementioned parties are available. The predominant reaction is to form an ad-hoc team to fight fires on a repeated basis.

Level 2. Customers, peer organizations, and users are still the primary detection methods. However, the organization has some data store from which to draw conclusions -- once the enterprise knows it must look for clues. Reaction involves more fire fighting, but the officers aren't quite as blind as they were at level 1 thanks to the availability of some logs.

Level 3. The Computer Incident Response Team (CIRT) is discovering incidents in concert with the parties listed at levels 1 and 2. Additional data sources augment those aggregated at level 2. The CIRT develops some degree of formal capability to detect and respond to intrusions.

Level 4. The CIRT is the primary means for detecting incidents. All or nearly all of the data sources one could hope to use for detection, response, and forensics are available. The CIRT exercises regularly and maintains dedicated personnel, tools, and resources for its mission.

Level 5. The CIRT is so advanced in its mission that it helps prevent incidents by identifying trends in the adversary community. The CIRT recommends defensive measures before the enterprise widely encounters the latest attacks. The CIRT operates a dedicated security intelligence operation to stay in tandem or even ahead of many threat agents.

Incident detection naturally leads to incident response, where actions are taken to contain, eradicate, and recover from intrusions.

These thoughts were on my mind as I worked with my team to build GE-CIRT during my four years at the General Electric Company (2007-2011).

Reader Questions on Network Security Monitoring

Sunday, January 18, 2009

A regular blog reader and Network Security Monitoring practitioner sent me these questions last month, so I'd like to answer them here.

1. Are all alert data created equal?

This question originates with my employment at an MSSP where we process many types of alert data from Dragon IDS, Cisco IPS and ISS. Snort and Sourcefire strangely are underrepresented. My question is if Dragon IDS, Cisco IPS, ISS, Snort and Sourcefire all looked at the same full-content data, would they all produce the same results? I think not and would like to empirically verify this theory.

Testing detection systems is a complicated topic. I am not sure what methodology a place like NSS Labs uses. I bet they get varying results depending on the product. If you read *A Tool for Offline and Live Testing of Evasion Resilience.* in *Network Intrusion Detection Systems* you will see big differences between Snort and Bro, for example.

2. When is an analyst no longer an analyzer of data but an analyzer of dashboards?

This question also originates with my employment at an MSSP because like I said, we process so many disparate alert types and there is only so much time in a shift that it is challenging for an analyst to really spend quality time with a piece of data and conclusively determine what happened. Therefore the analysts evolve into analyzers of dashboards instead of data in order to promptly assess alerts and determine if there was a legitimate attack or not.

I would say you are an analyzer of dashboards when you cannot do the following:

- Determine how a product generated an indicator
- See the underlying activity that produced the indicator, whether it is network traffic or raw log messages
- Research activity for which there is no indicator, i.e., you can only see indicators and not any activity for which an alert did not fire

3. If all you have is alert data, can you positively confirm that you have been compromised?

I know the answer to this one, but am including it for emphasis of the point that alert data alone does not lend itself to digital situational awareness. Alert data + session data is the bare minimum as far as I am concerned. At least with this combination you can observe the egress sessions, in other words, what did the attacker do next?

You are right. If you only have alert data, you cannot validate a security incident.

Thank you for your questions!

https://taosecurity.blogspot.com/2009/01/reader-questions-on-network-security.html

Commentary

This was an interesting question: **"When is an analyst no longer an analyzer of data but an analyzer of dashboards?"** Dashboards have become the primary means for many analysts to interact with security data. When I tried the Corelight Capture the Flight event this year, I completed all of the challenges using command line tools in a Secure Shell (SSH) session. I realized about halfway through that if I had a better command of SIEM functionality, I might have answered some of the questions faster. **The quality of the data is generally more important than the presentation system, unless the system also makes it easier to understand what the data means.**

Why Network Taps

Monday, January 26, 2009

My colleagues and I are spending some time justifying the installation of network taps, instead of using SPAN ports, to gain access to network traffic. This is an old discussion. See my Dec 07 post *Expert Commentary on SPAN and RSPAN Weaknesses*. For a different perspective see Scott Haugdahl's *Is Spanning Bad?* and *Is RSPAN Bad?*.

I'm using the following points when discussing the situation.

Taps free SPAN ports for tactical, on-demand monitoring, especially intra-switch monitoring. Many switches have only two ports capable of SPAN, and some offer only one. If you commit a SPAN port for permanent monitoring duties, and you need to reassign it for some sort of troubleshooting on a VLAN or other aspect of the traffic, you have to deny traffic to your sensor while the SPAN port is doing other work. Keep your SPAN ports free so you can do intra-switch monitoring when you need it.

Taps provide strategic, persistent monitoring. Installing a tap means you commit to a permanent method of access to network traffic. Once the tap is installed you don't need to worry about how you are going to access network traffic again. Taps should really be part of any network deployment, especially at key points in the network.

Selected taps do not permit injected traffic onto the monitored link. Depending on the tap you deploy, you will find that it will not be physically capable of transmitting traffic from the sensor to the monitored link. This is not true of SPAN ports. Yes, you can configure SPAN ports to not transmit traffic, and that is the norm. However, from my consulting days I can remember one location where I was told to deploy a sensor on a box with one NIC. Yes, one NIC. That meant the same NIC used for remote SSH access also connected to a switch SPAN port. Yes, I felt dirty.

What taps see is not influenced by configuration (as is the case with SPAN ports); i.e., what you see is really what is passing on the link. This is key, yet underestimated. If you own the sensor connected to a SPAN port, but not the switch, you are at the mercy of the switch owner. If the switch owner mistakenly or intentionally configures the SPAN port to not show all the traffic it should, you may or may not discover the misconfiguration. I have seen this happen countless times. With a network tap, there's no hiding the traffic passing on the monitored link. Many shops have been surprised by what is traversing a link when they finally take a direct look at the traffic.

Taps do not place traffic on a switch data plane, like a SPAN port does. This point is debatable. Depending on switch architecture, SPAN ports may or may not affect the switch's ability to pass traffic. By that I mean a SPAN port may not receive all traffic when the switch is loaded, because forwarding may take precedence over SPANning.

There are other reasons to prefer network taps, but I'll direct you to the links I provided. Those are good resources.

https://taosecurity.blogspot.com/2009/01/why-network-taps.html

I still prefer taps over SPAN ports wherever possible. Of course, you *must* use a powered, well-engineered tap, not an unpowered, "joke" tap. This is especially true when minimum link speeds are 1 Gbps. Why would you jeopardize network performance using a device that costs only a few dollars and looks like it was sold from a back street alley? If you can't afford a real tap, and don't have a switch with a SPAN port, buy a small managed switch with SPAN capability. Devices like the Netgear GS105Ev2 cost less than $50 and provide a SPAN port.

Black Hat Briefings Justify Supporting Retrospective Security Analysis

Sunday, February 22, 2009

One of the tenets of Network Security Monitoring, as repeated in *Network Monitoring: How Far?*, is to *collect as much data as you can, given legal, political, and technical means (and constraints)* because that approach gives you the *best chance to detect and respond to intrusions.* The Black Hat Briefings always remind me that such an approach makes sense. Having left the talks, I have a set of techniques for which I can now mine my logs and related data sources for evidence of past attacks.

Consider these examples:

- Given a set of memory dumps from compromised machines, search them using the "Snorting Memory" techniques for activity missed when those dumps were first collected.

- Review Web proxy logs for the presence of IDN [internationalized domain names] in URIs [uniform resource identifiers].
- Query old BGP [Border Gateway Protocol] announcements for signs of past MITM [man-in-the-middle] attacks.

You get the idea. The key concept is that *none of us are smart enough to know how a certain set of advanced threats are exploiting us right now*, or how they exploited us in the past. Once we get a clue to their actions, we can mine our security evidence for indicators of that activity. When we find signs of malicious activity we can focus our methods and expand our view until we have a better idea of the scope of an incident.

This strategy is the only one that has ever worked for digital intrusion victims who are constrained to purely defensive operations. A better alternative, as outlined in *The Best Cyber Defense*, is to conduct aggressive counterintelligence to find out what the enemy knows about you. Since that tactic is outside the scope for the vast majority of us, we should adopt a mindset, toolset, and tactics that enable *retrospective security analysis* -- the ability to review past evidence for indicators of modern attacks.

If you only rely on your security products to produce alerts of any type, or blocks of any type, you will consistently be "protected" from only the most basic threats. Advanced threats know how to evade many defenses because they test and hone their techniques before deploying them in the wild.

NSM has always implemented retrospective security analysis, but the idea applies to a wide variety of security evidence.

https://taosecurity.blogspot.com/2009/02/black-hat-briefings-justif y-supporting.html

This is integral to my philosophy: "The key concept is that *none of us are smart enough to know how a certain set of advanced threats are exploiting us right now*, or how they exploited us in the past. Once we get a clue to their actions, we can mine our security evidence for indicators of that activity. When we find signs of malicious activity we can focus our methods and expand our view until we have a better idea of the scope of an incident." If this mindset does not guide your security program, you will be in a world of hurt.

Network Security Monitoring Lives

Saturday, March 28, 2009

Every once in a while I will post examples of why Network Security Monitoring works in a world where Webbed, Virtual, Fluffy Clouds abound and people who pay attention to network traffic are considered stupid network security geeks.

One of the best posts I've seen on the worm-of-the-week, Conficker, is *Risk, Group Think and the Conficker Worm* by the Verizon Security Blog. The post says:

> With the exception of new customers who have engaged our Incident Response team specifically in response to a Conficker infection, Verizon Business customers have reported only isolated or anecdotal Conficker infections with little or no broad impact on operations. A very large proportion of systems we have studied, which were infected with Conficker in enterprises, were "unknown or unmanaged" devices. Infected systems were not part of those enterprise's configuration, maintenance, or patch processes.

In one study a large proportion of infected machines were simply discarded because a current user of the machines did not exist. This corroborates data from our DBIR which showed that a significant majority of large impact data breaches also involved "unknown, unknown" networks, systems, or data.

This, my friends, is the reality for anyone who defends a live network, rather than those who break them, dream up new applications for them, or simply talk about them. If a "very large proportion of systems" that are compromised are beyond the reach of the IT team to even know about them, what can be done? The answer is fairly straightforward: watch the network for them. How can you do that? Use NSM.

Generate and collect alert, statistical, session, and full content data. I've also started using the term *transaction data* to mean data which is application-specific but captured from the network, like DNS requests and replies, HTTP requests and replies, and so on. These five forms of data can tell you what systems live on the network and what they are doing. It is low-cost compared to the variety of alternatives (manual, physical asset control; network access control; scanning; etc.). Once a sensor is deployed in the proper place you can perform self-reliant (i.e., without the interference of other groups) NSM, on a persistent and consistent basis.

Where should you monitor? Watch at your trust boundaries. The best place to start is where you connect to the Internet. Make sure you can see the true source IP (e.g., a desktop's real IP address) and the true destination IP (e.g., a botnet C&C server). If that requires tapping two locations, do it. If you can approximate one or the other location using logs (proxy, NAT, firewall, whatever), consider that, but don't rely only on logs.

NSM lives, and it is working right now.

Commentary

I'm not sure if this is the first time I used the term "transaction data" rather than "session data," but it may be. When I first used session data, it referred to NetFlow-like details that contained information derived from layer 3 and 4 data, like IP addresses, ports, protocols, bytes transferred, and time components. Transaction data is the sort of information one enjoys when using software like Zeek. These days, the only reason to rely on session data is that it is the only information available in a constrained environment. Otherwise, session data should be replaced by transaction data.

NSM vs The Cloud

Sunday, March 29, 2009

A blog reader posted the following comment to my post *Network Security Monitoring Lives*:

> How do you use NSM to monitor the growing population of remote, intermittently connect mobile computing devices? What happens when those same computers access corporate resources hosted by a 3rd party such as corporate SaaS applications or storage in the cloud?

This is a great question. The good news is we are already facing this problem today. The answer to the question can be found in a few old principles I will describe below.

Something is better than nothing. I've written about this elsewhere: *computer professionals tend to think in binary terms, i.e., all or nothing.* A large number of people I encounter think 'if I can't get it all, I don't want anything." That thinking flies in the face of reality. There are no absolutes in digital security, or analog security for that matter. I already own multiple assets that do not strictly reside on any single network that I control. In my office I see my laptop and Blackberry as two examples.

Each could indeed have severe problems that started when they were connected to some foreign network, like a hotel or elsewhere. However, when they obtain Internet access in my office, I can watch them. Sure, a really clever intruder could program his malware to be dormant on my systems when I am connected to "home." How often will that be the case? It depends on my adversary, and his deployment model. (Consider malware that never executes on VMs. Hello, malware-proof hosts that only operate on VMs!)

The point is that *my devices spend enough time on a sufficiently monitored network for me to have some sense that I could observe indicators of problems.* Of course I may not know what those indicators could be *a priori*; cue *retrospective security analysis.*

What is the purpose of monitoring? Don't just monitor for the sake of monitoring. What is the goal? If you are trying to identify suspicious or malicious activity to high priority servers, does it make sense to try to watch clients? Perhaps you would be better off monitoring closer to the servers? This is where adversary simulation plays a role. Devise scenarios that emulate activity you expect an opponent to perform. Execute the mission, then see if you caught the red team. If you did not, or if your coverage was less than what you think you need, devise a new resistance and detection strategy.

Build visibility in. When you are planning how to use cloud services, build visibility in the requirements. This will not make you popular with the server and network teams that want to migrate to VMs in the sky or MPLS circuits that evade your NSM platforms. However, if you have an enterprise visibility architect, you can build requirements for the sort of data you need from your third parties and cloud providers. This can be a real differentiator for those vendors. Visibility is really a prerequisite for "security," anyway. If you can't tell what's happening to your data in the cloud via visibility, how are you supposed to validate that it is "secure"?

I will say that I am worried about attack and command and control channels that might reside within encrypted, "expected" mechanisms, like updates from the Blackberry server and the like. I deal with that issue by not handling the most sensitive data on my Blackberry. There's nothing novel about that.

https://taosecurity.blogspot.com/2009/03/nsm-vs-cloud.html

Commentary

To this day, there is a tendency for many members of the security community to think in terms of absolutes. If a critic can think of one case where an approach fails, then the approach itself is completely deficient. I prefer to think in terms of costs and benefits. At the point where the cost of deploying, maintaining, and operating NSM infrastructure exceeds the benefits, I would no longer advocate NSM as a methodology. I do not expect to meet that threshold given the prevalence of open source software and fairly simple network access technologies. However, I am open to new evidence and ways of thinking!

Elvis Presents IDS vs NSM

Tuesday, April 21, 2009

When I teach Network Security Monitoring I often introduce an image that shows what an analyst (here, Elvis Presley) might do if the only data he had to work with was an alert from something like a traditional intrusion detection system. I then compare that workflow with the possibilities provided by Network Security Monitoring.

Usually when I present this concept I take the opportunity to mention that Elvis studied American Kenpo with the founder of the style, Ed Parker. I also mention that Elvis frequently performed karate on stage, even doing so at someone else's concert!

I decided to track down a reference for that particular story, and through Shane Peterson's *Elvis and the Martial Arts*, I found this:

> Elvis attended the Tom Jones show on September 3rd [1974]. During the show he was introduced to the crowd by Tom. At that moment he was invited on stage and Tom asked him if he'd like to sing something. It wasn't possible, he [Elvis] said, as he had an exclusive contract with the Hilton. Instead he went into a Kata demonstration on the Caesar's Palace stage.

I would prefer to include links to the Web pages where I found these, but since they are hosted on Tripod pages I don't want to kill the owner's bandwidth through unnecessary click-throughs. If you want to find the sources please do a Google search.

https://taosecurity.blogspot.com/2009/04/elvis-presents-ids-vs-nsm.html

Commentary

When Bamm Visscher and I started our managed security service provider (MSSP) company in 2001, we nominated Elvis Presley as the patron saint of NSM. We named one of our first NSM sensors "elvis" and I had an "action figure" of "karate Elvis" at my desk. At the time I was studying American Kenpo (Ed Parker style) in San

Antonio, Texas, which was the style that Elvis trained. I have fond memories of that time.

Question on NSM Scaling

Wednesday, August 12, 2009

A long-time TaoSecurity Blog reader sent me the following question:

> I have a question about scaling NSM in regards to large, complex enterprises that transmit countless gigabytes of data per day.
>
> Last month I interviewed for a position with a large wireless company and the hiring manager was familiar with your work, so as I attempted to extol the value of NSM and explain how I thought that NSM could benefit this organization, I was told by the hiring manager that he felt that NSM worked with small organizations, but did not scale well with organizations of a certain size.
>
> I am curious if you have ever had to counter this type of argument and how you addressed it.

This is a common question. I'll need to address it concisely and precisely in an updated edition of *Tao*. A few recent posts come to mind, like *Requirements for Defensible Network Architecture: Monitored, NSM vs Encrypted Traffic, Plus Virtualization*, and *Network Security Monitoring Lives*. A few principles come to mind.

Concentrate on infrastructure you own, not necessarily infrastructure you support. In other words, I don't advocate full NSM for ISPs watching customer links. That may be the issue mentioned in the question, i.e., a wireless company might think NSM is inappropriate for watching customer traffic. I would probably agree with that.

Monitor at trust boundaries. The places where the infrastructure you own touches infrastructure you do not own is likely to be the place where you need additional visibility.

Monitor what you can, given your technical, political, and legal constraints. You may not be able to continuously capture full content data on 10 Gbps links with commodity hardware, or even specialized hardware. If that is too expensive, then don't do it. However, deploy the capability to capture at those locations when necessary. Better to be prepared than to struggle with workarounds or emergency deployments in a crisis.

Solutions can be engineered for almost any environment. I guarantee organizations larger than those in the question are already doing intense monitoring. If you don't believe me, look at the history of wiretapping during the last administration. Outside of that case, organizations like mine are deploying hundreds of sensors around the world. NSM can scale if you engineer it properly and hire people who know what they are doing!

Don't make NSM a hammer and every security problem a nail. NSM is one way to gain visibility and situational awareness. It may be worthless to deploy sensors doing traditional NSM on a link that only sees SSL-encrypted traffic between two point systems, or between the Internet and a SSL-only system. In cases like that, the first option might be to deploy host-centric monitoring and logging on the asset in question.

Thank you for questions like these -- please keep sending them. They make good sections for a new book.

https://taosecurity.blogspot.com/2009/08/question-on-nsm-scaling.html

I have heard the same complaints about scaling NSM for years. The more I interact with users, however, the more stories I hear about NSM scaled to the very largest scientific and educational network links. Accomplishing that feat might take a lot of investment in research or vendor solutions, but it is possible and is happening right now.

Build Visibility In

Thursday, August 13, 2009

Visibility has been a constant theme for this blog. Elsewhere I've used the phrase *build visibility in* to emphasize the need to integrate visibility requirements into the build and design phases of any technology project. Visibility should not be left as an afterthought. Building security in is required as well, but how can you determine how security is working if you have no visibility?

Based on my experiences with technology deployments since the late 1990s, I've realized that the following cycle defines just about every project I've ever seen.

The cycle is **Feature -> Management -> "Security" -> Visibility**.

I see this cycle at work in the mobile device space right now. Hardly anyone is thinking about how to determine if a mobile device (Blackberry, etc.) is compromised. The best we can do is imagine the sorts of attacks that might be happening to our mobile infrastructure, without visibility regarding how those devices might already be under attack.

I call this operating only within the *Decide -> Act* part of the OODA loop (*Observe -> Orient -> Decide -> Act*). We do it all the time in digital security. I called it *Soccer Goal Security* in 2005.

Does this cycle resonate with anyone?

https://taosecurity.blogspot.com/2009/08/build-visibility-in.html

Commentary

Nothing has changed in the 11 years since I wrote this post. A developer introduces a feature into an offering. When it becomes unwieldy on its own or in conjunction with other features, someone introduces a management layer. Eventually the software is important enough to attract the attention of intruders. Security is generally an afterthought, so as intruders exploit the software, "security" is added. It takes living through multiple iterations of this cycle for organizations to move security to the front of the queue. Some never do.

On "Advanced" Network Security Monitoring

Monday, December 04, 2017

My TaoSecurity News page says I taught 41 classes lasting a day or more, from 2002 to 2014. All of these involved some aspect of network security monitoring (NSM). Many times students would ask me when I would create the "advanced" version of the class, usually in the course feedback. I could never answer them, so I decided to do so in this blog post.

The short answer is this: *at some point, advanced NSM is no longer NSM*. If you consider my *collection - analysis - escalation - response* model, NSM extensions from any of those phases quickly have little or nothing to do with the network.

Here are a few questions I have received concerning "advanced NSM," paired with the answers I could have provided.

Q: "I used NSM to extract a binary from network traffic. What do I do with this binary?"

A: "Learn about reverse engineering and binary analysis."

Or:

Q: "I used NSM to extra Javascript from a malicious Web page. What do I do with this Javascript?"

A: "Learn about Javascript de-obfuscation and programming."

Or:

Q: "I used NSM to capture an exchange between a Windows client and a server. What does it mean?"

A: "Learn about Server Message Block (SMB) or Common Internet File System (CIFS)."

Or:

Q: "I used NSM to capture cryptographic material exchanged between a client and a server. How do I understand it?"

A: "Learn about cryptography."

Or:

Q: "I used NSM to grab shell code passed with an exploit against an Internet-exposed service. How do I tell what it does?"

A: "Learn about programming in assembly."

Or:

Q: "I want to design custom hardware for packet capture. How do I do that?"

A: "Learn about programming ASICs (application specific integrated circuits)."

I realized that I had the components of all of this "advanced NSM" material in my library. I had books on reverse engineering and binary analysis, Javascript, SMB/CIFS, cryptography, assembly programming, ASICs, etc.

The point is that eventually the NSM road takes you to other aspects of the cyber security landscape.

Are there *any* advanced area for NSM? One could argue that protocol analysis, as one finds in tools like Bro [Zeek], Suricata, Snort, Wireshark, and so on constitute advanced NSM. However, you could just as easily argue that protocol analysis becomes more about understanding the programming and standards behind each of the protocols.

In brief, to learn advanced NSM, expand beyond NSM.

https://taosecurity.blogspot.com/2017/12/on-advanced-network-se
curity-monitoring.html

Commentary

This is a great post to end this chapter. It's not quite saying that, in the end, "there is no spoon," but it's close. In the three years since I wrote this post, I've realized that in part I was focusing a bit too much on NSM as a collection methodology. Still, I maintain that augmenting your NSM knowledge requires working with topics that might be considered outside the mainstream model. I find that the farther I get from security, the more I learn about security.

Conclusion

Network security monitoring is a theme appearing in all three volumes of this work. However, these posts highlighted key aspects of my philosophy, sometimes showing how the data collected by NSM operations helps analysts make better decisions. NSM is not just "monitoring" the "network" for "security" reasons. NSM is a process and a model for conducting security operations, with elements applying to the tools, tactics, operations, and strategy levels of conflict.

Chapter 2. Technical Notes

Introduction

This chapter presents a selection of technical notes from TaoSecurity blog. It's a mixture of reports on experiments with various hardware, along with in-depth analysis of network traffic minutia. I included several of these posts because I have referred to them repeatedly over the years. Perhaps you can tell which ones they might be!

Running Four VMWare Guests Simultaneously

Friday, August 15, 2003

I installed Red Hat 9.0 on my IBM ThinkBrink (I mean ThinkPad) a20p yesterday. It has 384 MB RAM and a 20 GB hard drive. I then installed a trial version of VMWare 4 for Linux. Next, I installed images of Windows NT 4, Red Hat 7.0, FreeBSD 4.3, and Solaris 7 x86. I gave each OS 32 MB RAM and between 1-3 GB hard drive space. I was able to run all four OS simultaneously without a real problem, although I didn't run X in Linux and FreeBSD. Solaris offers a GUI by default but I began a command line session instead. This arrangement makes a decent lab environment, although more RAM would help. It's nice being able to run old operating systems in such small amounts of memory!

https://taosecurity.blogspot.com/2003/08/running-four-vmware-guests.html

Commentary

This post represents one of my quests as a system administrator in the late 1990s and early 2000s. The IBM ThinkPad a20p was my first laptop, which I bought in September 2000. I was still in the Air Force at that time, but this system was for personal use. It had a 6X/2X DVD-ROM, a 1.44 MB floppy disk drive, a 15" SXGA+ (1400x1050) LCD display, a first-generation USB port, a 10/100 EtherJet Mini PCI Adapter with 56K modem, and a PCMCIA slot which I used for WiFi NICs. Eventually I upgraded it to 512 MB RAM and a 60 GB hard drive!

I'm not sure everyone appreciates how revolutionary VMware was as a product. When I first started doing hands-on computer security work in 1998, there was no VMware. "Multibooting" was the pinnacle of achievement, whereby a power user installed two or more operating systems in different hard drive partitions. After making the appropriate sacrifices and chanting the correct incantations, one could run several operating systems, one at a time, on one piece of hardware. If I remember correctly, at one point before VMware I was multibooting four operating systems -- Linux, FreeBSD, Windows NT, and Solaris. I had to experiment quite a bit, and I even bought and read books dedicated to multibooting.

Once VMware arrived, running multiple operating systems on one platform was easy. It changed how I taught classes. My fellow instructors and I didn't need to reimage dozens of laptops simultaneously, the night before a class!

These days, of course, everyone uses VMware, Virtualbox, or just runs their workloads in the cloud. Below I have a post about quadruple-booting the same laptop.

Email Sent from Amateur Radio Network to Internet and Back

Saturday, August 16, 2003

Today I visited the Ham Radio Outlet in Woodbridge, VA and bought a Kantronics KPC-3+. This little beauty is a "Terminal Node Controller" (TNC) and it lets my HTX-202 2 meter amateur ("ham") radio talk to the "packet radio" network around the world.

Combine this equipment with an amateur radio license and you're ready to go! (I earned my Technician class license in 2001.)

I cabled my laptop to the KPC-3+, and cabled the KPC-3+ to my HTX-202. Next I used the Windows Hyper Terminal program to communicate with the KPC-3+. I told the TNC to connect to W4OVH, which is a geographically nearby packet node operated by the Ole Virginia Hams Amateur Radio Club. From there I hopped to a node which offers mail relay to Internet space from the packet network.

I composed a message, and sent it. I received the message on my Thunderbird Windows XP Internet email client. I replied to the message on my XP box and got the reply back through the packet radio network.

I think that's cool! Amateur radio operators can send email to each other without the use of the Internet. It's just like the old BBS days in the 1980s, and especially relevant in emergencies today. (The VA Digital Emergency Network operates using packet radio.)

My HTX-202 rig supports data transfer at 1200 baud, which is what I used with my Commodore 64 back in the day. Monday night I plan to attend a meeting of the amateur radio operators in my area and learn what else I can do with this technology.

https://taosecurity.blogspot.com/2003/08/email-sent-from-amateur-radio-network.html

Commentary

This might make an interesting covert communications channel. Hardly anyone checks for rogue communication equipment outside of WiFi bands. I imagine there are various intelligence agencies using technologies like these for close access operations.

Quadruple Boot Laptop

Wednesday, October 01, 2003

I own a Thinkpad a20p and I've decided to use it to test operating systems. I managed to quadruple-boot FreeBSD, NetBSD, OpenBSD. and Debian. Essentially I loaded FreeBSD 5.1 RELEASE, then OpenBSD 3.3, then NetBSD 1.6.1, and finally Debian 3.0.

I put OpenBSD first on its own primary partition/slice, followed by FreeBSD and NetBSD. I installed Debian in an extended partition with various logical partitions for /, swap, /var, /home, and /tmp. Thankfully I made a boot floppy when Debian asked, and used it to boot Debian and install lilo in the master boot record. I tried to use the advice in this post but found the various installs seemed to step on each other.

While installing I perused various reference materials. Darren Evans' *OpenBSD 3.3 Build Guide*, Matthew Charles' *OpenBSD: Updating source code and upgrading*, Gan Starling's *What Worked for Me on NetBSD*, Keith Parkansky's *About Debian*, and Daniel Roethlisberger's *FreeBSD on the IBM Thinkpad A20p* are helpful.

One post let me know NetBSD wouldn't cooperate when I tried to list the packages it was installing on the Thinkpad. In other words, the install would seg fault unless I hid the names of files it installed! NetBSD's installer found the wrong disk geometry but adjusted it when I told it to check the geometry.

https://taosecurity.blogspot.com/2003/10/quadruple-boot-laptop-i-own-thinkpad.html

Commentary

Several years later I again tried multi-booting on a new laptop, a Lenovo x60s. I ran Windows XP, Ubuntu 7.04, and FreeBSD 6.2 on that system in June 2007. I believe I wanted to have native operating system access to real hardware for testing various wireless applications.

TCP Sequence Numbers Explained

Monday, January 12, 2004

Today I was reading a new book on "intrusion detection and prevention" which repeats an often misinformed interpretation of TCP sequence numbers. The book said:

> "When either party wishes to send data to the other, it will send a packet with the ACK flag set, with an acknowledgement of the last sequence number (in the Acknowledgement field) received from the remote host, and with its own sequence number incremented to reflect the amount of data being transmitted."

This gets both the acknowledgement and sequence numbers wrong.

The following excerpt from my upcoming book *The Tao of Network Security Monitoring* explains how TCP sequence and acknowledgement numbers work by following a TCP session through Ethereal. 192.168.2.4 is a workstation named "caine" and 204.152.184.75 is ftp.netbsd.org, contracted to "netbsd" here.

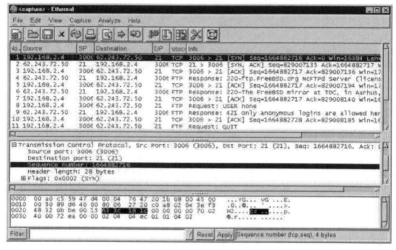

Figure 4. Frame 1

Packet 1 shows a SYN from caine to netbsd. The TCP segment's ISN is 1664882716. Directly to the right of the ISN is a 4 byte value of zeroes. This is where the acknowledgement number would reside, if the ACK flag were set.

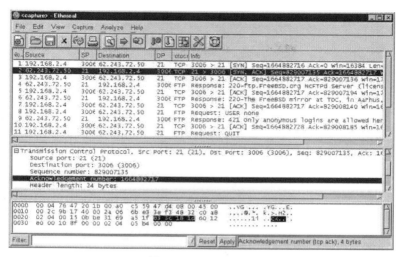

Figure 5. Frame 2

Packet 2 shows a SYN ACK from netbsd to caine. Netbsd sets an
Initial Response Number of 829007135 and an ACK value of
1664822717. ACK 1664822717 indicates that the next real byte of
application data netbsd expects to receive from caine will be number
1664822717. That ACK value also indicates netbsd received a "byte
of data" implied in the SYN packet caine sent, whose ISN was
1664822716. No bytes of data were actually sent. This is an example
of a sequence number being "consumed" in the three-way
handshake.

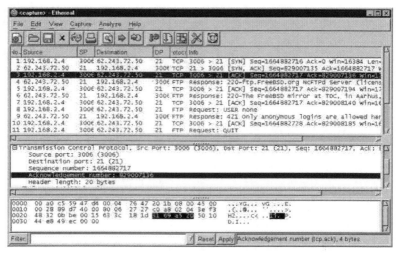

Figure 6. Frame 3

Packet 3 shows the completion of the three-way handshake. Caine sends an ACK 829007136, which acknowledges receipt of the one "byte of data" implied in the SYN ACK packet netbsd sent, whose IRN was 829007135. 829007136 indicates that the first real byte of data caine expects to receive from netbsd will be number 829007136. Again, no bytes of application data have actually been sent by either party. This is another example of a sequence number being "consumed" in the three-way handshake.

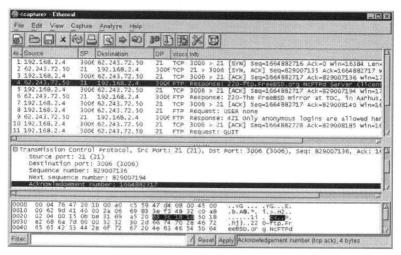

Figure 7. Frame 4

Packet 4 shows the first real bytes of application data sent from netbsd to caine. Netbsd still sends ACK 1664882717 because that is the sequence number of the first real byte of application data netbsd expects to receive from caine. Netbsd's sequence number is 829007136, meaning the first byte of application data in packet 4 is numbered 829007136. That is the byte with hexadecimal value 0x32, which is ASCII 2 of the first digit in the "220" status code sent by Netbsd's FTP service. "32 32 30," or ASCII 220, appears in the line below the acknowledgement number.

Observe that this packet bears a sequence number indicating the sequence number of the first byte of application data in the packet. The value of this sequence number bears no relationship with the amount of application data in the packet. If netbsd sends 58 bytes or 580 bytes, it still uses sequence number 829007136, because that is the number of the first byte of data it promised to send to caine.

Ethereal reports the "next sequence number" to be 829007194. This value does not specifically appear anywhere in the packet. It is calculated by adding the number of bytes of application data in the packet (58) to the sequence number of the first byte of data in the packet (829007136). This does not mean the last sequence number of data in this packet is 829007194. Rather, the sequence number of the last byte of data is 829007193. How is this so? The following table tracks the sequence numbers of the bytes of application data in this packet.

```
Seq Num      Hex   ASCII
829007136    32    2
829007137    32    2
829007138    30    0
829007139    2d    -
...50 bytes omitted...
829007190    79    y
829007191    2e    .
829007192    0d    carriage return
829007193    0a    new line
```

This fact probably accounts for most of the misunderstandings regarding the relationship between sequence numbers and byte counts of application data.

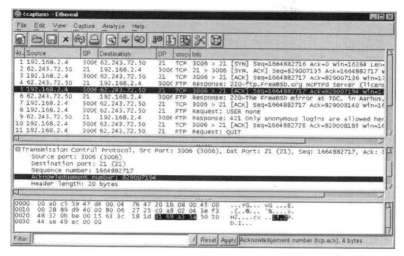

Figure 8. Frame 5

Packet 5 shows caine acknowledges receipt of bytes 829007136
through 829007193 from netbsd by sending ACK 829007194. This
means the next byte of application data caine expects to receive from
netbsd will be number 829007194. Caine's own sequence number
1664882717 is unchanged as it has not yet sent any application data.

105

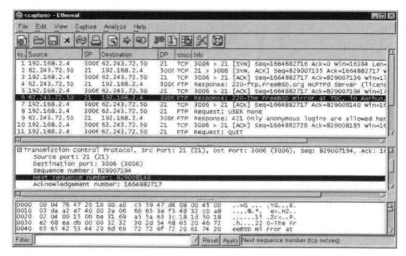

Figure 9. Frame 6

Packet 6 shows netbsd sending more data to caine. The "next sequence number field" shows there is no corresponding real field in the TCP header of the bottom pane. The value 829008140 means netbsd sent 946 bytes of application data. Netbsd sets its sequence number as 829007194 to represent the first byte of data in this packet. The sequence number of the last byte of application data is 829008139. Its acknowledgement number remains at 1664882717 because caine still has not sent any application data.

106

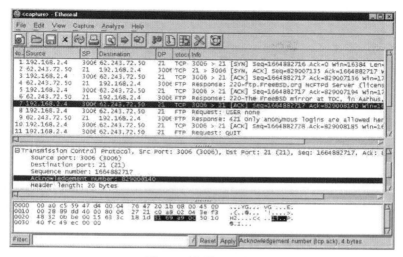

Figure 10. Frame 7

Packet 7 shows caine acknowledges receipt of 946 bytes of application data with an ACK 829008140. This means the last byte of data caine received was number 829008139. Caine expects to receive 829008140 next from netbsd. Caine's sequence number is still set at 1664882717 because it has not yet sent any application data to netbsd.

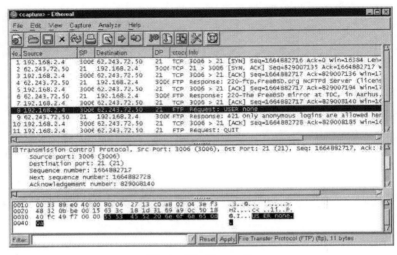

Figure 11. Frame 8

In packet 8 caine finally sends its own application data to netbsd. Caine transmits 11 bytes, starting with sequence number 1664882717 (0x55, or ASCII U) and ending with 1664882727 (0x0a, or new line). Caine's acknowledgement number stays at 829008140 because that is the number of the next byte of application data caine expects from netbsd. Should caine send more application data, the first byte will be number 1664882728, as depicted in the "next sequence number" calculated by Ethereal.

As we saw earlier when netbsd sent application data, the sequence number carried in the packet is the number of the first byte of application data. Here it is 1664882717, which is what caine promised to send netbsd way back in packet 2.

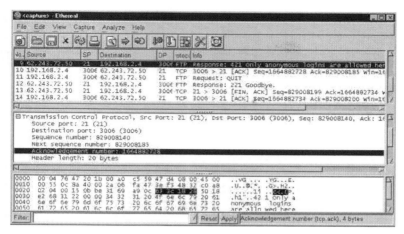

Figure 12. Frame 9

Packet 9 shows netbsd acknowledges bytes 1664882717 through
1664882727 by sending an ACK 1664882728. Netbsd sends 45
bytes of its own application data, demonstrating that TCP allows
acknowledging data sent by another party while transmitting new
data to that party.

By now you should have a good understanding of how TCP
sequence numbers work. We skip packets 10, 11, and 12 as they offer
nothing new in terms of watching sequence numbers.

109

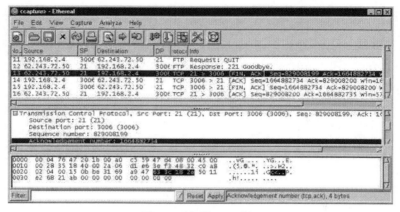

Figure 13. Frame 13

Packet 13 begins the TCP "graceful close" or "orderly release," by which each side of the conversation closes the session. We can inspect the one-line summary of the sequence and acknowledgement numbers to follow the closing of the session.

Packet 13 shows netbsd terminates the session by sending a FIN ACK packet. Netbsd sets its ACK number at 1664882734, indicating it has received bytes of data through 1664882733 from caine. Packet 13 bears a sequence number of 829008199.

Packet 14 shows caine's response, an ACK 829008200. This acknowledges receipt of the "byte of data" implied by packet 13 from netbsd. This is similar to the way sequence numbers were "consumed" during the three-way handshake to confirm acknowledgement of SYN and SYN ACK packets. Packet 14 is caine's way of saying it received the FIN ACK from netbsd.

Packet 15 is caine's own FIN ACK. Caine uses ACK 829008200, the same as it used in packet 14. Caine sets its own sequence number at 1664882734. Netbsd will use this as the basis for its own acknowledgement in packet 16.

110

Why doesn't caine combine packets 14 and 15 into a single FIN ACK? The reason lies with the work being done at different levels of the OSI model. Packet 14 shows the TCP layer talking. By immediately replying with an ACK to netbsd's FIN ACK, caine indicates its receipt of packet 13. Caine's TCP/IP stack then needs to check with its FTP client application to see if it has any more application data to send. When the stack learns the FTP client is done with the session, caine sends its own FIN ACK in packet 15.

Packet 16 is netbsd's acknowledgement of caine's FIN ACK. Netbsd sets its ACK value to 1664882735, indicating it received the "byte of data" implied by packet 15 from caine. This is another consumption of a sequence number used to complete the TCP graceful close.

I hope this helps dispel the fog surrounding TCP sequence numbers.

https://taosecurity.blogspot.com/2004/01/tcp-sequence-numbers-explained-today-i.html

Commentary

I included this post because many people do not understand how sequence numbers work in TCP. I lightly edited the original text in the event the reader could not see the images. They are not critical to understanding the main points. If you happen to have a very early print copy, perhaps from the first run, you will notice the figure captions for this section are off by one in that edition. Somehow that error appeared in the production process, but Addison-Wesley corrected it in the later printings.

Comments on TCP Reset Worries

Saturday, April 24, 2004

I attended Paul Watson's talk at CanSecWest this week on "Slipping in the Window." Paul was inspired by last year's Black Hat 2003 Las Vegas talk "BGP Vulnerability Testing" by Matthew Franz & Sean Convery. I attended that presentation as well, and found Matt and Sean's conclusion to be accurate: why bother with lower layer attacks when you can own the router? In other words, so many routers are misconfigured, it's not necessary to resort to spoofing or other elaborate games to disrupt global routing.

Paul decided to focus on the likelihood of successful reset attacks against routers speaking BGP. He found that Matt and Sean's estimates for the time needed to guess the right TCP sequence number to reset a TCP connection were overstated. Matt and Sean did not take into account TCP receive windows, meaning a reset with a sequence number within the window would be accepted by the target. This makes it easier to reset a persistent connection, and TCP implementations with large windows are even easier to disrupt.

Matt and Sean posted an updated version of their paper acknowledging Paul's finds.

A well-written advisory by the UK's NISCC states "an established connection will abort by sending a RST if it receives a duplicate SYN packet with initial sequence number within the TCP window." This means tearing down established connections can be done with SYN packets, not just RST packets.

CIsco published an advisory titled *TCP Vulnerabilities in Multiple IOS-Based Cisco Products* explaining the issue and listing fixes. It's important to note that since Cisco IOS 10.2 (very old!), IOS rate-limits RST packets by default. According to Cisco, "in the case of a storm of RST packets, they are effectively limited to one packet per second." This countermeasure effectively renders Paul's reset attack too slow to be workable. However, SYN packets are not rate-limited.

Cisco's rate limiting is not the only way to mitigate this attack. Anti-spoofing measures and not letting arbitrary traffic to inject itself between BGP speaking routers are other countermeasures.

I don't foresee the Internet dying at any time in the near future due to this discovery. Owning the target routers would probably be easier. Remember this is mainly a threat to persistent connections. No one is going to kill your Web browsing sessions with this sort of attack, but they would make your life miserable if you tried to download an .iso via FTP. Of course, how are attackers going to know what sessions to target?

Incidentally, while browsing Cisco's site I learned their IOS Upgrade Planner and Feature Navigator appears to be working again.

Update: Raven Adler spoke to the DC Security Geeks on 27 April about the BGP issue. Her talk was professional and informative. She worked on the same issue several years before Paul Watson's discoveries. She reported being involved in an incident response where an intruder physically attached a rogue laptop to a public peering point switch to disrupt and/or inject routing.

https://taosecurity.blogspot.com/2004/04/comments-on-tcp-reset-worries-i.html

Commentary

My favorite line from this post is "I don't foresee the Internet dying at any time in the near future due to this discovery." Probably once a year we read reports of some exploit or vulnerability that threatens to destroy the Internet, and yet we invariably survive. Criminals and other threat actors benefit from the Internet far too much to make destroying it worthwhile.

Understanding Tcpdump's -d Option

Thursday, September 30, 2004

Have you ever used Tcpdump's -d option? The man page says:

-d Dump the compiled packet-matching code in a human readable form
     to standard output and stop.

I've never used that option before, but I just saw a Tcpdump developer use it to confirm a Berkeley packet filter in this thread. The user in the thread is trying to see TCP or UDP packets with a source address of "centernet.jhuccp.org" (162.129.225.192). First he specifies an incorrect BPF filter, which the developer then corrects. This is mildly interesting, but the useful information on the -d option appears in this post.

Tcpdump developer Guy Harris interprets output from the -d option:

```
> www:~# tcpdump -d src host centernet.jhuccp.org and
\( ip proto \\tcp
> or \\udp \)
> (000) ldh       [12]
> (001) jeq       #0x800                jt 2    jf 8
> (002) ld        [26]
> (003) jeq       #0xa281e1c0           jt 4    jf 8
> (004) ldb       [23]
> (005) jeq       #0x6                  jt 7    jf 6
> (006) jeq       #0x11                 jt 7    jf 8
> (007) ret       #96
> (008) ret       #0
```

OK, that code:

loads the 2-byte big-endian quantity at an offset of 12 from the beginning of the packet - which, on an Ethernet packet, is the type/length field in the Ethernet header - and compares it with 0x0800 - which is the type code for IPv4 - and, if it's not equal, jumps to instruction 8, which returns 0, meaning "reject this packet" (i.e., it rejects all packets other than IPv4 packets);

loads the 4-byte big-endian quantity at an offset of 26 from the beginning of the packet - which, for an IPv4-over-Ethernet packet, is the source IP address in the IPv4 header - and compares it with 0xa281e1c0 - which is 162.129.225.192, or "centernet.jhuccp.org" - and, if it's not equal, jumps to instruction 8 (i.e., it rejects all packets that don't have a source IP address of 162.129.225.192);

loads the one-byte quantity at an offset of 23 from the beginning of the packet - which, for an IPv4-over-Ethernet packet, is the protocol type field in the IPv4 header - and, if it's equal to 6 - i.e., if it's a TCP packet - jumps to instruction 7, which returns 96, meaning "accept this packet and get its first 96 bytes", and, if it's not 6, jumps to instruction 6, which does the same check for 17, i.e. UDP.

I found this explanation very enlightening and I appreciate Guy taking the time to discuss it.

https://taosecurity.blogspot.com/2004/09/understanding-tcpdump-s-d-option-have.html

Commentary

This was my first real introduction to the inner workings of the Tcpdump Berkeley Packet Filter. Please see the next post for more details.

Understanding Tcpdump's -d Option, Part 2

Tuesday, December 21, 2004

In September I referenced a post by libpcap guru Guy Harris explaining output from Tcpdump's -d switch. After looking at the original 1992 BSD Packet Filter (.pdf) paper and the subsequent 1999 *BPF+* paper, I understand the syntax for the compiled packet-matching code generated by the tcpdump -d switch. For example:

```
fedorov:/usr/local/etc/nsm# tcpdump -n -i em1 -d tcp

tcpdump: WARNING: em1: no IPv4 address assigned

(000) ldh       [12]

(001) jeq       #0x86dd           jt 2    jf 4

(002) ldb       [20]

(003) jeq       #0x6             jt 7    jf 8

(004) jeq       #0x800           jt 5    jf 8

(005) ldb       [23]

(006) jeq       #0x6             jt 7    jf 8

(007) ret       #96

(008) ret       #0
```

Here is what each instruction means:

000 says load (using 'ldh') the "half word" or two bytes starting at offset 12 of the Ethernet header. Since we begin counting at 0, bytes 0 to 5 are the destination MAC address and bytes 6 to 11 are the source MAC address. The name of the two bytes beginning at offset 12 differs according to the Ethernet format used.

001 compares the two bytes loaded in 000 with the value 0x86dd. That is the Ethertype of IPv6. A comparison is made (using 'jeq'); if equality is true, jump ('jt') to instruction 002. If false, jump ('jf') to 004.

002 loads the byte found at offset 20. If we are evaluating this instruction we are in an IPv6 header. Offset 20 holds the "next header" value.

003 compares the byte loaded in 002 with the value 0x6. This is the IP protocol code for TCP. A comparison is made (using 'jeq'); if equality is true, jump ('jt') to instruction 007. If false, jump ('jf') to 008.

004 compares the byte loaded in 000 with the value 0x800. That is the Ethertype of IPv4. A comparison is made (using 'jeq'); if equality is true, jump ('jt') to instruction 005. If false, jump ('jf') to 008.

005 loads the byte found at offset 23. If we are evaluating this instruction we are in an IPv4 header. Offset 20 holds the "protocol" value for the protocol following the IP header.

006 compares the byte loaded in 005 with the value 0x6. That is the protocol value for TCP. A comparison is made (using 'jeq'); if equality is true, jump ('jt') to instruction 007. If false, jump ('jf') to 008.

007 is the equivalent of "TRUE", meaning that the indicated number of bytes (96) of packet data will be copied to the calling application (in this case, Tcpdump). You reach this point if the packet being inspected is TCP, either using IPv4 or IPv6.

008 is the equivalent of "FALSE", meaning zero bytes of packet data will be copied to the application. You reach this point if the packet being inspected is not TCP.

Understanding this syntax is a way to troubleshoot BPFs that don't behave as you expect. You can run 'tcpdump -d' and inspect the code as explained above to see if it performs as you want.

For those of you wanting a definition of a packet filter, here is what I've come up with based on the original paper, *The Packet Filter: An Efficient Mechanism for User-level Network Code*: a packet filter is a kernel-resident packet demultiplexer that provides a way for userland processes to tell the kernel what packets they want.

For more detail, I recommend reading the three papers mentioned in this story. Guy Harris also posted a message to tcpdump-workers explaining BPF.

https://taosecurity.blogspot.com/2004/12/understanding-tcpdumps-d-option-part-2.html

Commentary

In this post I showed how to understand one of the simplest BPF syntax statements one could choose -- filtering for TCP traffic. I liked how logical this system was. It's a powerful way to determine if the syntax you are using works as you think it does. This logic still applies today.

Generating Multicast Traffic

Friday, September 22, 2006

If you're a protocol junkie like me, you probably enjoy investigating a variety of network traffic types. I don't encounter multicast traffic too often, so the following caught my eye.

I'm using Iperf for some simple testing, and I notice it has a multicast option. Here's how I used it.

In the following scenario, I have two hosts (cel433 and cel600) on the same segment. This is important because the router(s) in this test network are not configured to support multicast.

I set up cel433 as a Iperf server listening on multicast address 224.0.55.55.

```
cel433:/root# iperf -s -u -B 224.0.55.55 -i 1
------------------------------------------------------------
Server listening on UDP port 5001
Binding to local address 224.0.55.55
Joining multicast group  224.0.55.55
Receiving 1470 byte datagrams
UDP buffer size: 41.1 KByte (default)
```

Now I generate multicast traffic from cel600.

```
cel600:/root# iperf -c 224.0.55.55 -u -T 32 -t 3 -i 1
------------------------------------------------------------
Client connecting to 224.0.55.55, UDP port 5001
Sending 1470 byte datagrams
Setting multicast TTL to 32
UDP buffer size: 9.00 KByte (default)
------------------------------------------------------------
[  3] local 10.1.10.3 port 51296 connected with 224.0.55.55
port 5001
[  3]  0.0- 1.0 sec    129 KBytes  1.06 Mbits/sec
[  3]  1.0- 2.0 sec    128 KBytes  1.05 Mbits/sec
```

```
[  3]   2.0- 3.0 sec    128 KBytes  1.05 Mbits/sec
[  3]   0.0- 3.0 sec    386 KBytes  1.05 Mbits/sec
[  3] Sent 269 datagrams
```

Here is what cel433 sees:

```
------------------------------------------------------------
[  3] local 224.0.55.55 port 5001 connected with 10.1.10.3
port 51296
[  3]   0.0- 1.0 sec    128 KBytes  1.05 Mbits/sec  0.146 ms
0/    89 (0%)
[  3]   1.0- 2.0 sec    128 KBytes  1.05 Mbits/sec  0.100 ms
0/    89 (0%)
[  3]   2.0- 3.0 sec    128 KBytes  1.05 Mbits/sec  0.110 ms
0/    89 (0%)
[  3]   0.0- 3.0 sec    386 KBytes  1.05 Mbits/sec  0.098 ms
0/   268 (0%)
[  3]   0.0- 3.0 sec  1 datagrams received out-of-order
```

The traffic looks like this:

```
cel433:/root# tcpdump -n -i xl0 -s 1515 udp
tcpdump: verbose output suppressed, use -v or -vv for full
protocol decode
listening on xl0, link-type EN10MB (Ethernet), capture size
1515 bytes
15:29:53.669508 IP 10.1.10.3.51296 > 224.0.55.55.5001: UDP,
length 1470
15:29:53.680789 IP 10.1.10.3.51296 > 224.0.55.55.5001: UDP,
length 1470
15:29:53.691934 IP 10.1.10.3.51296 > 224.0.55.55.5001: UDP,
length 1470
...truncated...
```

This is a simple way to generate multicast traffic and ensure a
member of the multicast group actually receives it.

Update: I forgot to show the IGMP messages one would see when
starting a multicast listener.

This is the interface listening for multicast:

```
cel433:/root# ifconfig xl0
xl0: flags=8843 mtu 1500
        options=9
        inet6 fe80::2c0:4fff:fe1c:102b%xl0 prefixlen 64 scopeid 0x6
        inet 10.1.10.2 netmask 0xffffff00 broadcast 10.1.10.255
        ether 00:c0:4f:1c:10:2b
        media: Ethernet autoselect (100baseTX )
        status: active
```

Here are IGMP report and leave messages.

```
cel433:/root# tcpdump -nevv -i xl0 -s 1515 igmp

tcpdump: listening on xl0, link-type EN10MB (Ethernet),
capture size 1515 bytes

06:28:40.887868 00:c0:4f:1c:10:2b > 01:00:5e:00:37:37,
ethertype IPv4 (0x0800),length 46: (tos 0x0, ttl  1, id
59915, offset 0, flags [none], proto: IGMP (2), length: 32,
options ( RA (148) len 4 )) 10.1.10.2 > 224.0.55.55: igmp v2
report 224.0.55.55

06:28:42.196233 00:c0:4f:1c:10:2b > 01:00:5e:00:00:02,
ethertype IPv4 (0x0800), length 46: (tos 0x0, ttl  1, id
59920, offset 0, flags [none], proto: IGMP (2), length: 32,
options ( RA (148) len 4 )) 10.1.10.2 > 224.0.0.2: igmp
leave 224.0.55.55
```

I used the -e option to show the MAC addresses. Notice the
destination MAC for these multicast packets.

```
06:31:21.467919 00:b0:d0:14:b2:11 > 01:00:5e:00:37:37,
ethertype IPv4 (0x0800), length 1512: (tos 0x0, ttl  32, id
1652, offset 0, flags [none], proto: UDP (17), length:
1498) 10.1.10.3.58479 > 224.0.55.55.5001: [udp sum ok] UDP,
length 1470
```

The 01:00:5e:00:37:37 MAC address is a mapping derived from the
24-bit IANA multicast OUI 01:00:5e and the multicast IP address
224.0.55.55.

https://taosecurity.blogspot.com/2006/09/generating-multicast-traf
fic.html

Commentary

This little post was one of the top traffic generators for TaoSecurity blog. I guess readers could not find resources on how to generate multicast traffic, so their searches ended up sending them to this post.

Simpler IP Range Matching with Tshark Display Filters

Sunday, June 28, 2009

In today's SANS ISC journal, the story IP Address Range Search with libpcap wonders how to accomplish the following:

> ...how to find SYN packets directed to natted addresses where an attempt was made to connect or scan a service natted to an internal resource. I used this filter for addresses located in the range 192.168.25.6 to 192.168.25.35.

The proposed answer is this:

```
tcpdump -nr file '((ip[16:2] = 0xc0a8  and ip[18] =
0x19 and ip[19] > 0x06)\
and (ip[16:2] = 0xc0a8 and ip[18] = 0x19 and ip[19] <
0x23) and tcp[13] = 0x02)'
```

I am sure it's clear to everyone what that means!

Given my low success rate in getting comments posted to the SANS ISC blog, I figured I would reply here.

Last fall I wrote Using Wireshark and Tshark display filters for troubleshooting. Wireshark display filters make writing such complex Berkeley Packet Filter syntax a thing of the past.

Using Wireshark display filters, a mere mortal could write the following:

```
tshark -nr file 'tcp.flags.syn and (ip.dst >
192.168.25.6 and ip.dst < 192.168.25.35)'
```

Note that if you want to be inclusive, change the > to >= and the < to <= .

To show that my filter works, I ran the filter against a file with traffic on my own 192.168.2.0/24 network, so I altered the last two octets to match my own traffic.

```
$ tshark -nr test.pcap 'tcp.flags.syn and (ip.dst >
192.168.2.103 and ip.dst < 192.168.2.106)'

137 2009-06-28 16:21:44.195504 74.125.115.100 ->
192.168.2.104 HTTP Continuation or non-HTTP traffic
```

You have plenty of other options, such as ip.src and ip.addr.

https://taosecurity.blogspot.com/2009/06/simpler-ip-range-matching-with-tshark.html

Commentary

I never understood the SANS ISC's devotion, at least in the 2000s, to Tcpdump and BPF. Gerald Combs released Ethereal, later renamed as Wireshark, to the world in 1998. With its robust, human-friendly syntax, it made complicated BPF obsolete for many analysis tasks. Chances are if you are trying to do packet matching, especially in saved traces, it makes sense to use Tshark or Wireshark filters, not Tcpdump BPF.

Conclusion

Did you guess which posts are some of my go-to reference materials? I've used the Tcpdump -d post several times as a way to understand BPF syntax and its effects. I've also referred to the TCP sequence number post when I come across an author's "explanation" of how he or she thinks sequence numbers change. A lesson I learned from reading the original edition of *TCP/IP Illustrated, Volume 1: The Protocols*, by W. Richard Stevens, is that there is no better way to learn networking than to watch real traffic.

Chapter 3. Research

Introduction

This chapter is a collection of research topics. In some cases, like the next post, it is an investigative journey to determine if a claim is true. In other cases, I assess various aspects of the digital security field. This chapter addresses many themes and includes some of my favorite posts.

Is Earth Station Five a Hoax?

Thursday, August 28, 2003

Is Earth Station Five a media industry sting operation? A few friends told me about this site today, so I poked around a bit. ES5 appears to be some sort of file-sharing network which thumbs its nose to the Recording Industry Association of America and the Motion Picture Association of America.

ES5 seems to have made its biggest splash in a CNET News.com article where ES5 "President" "Ras Kabir" claims "We're in Palestine, in a refugee camp."

The earliest reference I found dates from 18 March 2003 in a post at a digital music site. It was also discussed on 25 June 2003 at the file sharing site Zeropaid.com. Prior to the News.com story, I found press releases which appear to be from 27 June 2003, 1 July 2003 and 7 July 2003.

The News.com story states:

"According to Earthstation 5 founder Kabir, the company was formed after a conversation with his brother Nasser in Ramallah two years ago, as Napster was circling toward its nadir. Over time, they won the financial backing of investors in Israel, Saudi Arabia and Russia, who have asked to remain anonymous. Those funds were used in part to pay contract programmers, largely in Russia, to help build the basic software.

The 35-year-old Kabir, who speaks fluent English, says he is Palestinian but spent much of his childhood in Manchester, England, with his mother. He now has homes in Jenin and elsewhere in Palestine, where Earthstation 5 is based, he said."

It's convenient that someone presenting himself as a Palestinian speaks fluent English. Next ES5 issued a "declaration of war" via press release, claiming:

"In response to the email received today from the Motion Picture Association of America (MPAA) to Earthstation 5 for copyright violations for streaming FIRST RUN movies over the internet for FREE, this is our official response! Earthstation 5 is at war with the Motion Picture Association of America (MPAA) and the Record Association of America (RIAA), and to make our point very clear that their governing laws and policys [sic] have absolutely no meaning to us here in Palestine, we will continue to add even more movies for FREE."

I uncovered some "investigative reporting" at slyck.com, whereby the site owner interviewed "Ras Kabir," ES5 "president." He focused mainly on usage statistics:

"Slyck asked Ras Kabir to explain how his program could possibly have 3 times the level of usage of FastTrack and be one of the most downloaded software applications in such a short period. This especially seems hard to explain given the fact that it is difficult to find content for some artists. Surely these figures are inflated?"

I'm more concerned with the odd language used by the site. I have two explanations. First, it's the sort of "wanna-be-cool, fight-the-man" language used by a marketing-drone-turned-sting operator. For example, the ES5 Chronicles page uses terms like "evil empire" and "enemy hands" too many times for my tastes. Other people have also expressed doubts about ES5's authenticity.

Putting on my intel officer hat, I did some cursory research on the "Jenin refugee camp" from where ES5 allegedly operates. After seeing the pictures on this site, I wondered what kind of infrastructure is there to support major file sharing operations! Still, lots of rebuilding is going on. You can check the United Nations Relief and Works Agency for Palestine Refugees in the Near East site for information. I couldn't find anything specifically mentioning a "Jenin refugee camp 23."

For the sake of research, here's some ownership information on the domains associated with ES5:

```
Checking server [whois.crsnic.net]
Checking server [whois.namescout.com]
Results:
Domain earthstation5.com
```

Date Registered: 2002-2-26
Date Modified: 2002-6-13
Expiry Date: 2005-2-26
DNS1: ns1.earthstationv.com
DNS2: ns2.earthstationv.com

Registrant

Earthstationv Ltd, A Vanuatu Corporation
Jenin refugee camp #23
Jenin
PS
NONE

Administrative Contact

EarthstationV Ltd., A Vanuatu Corporation
Mr Domain Administrator
Jenin refugee camp #23
Jenin
NONE
PS
067351065
67351065
ras@earthstationv.com

Technical Contact

EarthstationV Ltd., A Vanuatu Corporation
Mr Domain Administrator
Jenin refugee camp #23
Jenin
NONE
PS
067351065
67351065
ras@earthstationv.com

Registrar: NameScout.com

Register your domain now at www.namescout.com

===

```
Checking server [whois.crsnic.net]
Checking server [whois.namescout.com]
Results:
```

Domain es5.com

Date Registered: 12/9/2001
Date Modified: 3/28/2003
Expiry Date: 12/9/2004
DNS1: NS1.EARTHSTATIONV.COM
DNS2: NS2.EARTHSTATIONV.COM

Registrant

Earthstationv Ltd., A Vanuatu Corporation
Jenin refugee camp #23
Jenin (PS)
NONE

Administrative Contact

EarthstationV Ltd., A Vanuatu Corporation
Mr Domain Administrator
Jenin refugee camp #23
Jenin (PS)
NONE
067351065
67351065
N-88532yfvx@usersa5.namescout.com

Technical Contact

EarthstationV Ltd., A Vanuatu Corporation
Mr Domain Administrator
Jenin refugee camp #23
Jenin (PS)
NONE
067351065
67351065
N-88532yfvx@usersa5.namescout.com

Registrar: NameScout.com

Register your domain now at www.namescout.com

===

129

```
Checking server [whois.crsnic.net]
Checking server [whois.namescout.com]
Results:
Domain earthstationv.com
```

Date Registered: 3/10/2002
Date Modified: 2002-6-13
Expiry Date: 2005-3-10
DNS1: NS1.EARTHSTATIONV.COM
DNS2: NS2.EARTHSTATIONV.COM

Registrant

Earthstationv Ltd, A Vanuatu Corporation
Jenin refugee camp #23
Jenin
PS
NONE

Administrative Contact

EarthstationV Ltd., A Vanuatu Corporation
Mr Domain Administrator
Jenin refugee camp #23
Jenin
PS
NONE
067351065
67351065
ras@earthstationv.com

Technical Contact

EarthstationV Ltd., A Vanuatu Corporation
Mr Domain Administrator
Jenin refugee camp #23
Jenin
NONE
PS
067351065
67351065

ras@earthstationv.com

Registrar: NameScout.com

Register your domain now at www.namescout.com

==

```
Checking server [whois.crsnic.net]
Checking server [whois.namescout.com]
Results:
Domain earthstationfive.com
```

Date Registered: 2002-2-26
Date Modified: 2002-6-10
Expiry Date: 2005-2-26
DNS1: NS1.EARTHSTATIONV.COM
DNS2: NS2.EARTHSTATIONV.COM

Registrant

Earthstationv Ltd, A Vanuatu Corporation
Jenin refugee camp #23
Jenin
PS
NONE

Administrative Contact

EarthstationV Ltd., A Vanuatu Corporation
Mr Domain Administrator
Jenin refugee camp #23
Jenin (PS)
NONE
067351065
67351065
ras@earthstationv.com

Technical Contact

EarthstationV Ltd., A Vanuatu Corporation
Mr Domain Administrator

Jenin refugee camp #23
Jenin (PS)
NONE
067351065
67351065
ras@earthstationv.com

Registrar: NameScout.com

Register your domain now at www.namescout.com

Here is a query against ns1.earthstationv.com for DNS records:

; <<>> DiG 8.2 <<>> @ns1.earthstationv.com earthstationv.com ANY
; (1 server found)
;; res options: init recurs defnam dnsrch
;; got answer:
;; ->>HEADER<<- opcode: QUERY, status: NOERROR, id: 6
;; flags: qr aa rd; QUERY: 1, ANSWER: 5, AUTHORITY: 0, ADDITIONAL: 2
;; QUERY SECTION:
;; earthstationv.com, type = ANY, class = IN

;; ANSWER SECTION:
earthstationv.com. 1H IN SOA earthstationv.com.earthstationv.com.
root.earthstationv.com. (
    200350918 ; serial
    3H ; refresh
    1H ; retry
    1W ; expiry
    1D) ; minimum

earthstationv.com. 1H IN NS ns2.earthstationv.com.
earthstationv.com. 1H IN NS ns1.earthstationv.com.
earthstationv.com. 1H IN A 213.152.100.163
earthstationv.com. 1H IN MX 10 earthstationv.com.

;; ADDITIONAL SECTION:
ns1.earthstationv.com. 1H IN A 213.152.100.163
ns2.earthstationv.com. 1H IN A 213.152.119.35

;; Total query time: 262 msec

;; FROM: gp.centergate.com to SERVER: ns1.earthstationv.com 213.152.100.163
;; WHEN: Thu Aug 28 21:12:19 2003
;; MSG SIZE sent: 35 rcvd: 194

Here's traceroute output, first to the site's home page in Israel and then to its movie download page, also in Israel. How can that be? Well, the last resolved router name in the first trace is 212.199.218.130.forward.012.net.il, which makes us think the end node is in Israel. The last resolved router name in the second trace is unknown.Level3.net, which tells us nothing. The prior router is gige10-2.ipcolo1.Amsterdam1.Level3.net, which makes us think the end node might be in Amsterdam too. This is not the case.

We'll see in the BGP data later that Level 3 is listed as an "adjacent" AS, which might indicate its placement in the traceroute data. Both end nodes, the web site and the download site, belong to the same company (ES5). ES5 receives its connectivity from "SpeedNet," which we'll learn about later. First, traceroutes from a publicly available traceroute server to each host:

```
FROM www.above.net TO www.earthstationv.com.

traceroute to www.earthstationv.com (213.152.100.163), 30
hops max, 40 byte packets
 1  inside.fw1.sjc2.mfnx.net (208.184.213.129)  0.311 ms
0.245 ms  0.219 ms
 2  99.ge-5-1-1.er10a.sjc2.us.above.net (64.124.216.10)
0.534 ms  0.545 ms  0.500 ms
 3  so-2-0-0.mpr3.sjc2.us.above.net (64.125.30.89)  0.569 ms
0.513 ms  0.500 ms
 4  so-5-1-0.cr1.dca2.us.above.net (208.184.233.134)  66.905
ms  66.742 ms  66.736 ms
 5  so-6-0-0.cr1.lhr3.uk.above.net (64.125.31.185)  138.525
ms  138.568 ms  138.596 ms
 6  pos9-0.cr1.ams2.nl.above.net (64.125.31.154)  144.160 ms
144.232 ms  144.174 ms
 7  pos14-0.mpr1.ams1.nl.above.net (208.184.231.53)  144.717
ms  144.756 ms  144.712 ms
 8  so-1-3-0.cr2.fra1.de.above.net (64.125.30.149)  151.540
ms  151.440 ms  151.498 ms
```

```
 9  pos3-0.pr1.fra1.de.mfnx.net (216.200.116.210)  151.395
ms  151.640 ms  151.411 ms
10  decix-abovenet-us.fra.seabone.net (195.22.211.45)
151.487 ms  151.320 ms  151.478 ms
11  pal6-pal8-racc1.pal.seabone.net (195.22.218.229)
180.994 ms  181.401 ms  180.925 ms
12  goldenlines-1-il-pal6.seabone.net (195.22.196.194)
206.393 ms  206.489 ms  206.300 ms
13  212.199.28.65 (212.199.28.65)  221.834 ms  206.473 ms
206.520 ms
14  212.199.28.242 (212.199.28.242)  208.880 ms  208.337 ms
208.309 ms
15  212.199.26.35 (212.199.26.35)  210.346 ms  210.450 ms
210.242 ms
16  212.199.218.130.forward.012.net.il (212.199.218.130)
211.823 ms  210.629 ms  210.658 ms
17  213.152.100.254 (213.152.100.254)  208.999 ms  209.503
ms  209.039 ms
18  213.152.100.163 (213.152.100.163)  211.880 ms *  212.004
ms


===


FROM www.above.net TO movies.earthstationv.com.

traceroute to movies.earthstationv.com (213.152.119.82), 30
hops max, 40 byte packets
 1  inside.fw1.sjc2.mfnx.net (208.184.213.129)  0.301 ms
0.533 ms  0.227 ms
 2  99.ge-5-1-1.er10a.sjc2.us.above.net (64.124.216.10)
0.573 ms  0.496 ms  0.467 ms
 3  so-1-0-0.mpr4.sjc2.us.above.net (64.125.30.93)  0.506 ms
0.519 ms  0.484 ms
 4  pos-1-0.mpr2.pao1.us.above.net (209.249.0.125)  0.932 ms
0.894 ms  0.834 ms
 5  GigabitEthernet6-0.edge1.paix-sjo1.Level3.net
(209.245.146.157)  0.877 ms  1.041 ms  0.799 ms
 6  GigabitEthernet3-1.core1.SanJose1.Level3.net
(209.244.3.249)  1.213 ms  1.185 ms  1.188 ms
 7  ae0-55.mp1.SanJose1.Level3.net (64.159.2.129)  1.692 ms
1.622 ms  1.680 ms
 8  so-0-1-0.bbr1.Washington1.level3.net (64.159.0.229)
80.943 ms  79.589 ms  79.546 ms
 9  so-2-0-0.mp1.London2.Level3.net (212.187.128.137)
147.371 ms  147.342 ms  147.247 ms
10  so-2-0-0.mp1.Amsterdam1.Level3.net (212.187.128.26)
160.888 ms  160.546 ms  160.582 ms
```

```
11  gige10-2.ipcolo1.Amsterdam1.Level3.net (213.244.165.99)
160.796 ms  160.925 ms  160.833 ms
12  unknown.Level3.net (213.244.164.18)  160.973 ms  161.061
ms  161.095 ms
13  213.152.119.253 (213.152.119.253)  161.885 ms  161.306
ms  161.367 ms
14  213.152.119.82 (213.152.119.82)  161.864 ms  161.294 ms
162.110 ms
```

RIPE reports that ES5 owns the following netblocks:

213.152.100.0 - 213.152.101.255

213.152.102.0 - 213.152.102.127

213.152.102.128 - 213.152.102.192

213.152.102.193 - 213.152.102.209

213.152.119.0 - 213.152.120.255

213.152.121.0 - 213.152.121.63

213.152.123.0 - 213.152.123.128

Both "Nasser" and "Ras" Kabir are listed as owners. Here are the
details on netblocks owned by earthstationv, as returned by RIPE:

```
inetnum:   213.152.119.0 - 213.152.120.255
netname:   EARTHSTATIONV
descr:     Employee's VOIP and workstations in the
           Jenin refugee camp #23
country:   PS
admin-c:   RAS9905-RIPE
tech-c:    NKA9905-RIPE
remarks:   Speednet's # 2002122740
status:    ASSIGNED PA
mnt-by:    SPEEDNET-MNT
notify:    admin@earthstationv.com
mnt-routes: EARTHSV-MNT
mnt-lower: EARTHSV-MNT
changed:   speednet@email.com 20021231
source:    RIPE

inetnum:   213.152.102.0 - 213.152.102.127
netname:   EARTHSTATIONV
```

```
descr:      VOIP Dialup Gateway
country:    PS
admin-c:    RAS9905-RIPE
tech-c:     NKA9905-RIPE
status:     ASSIGNED PA
notify:     admin@earthstationv.com
remarks:    Speednet's #2002122740
mnt-by:     SPEEDNET-MNT
mnt-routes: EARTHSV-MNT
mnt-lower:  EARTHSV-MNT
changed:    speednet@email.com 20021231
source:     RIPE


inetnum:    213.152.121.0 - 213.152.121.63
netname:    EARTHSTATIONV
descr:      Peer to Peer IP network
country:    PS
admin-c:    RAS9905-RIPE
tech-c:     NKA9905-RIPE
status:     ASSIGNED PA
notify:     admin@earthstationv.com
remarks:    Speednet's #2002122740
mnt-by:     SPEEDNET-MNT
mnt-routes: EARTHSV-MNT
mnt-lower:  EARTHSV-MNT
changed:    speednet@email.com 20021231
source:     RIPE


inetnum:    213.152.102.128 - 213.152.102.192
netname:    EARTHSTATIONV
descr:      Internet Café in Hebron, Gaza City and Jenin
            Palestine
country:    PS
admin-c:    RAS9905-RIPE
tech-c:     NKA9905-RIPE
status:     ASSIGNED PA
notify:     admin@earthstationv.com
remarks:    Speednet's #2002122740
mnt-by:     SPEEDNET-MNT
mnt-routes: EARTHSV-MNT
mnt-lower:  EARTHSV-MNT
changed:    speednet@email.com 20021231
```

source: RIPE

inetnum: 213.152.102.193 - 213.152.102.209
netname: EARTHSTATIONV
descr: Video and sound Broadcasting
            from the El-Bureij Refugee Camp in Gaza, Palestine
country: PS
admin-c: RAS9905-RIPE
tech-c: NKA9905-RIPE
status: ASSIGNED PA
notify: admin@earthstationv.com
remarks: Speednet's #2002122740
mnt-by: SPEEDNET-MNT
mnt-routes: EARTHSV-MNT
mnt-lower: EARTHSV-MNT
changed: speednet@email.com 20030102
source: RIPE

inetnum: 213.152.100.0 - 213.152.101.255
netname: EARTHSTATIONV
descr: Peer to Peer Ebay Web Pages
country: PS
admin-c: RAS9905-RIPE
tech-c: NKA9905-RIPE
status: ASSIGNED PA
notify: admin@earthstationv.com
remarks: Speednet's #2002122740
mnt-by: SPEEDNET-MNT
mnt-routes: EARTHSV-MNT
mnt-lower: EARTHSV-MNT
changed: speednet@email.com 20021231
source: RIPE

inetnum: 213.152.123.0 - 213.152.123.128
netname: EARTHSTATIONV
descr: DialUP Palestine
country: PS
admin-c: RAS9905-RIPE
tech-c: NKA9905-RIPE
status: ASSIGNED PA
mnt-by: SPEEDNET-MNT
changed: speednet@email.com 20030325

source: RIPE

role: Earthstationv Hostmaster
address: Jenin refugee camp #23
         Palestine
notify: raskabir@gaza.net
trouble: If you have a problem you can email us at
         help@earthstationv.com For sales contact
         sales@earthstationv.com
phone: +972 673 51065
e-mail: admin@earthstationv.com
admin-c: RAS9905-RIPE
tech-c: NKA9905-RIPE
nic-hdl: EAR0007-RIPE
mnt-by: SPEEDNET-MNT
changed: raskabir@gaza.net 20021231
source: RIPE

person: Ras Kabir
address: 121 Gaza
address: Gaza, Palestine
phone: +972 673 51065
fax-no: +972 673 51065
mnt-by: SPEEDNET-MNT
e-mail: ras@earthstationv.com
nic-hdl: RAS9905-RIPE
changed: ras@earthstationv.com 20030717
source: RIPE

person: Nasser Kabir
address: 121 Gasa
address: Gaza, Palestine
phone: +972 673 51065
fax-no: +972 673 51065
mnt-by: SPEEDNET-MNT
e-mail: ras@earthstationv.com
nic-hdl: NKA9905-RIPE
changed: ras@earthstationv.com 20030717
source: RIPE

The records show SpeedNet is the provider:

138

```
mntner:      SPEEDNET-MNT
descr:       SPEEDNET maintainer
admin-c:     MM9905-RIPE
tech-c:      MO2551-RIPE
upd-to:      domain@17q.com
mnt-nfy:     domain@17q.com
auth:        MD5-PW $1$hlXT6LEy$iBPFGRF8VXAjVUVBVkdZG1
mnt-by:      SPEEDNET-MNT
referral-by: RIPE-DBM-MNT
changed:     speednet@email.com 20020924
changed:     ripe-dbm@ripe.net 20030508
source:      RIPE

person:      Moshe Maimone
address:     63 Saudia Gaon
        Hertzlya, Israel
phone:       +39247585
nic-hdl:     MM9905-RIPE
mnt-by:      SPEEDNET-MNT
changed:     Speednet@email.com 20030508
source:      RIPE

person:      Motti Oran
address:     25 Hasivin Street
        Petach Tikva, Israel 49170
phone:       +039247585
fax-no:      +039247736
mnt-by:      SPEEDNET-MNT
notify:      speednet@email.com
e-mail:      motti@speed-net.com
nic-hdl:     MO2551-RIPE
changed:     speednet@email.com 20030105
source:      RIPE
```

I determined SpeedNet's Autonomous System Number (ASN)
using a route server:

```
route-server.he.net>show ip bgp 213.152.100.163

BGP routing table entry for 213.152.100.0/24, version
245489010
Paths: (7 available, best #6, table
Default-IP-Routing-Table)
  Not advertised to any peer
  7911 6762 9116 25276
    64.200.150.105 from 216.218.252.147 (216.218.252.147)
      Origin IGP, metric 46, localpref 100, valid, internal
      Originator: 216.218.252.146, Cluster list:
216.218.252.147
  7911 6762 9116 25276
    64.200.150.105 from 216.218.252.149 (216.218.252.149)
      Origin IGP, metric 46, localpref 100, valid, internal
      Originator: 216.218.252.146, Cluster list:
216.218.252.149
  7911 6762 9116 25276
    216.218.252.146 from 216.218.252.146 (216.218.252.146)
      Origin IGP, metric 46, localpref 100, valid, internal
  7911 6762 9116 25276
    64.200.150.105 from 216.218.252.151 (216.218.252.151)
      Origin IGP, metric 60, localpref 100, valid, internal
      Originator: 216.218.252.146, Cluster list:
216.218.252.151
  7911 6762 9116 25276
    64.200.150.105 from 216.218.252.145 (216.218.252.145)
      Origin IGP, metric 46, localpref 100, valid, internal
      Originator: 216.218.252.146, Cluster list:
216.218.252.145
  6461 6762 9116 25276
    216.66.23.99 from 216.66.23.99 (216.66.23.99)
      Origin IGP, metric 45, localpref 100, valid,
internal, best
  6461 6762 9116 25276
    216.200.56.53 from 216.218.252.152 (216.218.252.152)
      Origin IGP, metric 45, localpref 100, valid, internal
      Originator: 216.66.23.99, Cluster list:
216.218.252.152
```

SpeedNet's ASN was the last number in each list, meaning '25276'. I
then queried cidr-report.org for more information on ASN 25276. I
could have also queried ARIN for similar information.

Report for AS25276
SPEEDNET-AS Speednet Ltd, An Israel Corporation

Whois Entry
IANA has recorded AS25276 as originally allocated by RIPE
RIRs have AS25276 whois information provided by RIPE
-No Whois Entry Obtained-

AS Adjancency Report

In the context of this report "Upstream" indicates that there is an adjacent AS that
lies between the BGP table collection point (in this case at AS4637) as the specified
AS. Similarly, "Downstream" refers to an adjacent AS that lies beyond the specified
AS. This upstream / downstream categorisation is strictly a description relative
topology, and should not be confused with provider / customer / peer inter-AS
relationships.

5963 AS25276 SPEEDNET-AS Speednet Ltd, An Israel Corporation
Adjacency: 2 Upstream: 2 Downstream: 0
Upstream Adjacent AS list
AS3356 LEVEL3 Level 3 Communications, LLC
AS9116 AS9116 Goldenlines main autonomous system

Announced Prefixes
Rank AS Type Originate Addr Space (pfx) Transit Addr space (pfx) Description
9865 AS25276 ORIGIN Originate: 1280 /21.68 Transit: 0 /0.00 SPEEDNET-AS
Speednet Ltd, An Israel Corporation

Aggregation Suggestions

This report does not take into account conditions local to each origin AS in terms of
policy or traffic engineering requirements, so this is an approximate guideline as to
aggregation possibilities.

Rank AS AS Name Current Wthdw Aggte Annce Redctn %
3730 AS25276 SPEEDNET-AS Speednet Ltd, An Israel Cor 5 2 1 4 1 20.00%

AS25276: SPEEDNET-AS Speednet Ltd, An Israel Corporation
Prefix (AS Path) Aggregation Action
213.152.96.0/24 6762 9116 25276
213.152.99.0/24 3356 25276

213.152.100.0/23 6762 9116 25276 + Announce - aggregate of 213.152.100.0/24
(6762 9116 25276) and 213.152.101.0/24 (6762 9116 25276)
213.152.100.0/24 6762 9116 25276 - Withdrawn - aggregated with
213.152.101.0/24 (6762 9116 25276)
213.152.101.0/24 6762 9116 25276 - Withdrawn - aggregated with
213.152.100.0/24 (6762 9116 25276)
213.152.119.0/24 3356 25276

What does this all mean? I'm not sure, but I hope you followed along and discovered all the different sorts of information you can learn given only a few IP addresses and domain names. I didn't touch ES5 to get any of this, other than visiting their web site to grab a few screenshots. I'd like to download their software and test it in the lab next.

https://taosecurity.blogspot.com/2003/08/is-earth-station-five-hoax-is-earth.html

Commentary

Years later it became clear that ES5 was run by one or more shady characters with no relationship to the Middle East. It was gone by 2005. This February 2005 story by reporter Thomas Mennecke captures the gory details.

https://web.archive.org/web/20050224160315/http://www.slyck.com/news.php?story=678

Apparently ES5 was a file sharing network that used Palestine as a cover story to obscure its operators.

I included this post to demonstrate some of what can be learned from IP addresses and domain names. These days, analysts don't have easy access to as many details on domain names, thanks to so-called "privacy enhancements" affecting domain name registrations.

Problems with Signature and Protocol Anomaly Detection Methods

Monday, April 04, 2005

I often have to describe what differentiates network security monitoring from traditional intrusion detection. Now that "intrusion prevention" is all the rage (when was preventing intrusions not popular?), I have to think in terms of blocking traffic that is potentially suspicious or malicious. Recently while performing network security monitoring, I received the following Snort alert, as reported by Sguil. I had never seen an alert like this before. Here is a text-based representation of what Sguil displayed in its GUI:

```
Count:1 Event#3.57183 2005-03-31 23:24:14
FTP invalid MODE
1.30.163.130 -> 2.35.23.101
IPVer=4 hlen=5 tos=0 dlen=48 ID=42411 flags=2
 offset=0 ttl=117 chksum=0
Protocol: 6 sport=9542 -> dport=21

Seq=3804195312 Ack=735521810 Off=5 Res=0
 Flags=***AP*** Win=63842 urp=23116 chksum=0
Payload:
4D 4F 44 45 20 5A 0D 0A                    MODE Z..
```

That looks odd. What is "MODE Z"? Here is the Snort rule that produced this alert:

```
alert tcp $EXTERNAL_NET any -> $HOME_NET 21
  (msg:"FTP invalid MODE"; flow:to_server,established;
  content:"MODE"; nocase;
pcre:"/^MODE\s+[^ABSC]{1}/msi";
  classtype:protocol-command-decode; sid:1623; rev:6;)
```

I am no PCRE expert, but I can see that "MODE Z" will trigger this rule. The Snort rule documentation doesn't shed any real light on

143

the subject. A Google search result reveals that "MODE Z" enables dynamic data compression via the zlib library.

If we were using a Web-based alert browser, this would be the end of the line. There would be no other data to review other than the packet that tripped the rule and the rule itself. How did the Web server respond? Did it respond at all? What FTP server is running? These and other questions remain unanswered when you use an IDS whose chief purpose in life is to generate alert data.

Fortunately, we're using Sguil. We recognize there's more to life than alert data; there's session, full content, and statistical data. We can generate a transcript of their entire conversation between the FTP client and server if we collected the full content data between both parties. Here is that transcript:

Sensor Name: bej-sensor-fl
Timestamp: 2005-03-31 23:24:14
Connection ID: .bej-sensor-fl_57183
Src IP: 1.30.163.130 (mail.example.com)
Dst IP: 2.35.23.101 (Unknown)
Src Port: 9542
Dst Port: 21
OS Fingerprint: 1.30.163.130:9542 - Windows XP Pro SP1, 2000 SP3
OS Fingerprint: -> 2.35.23.101:21 (distance 11, link: ethernet/modem)

DST: 220 Serv-U FTP Server v5.1 for WinSock ready...
DST:
SRC: USER example
SRC:
DST: 331 User name okay, need password.
DST:
SRC: PASS example
SRC:
DST: 230 User logged in, proceed.
DST:
SRC: SYST
SRC:
DST: 215 UNIX Type: L8

DST:
SRC: FEAT
SRC:
DST: 211-Extension supported
DST:
DST: AUTH TLS
DST: SSCN
DST: PBSZ
DST: PROT
DST: CCC
DST: CLNT
DST: MDTM
DST: MDTM YYYYMMDDHHMMSS[+-TZ];filename
DST: SIZE
DST: SITE PSWD;EXEC;SET;INDEX;ZONE;CHMOD;MSG
DST: REST STREAM
DST: XCRC filename;start;end
DST: MODE Z
DST: 211 End
DST:
SRC: CLNT SmartFTP 1.1.984
SRC:
DST: 200 Noted.
DST:
SRC: PWD
SRC:
DST: 257 "/" is current directory.
DST:
SRC: MODE Z
SRC:
DST: 200 MODE Z ok.
DST:
SRC: PASV
SRC:
DST: 227 Entering Passive Mode (2,35,23,101,9,24)
DST:
SRC: LIST -aLT
SRC:
DST: 150 Opening ASCII mode data connection for /bin/ls.
DST:
DST: 226 Transfer complete.
DST:

```
SRC: TYPE I
SRC:
DST: 200 Type set to I.
DST:
SRC: PASV
SRC:
DST: 227 Entering Passive Mode (2,35,23,101,9,25)
DST:
SRC: STOR test.txt.asc
SRC:
DST: 150 Opening BINARY mode data connection for test.txt.asc.
DST:
DST: 226 Transfer complete.
SRC: QUIT
SRC:
DST: 221 Goodbye!
DST:
```

Based on the transcript, we see the Serv-U FTP Server v5.1 for
WinSock offer MODE Z, and the client decides to use it before
transferring several files. There is nothing suspicious or malicious
about this exchange. It is completely within business norms.

This example highlights the use of a signature to implement protocol
anomaly detection. The signature provided a "white list" of
acceptable MODEs. These MODEs were believed to represent
normal use of the FTP protocol. Deviations from these norms were
thought to be anomalies that indicate intrusion.

This is a fine approach to detecting intrusions, but it highlights a
problem that I constantly debate with security developers. I contend
that the Internet and its protocols are too dynamic to code into
highly reliable systems. Application developers will forever be ahead
of security developers. Application developers will always be crafting
new protocols or bending and breaking old protocols. Security
developers will constantly try to keep redefining what is "normal"
and "abnormal" to enforce access control, detect intrusions, and so
on.

The consequences of firing an alert for the MODE Z case are minimal when an IDS is involved. If the IDS were replaced by an inline, so-called "IPS," it may have dropped the traffic. The layer 7 firewall -- sorry, "IPS" -- might believe MODE Z is an attack, thereby denying legitimate business functions. Sure, you can "tune it," but there's another application developer out there creating another twist on what the security developer considers normal. So, in addition to the never-ending battle with intruders, security staff face a never-ending battle with developers!

What is my answer? Block what you can, as smartly as you can, and then keep track of everything else via a network audit system. Content-neutral systems store session and full content data to provide network audit. If you ever forget the network audit piece of the IDS/"IPS" puzzle, and concentrate on alert data, you will lose.

https://taosecurity.blogspot.com/2005/04/problems-with-signature-and-protocol.html

Commentary

Detection engineers like to talk about using so-called "allow" lists rather than "deny" lists when creating signatures... I mean "analytics." In this case, any FTP mode other than A, B, S, or C was assumed to be suspicious or malicious. "ABSC" constituted the allow list. When mode "Z" appeared, this alert fired. Thankfully, FTP was a clear text protocol, and I was able to use type III NSM to see the exact nature of the data exchanged between the FTP client and the server, and determine that nothing untoward occurred.

These days, with so many more encrypted protocols, I would likely not get a signature-based alert. The command channel would be encrypted. Type I NSM might indicate something suspicious was occurring, and I could use type II NSM to identify its general characteristics. Determining ground truth might require investigating infrastructure or application logs, or even querying a host-based agent for evidence.

How Do You Fit Into the Security Community?

Monday, July 17, 2006

I've spent some time beefing up my RSS feeds. As I look for people with ideas that could be useful, I'm reminded of the vast differences among those who would all presumably claim to be "security professionals." I am acutely aware of these differences when I visit security conferences, and I wrote about this phenomenon after attending USENIX 2003, Black Hat 2003, and SANS NIAL 2003 within a span of 30 days.

At the risk of being attacked for promoting stereotypes or hurting feelings, I decided to share a few thoughts on this subject. What group describes you?

Academics: This group consists of undergraduates, graduates, PhD candidates, and faculty. They tend to frequent USENIX conferences where they will be talking about the latest security protocol. They have ties to government organizations because that is the source of grant money. They write papers, mostly speak in front of other academics, and take deep looks at improving security technologies in formal and peer-reviewed ways. Academics obviously have formal training and they tend to have tinkered with security before joining this group.

Policemen: (Police women also fit here!) Policemen enforce the law. They like to talk about who they have "busted." They seem to often assume duties for which they are not prepared. They are overwhelmed by the amount of work they face, even though they are one of the few groups who can eliminate threats. Their organizations usually consider their work to be secondary to "real law enforcement." Sometimes their bosses don't even read email. Policemen tend to struggle to understand technology because they usually come from traditional police backgrounds, and their workload ensures no free time to tinker. Policemen often concentrate on host-based forensics, and they attend HTCIA and InfraGard conferences.

Government civilians and contractors: Government civilians and contractors obsess over certifications. They are most likely to be talking about CISSP, PMP, ISSAP, ISSEP, GIAC, and so on at ISSA meetings. They often perform certification and accreditation and don't understand why those processes are broken. Some of them are trying very hard to fix their agencies, but they struggle with political infighting and bureaucratic inertia. This group likes SANS and CSI conferences.

Warfighters: This is the uniform-wearing military. This group is youngish and skilled. Many of them would fit into the "hacker" category (see below) but they are definitely on the white hat side. They are sharp because their infrastructures are under constant assault. Unfortunately the military personnel system generally offers no career path to develop their skills and interests. This group tends to leave the military for the commercial or government worlds just when they are becoming real experts. Warfighters attend their own closed conferences but they also try to learn from their opponents at offensive-minded conferences like Black Hat or CanSec.

Hackers: To some degree all of the groups here would want to consider themselves "hackers," with the exception of policemen and some government civilians. (Being a hacker is supposed to be cool, but some consider it to be bad.) In reality, you know a hacker when you talk to him or her. Hackers tend to have extremely deep technical knowledge in very specific areas. A hacker might write his own compiler or debugger, but not practice sound system administration practices. (For example, a hacker might think it's ok to put all system files in a single partition on a production server.) Hackers are the source of real public innovation in attack methodologies and they are extremely creative and unpredictable. Hackers are more likely to speak at conferences like Black Hat or CanSec, but they seem to be migrating to smaller or private gatherings. Hackers are some of the youngest members of the security community, but as they build families and get older they migrate to another group. When young they are either in high school or college. Upon graduation (from either place), hackers usually work as consultants. Sometimes they work directly for governments or the military.

Consultants/Corporates: This group includes those who work for security companies, and those who provide security services within non-security companies. Consultants and corporates are a very diverse group, drawing upon most of the earlier categories. Many corporates have general IT backgrounds and "end up" in security because they staff a one- or two-person IT shop. If they are serious about providing good services, and their employers agree, they tend to specialize in one or two areas. (Companies who expect consultants and corporates to be experts in everything should expect disaster.) This group is second to the government civilians and contractors in pursuing certifications, because they think clients will value them or their employers will reward them.

Developers: The last group creates security products, but I prefer to concentrate on those who participate in the design process. (Code monkeys who implement without consideration for underlying security principles aren't really security people.) Security developers are usually former members of the other groups, since serving two roles is too tough. Developers have decided they want to solve a problem encountered in their previous lives. They are very skilled in their work area, with depth of knowledge rivalling the hackers. Some developers are older hackers.

Did I miss anyone?

Keep in mind that some people may fit in one category while working in another category. For example, I know many "hackers" who are government contractors during their day jobs. Many consultants are like government civilians or contractors. Also note I do not consider any of these people to be the adversary. I will not be discussing threats.

I wanted to record these thoughts, because you can probably imagine the diversity of opinion suggested by this list. I have some ties to each of these groups, and they approach problems from very different angles. I have no way of knowing the sorts of people who read my blog, but in some ways I'm guessing few hackers, developers, or policemen read it. I could be wrong though.

I would be interested in hearing your thoughts, especially if you can help refine/define these categories. This is not some sort of formal taxonomy, just some ideas.

https://taosecurity.blogspot.com/2006/07/how-do-you-fit-into-security-community.html

Commentary

This is a look into my mindset and perceptions concerning information security practitioners, circa 2006. At this point I was working for myself at TaoSecurity LLC, so I came into contact with many sorts of security people. Since this time, the intelligence community has become a major player in the information security scene, so I would add them to my list. I did not discuss the gray or criminal communities in this post, as that was neither my audience nor my interest.

Bloom's Hierarchy for Digital Security Learning

Tuesday, October 17, 2006

Twenty years ago, when some of my readers were busy being born, I was a high school freshman. My favorite instructor, Don Stavely, taught history. One of the educational devices he used was Bloom et al.'s *Taxonomy of the Cognitive Domain*. This hierarchy, which travels from bottom to top, is a way to describe a student's level of understanding of a given subject.

These descriptions from Purdue are helpful. They start at the bottom of the hierarchy and progress to the top.

Knowledge entails the ability to recall or state information.

Comprehension entails the ability to give meaning to information.

Application entails the ability to use knowledge or principles in new or real-life situations.

Analysis entails the ability to break down complex information into simpler parts and to understand the relationships among the parts.

Synthesis entails the act of creating something that did not exist before by integrating information that had been learned at lower levels of the hierarchy.

Evaluation entails the ability to make judgments based on previous levels of learning to compare a product of some kind against a designated standard.

I find this to be a useful way to evaluate mastery of a given subject.

For example, I propose that many people detest technical certifications because they perceive the candidates as simply working at the *knowledge* level.

I think many people were disappointed by the removal of the SANS practical requirement, because meeting that challenge required work at the *synthesis* level -- a very high mark indeed.

I keep this hierarchy in mind when I review books. If I am reading material related to network security monitoring, I can absolutely make judgements not only about accuracy but also about relevance and worth. That's an *evaluation* level activity. On the other hand, books about reverse engineering malicious code might strain my ability to review at the *comprehension* or even the *knowledge* level when discussing assembly language.

If you're responsible for hiring people, you might consider using some of these ideas in your interviews. A security architect should demonstrate skills at the *synthesis* or *evaluation* levels, while those on the entry level should function at least at the *knowledge* level.

https://taosecurity.blogspot.com/2006/10/blooms-hierarchy-for-digital-security.html

Commentary

Dr. Benjamin S. Bloom (1913-1999) was an educator and researcher. The 1948 Convention of the American Psychological Association prompted Dr. Bloom to "develop a method of classification for thinking behaviors that were believed to be important in the processes of learning." In 1956 Dr. Bloom and his colleagues published Bloom's Taxonomy, which formed the basis for this post.

In 1995, one of Dr. Bloom's colleagues, Dr. Lorin Anderson (b. 1945) led a new group tasked with updating the taxonomy. They published their work in 2001. Two of the more significant changes include the following.

First, the six major categories were changed from nouns to verbs. Second, the top two elements were switched in position, making the creation of knowledge (previously "synthesis") higher than the evaluation of knowledge.

In her summary of the new 2001 edition of the taxonomy, Mary Forehand cites a 2001 source by Anderson and Krathwohl, providing the following description of each level, from lowest to highest:

- **Remembering**: Retrieving, recognizing, and recalling relevant knowledge from long-term memory.
- **Understanding**: Constructing meaning from oral, written, and graphic messages through interpreting, exemplifying, classifying, summarizing, inferring, comparing, and explaining.
- **Applying**: Carrying out or using a procedure through executing, or implementing.
- **Analyzing**: Breaking material into constituent parts, determining how the parts relate to one another and to an overall structure or purpose through differentiating, organizing, and attributing.
- **Evaluating**: Making judgments based on criteria and standards through checking and critiquing.
- **Creating**: Putting elements together to form a coherent or functional whole; reorganizing elements into a new pattern or structure through generating, planning, or producing.

There are other changes to the taxonomy. Those who would like to learn more would enjoy reading this document:

http://epltt.coe.uga.edu/index.php?title=Bloom%27s_Taxonomy#Bloom_-_Biography

Could you imagine using these terms in job descriptions?

"Demonstrate *knowledge* of the TCP/IP networking" vs "demonstrate the ability to *evaluate* implementations of TCP/IP networking."

Hardly anything in the security industry is standardized, but using these terms might be useful.

Digital Security Lessons from Ice Hockey

Friday, November 24, 2006

I'm struck by the amount of attention we seem to be paying to discovering vulnerabilities and writing exploits. I call this "offensive" work, in the sense that the fruits of such labor can be used to attack and compromise targets. This work can be justified as a defensive activity if we accept the full disclosure argument that truly bad guys already know about these and similar vulnerabilities, or that so-called responsible disclosure motivates vendors to fix their software. This post isn't about the disclosure debate, however. Instead, I'm wondering what this means for those of us who don't do offensive work, either due to lack of skills or opportunity/responsibility.

It occurred to me today that we are witnessing the sort of change that happened to the National Hockey League in the late 1960s and early 1970s. During that time, Bobby Orr changed the game of ice hockey forever. For those of you unfamiliar with hockey, teams field six players: one goalie, who guards the net; two defensemen, who try to stop opposing players; and three forwards (one center and two wings), who try to score goals.

Prior to Orr, defensemen almost never took offensive roles. (Forwards didn't pay much attention to defense, either. Only in 1978 did the Selke Trophy, for best defensive forward, start being awarded.) When Orr began playing, he wasn't satisfied to control the puck in his defensive end and then hand it off to one of his forwards. He jumped into the play, sometimes carrying the puck end-to-end, finishing by scoring himself. Twice in his ten year career he even led the league in scoring -- scoring more goals than forwards. He didn't neglect his defensive duties, either. He was named league best defenseman eight years straight.

What does this mean for digital security? It's easy to identify the forwards in our game. They discover and write exploits. Some of them can play defense, while others cannot. Many of us are traditional defensemen. We know how to impede the opposing team, and we know enough offense to understand how the enemy forwards operate. A few of us are goalies. Aside from clearing the zone or maybe making a solid pass to a forward, goalies have near-zero ability to score goals. (Yes, I remember Ron Hextall.) That's the nature of their position -- they can't skate to the other end of the ice!

Anyone who plays a sport will probably recognize the term "well-rounded." Being well-rounded means knowledge and capability in offense and defense. I think it applies very well to ice hockey and basketball, less so to soccer, somewhat well to baseball, and not at all to football. I see well-roundedness as the proper trait for the general security practitioner, i.e., the sort of person who expects to work in a variety of roles during a career. This is the ice hockey model.

I do not recommend following what might be called the [American] football model. Football players are exceptionally specialized and usually ineffective when told to play out of position. (Could you imagine the kicker playing on the defensive line, or the center as a wide receiver?)

Returning to the hockey model, remember that there are three positions, with varying degrees of offensive and defensive responsibilities. Goalies focus almost exclusively on defense, but they try to make smart plays that lead to break-outs. Defensemen concentrate on defense but should contribute offensively where possible. Forwards concentrate on offense, but help the defensemen as well. How does this model apply to my position in digital security? I consider myself a defenseman, but I'm trying to develop my offensive skills. (At the very least, better knowledge of offensive tools and techniques helps me better defend against them.) I have no interest in being a goalie. Being a forward would be exciting, but I'm not sure I'll have an opportunity or job responsibility to fully develop those skills.

I suppose it's even possible to become a coach or trainer (like skating guru Laura Stamm). You don't have to actually play the game, but you quickly become irrelevant if you lose touch with the game.

Does the extreme specialization of the football model apply? I think it may apply for large consultancies (or perhaps for the security market as a whole). In a large consultancy, you can be the "Web app guy" or the "incident response gal" and make a living. Outside of that environment, perhaps at a general security job for a company, you're expected to be good at almost everything.

I've written before that it's unreasonable to be good at everything, despite the unrealistic desire of CIOs to hire so-called "multi-talented specialists." I recommend choosing to be a goalie, defenseman, forward, or coach/trainer. Be solid in your core responsibilities, but remember Bobby Orr's example.

How do you fit into my hockey model?

Commentary

One of the best developments in the security field during the last two decades was the concept and terminology around "threat hunting." Suddenly there was a cool name for the sort of work that some defenders had been conducting for years. It's almost as cool to be a "threat hunter" as it is to be a "hacker!"

Regarding the main point of this post, I believe it still holds. Security is too broad a field to be an expert in one or two defined areas, at most. It's important to have at least some *knowledge* and *comprehension* (to channel the last post) of other areas, but expecting *synthesis* or beyond for many areas is plainly unrealistic.

Lessons from Analog Security

Friday, December 29, 2006

As a security person I try to take notice of security measures in non-digital settings. These are a few I noticed this week.

When visiting a jewelry store, I saw a sign say the following: "Our insurance policy does not permit us to remove more than one item at a time from this display case." This sign was attached to a case containing the store's most valuable jewelry. This is an example of *limiting exposure by restricting access to one asset at a time.* In a more generic sense, the digital version might involve following guidelines applied by an insurance company. Perhaps they would require WPA2 for wireless networks, etc.

I received a check from a client. Underneath the signature line I read "Two signatures required for amounts over $75,000." This is an example of *dual accountability*. It requires someone writing fraudulent checks to have an accomplice. The digital version involves requiring two privileged users acting together to accomplish a particularly sensitive task.

At many stores I saw video cameras directly above the cash register. While these might be useful for recording thieves, it is probably in place to *deter employees from stealing*. The digital version is comprehensive host- and network-centric monitoring.

I think one of the fundamental problems of digital security is the inability to translate historically sound analog security practices into digital forms. Traditional computer scientists are not security experts. Traditional security experts are usually not computer scientists. Addressing this gap would be beneficial to both communities.

Can you think of other examples of security measures in the analog world that could be applied to the digital world?

https://taosecurity.blogspot.com/2006/12/lessons-from-analog-security.html

Commentary

I strongly believe that the digital security world has a lot to learn from the physical or analog security worlds. While "cyber" is unique in some respects, the way people think about elements of the risk equation -- threats, vulnerability, and assets -- transcends the domain.

Operational Traffic Intelligence System Woes

Monday, January 15, 2007

Recently I posted thoughts on Cisco's Self-Defending Network. Today I spent several hours on a Cisco Monitoring, Analysis and Response System (MARS) trying to make sense of the data for a client. I am disappointed to report that I did not find the experience very productive. This post tries to explain the major deficiencies I see in products like MARS.

Note: I call this post *Operational Traffic Intelligence System Woes* because I want it to apply to detecting and resisting intrusions. As I mentioned earlier, hardly anyone builds real intrusion detection systems. So-called "IDS" are really attack indication systems. I also dislike the term intrusion prevention system ("IPS"), since anything that seeks to resist intrusion could be considered an "IPS."

Most available "IPS" are firewalls in the sense that anything that denies activity is a policy enforcement system. I use the term traffic intelligence system (TIS) to describe any network-centric product which inspects traffic for detection or resistance purposes. That includes products with the popular labels "firewall," "IPS," and "IDS."

Three main criticisms can be made against TIS. I could point to many references but since this is a blog post I'll save that heavy lifting for something I write for publication.

Failure to Understand the Environment: This problem is old as dirt and will never be solved. The root of the issue is that in any network of even minimal size, it is too difficult for the TIS to properly model the states of all parties. The TIS can never be sure how a target will decipher and process traffic sent by an intruder, and vice versa. This situation leaves enough room for attacks to drive a Mack truck, e.g., they can fragment at the IP / TCP / SMB / DCE-RPC levels and confuse just about every TIS available, while the target happily processes what it receives. Products that gather as much context about targets improve the situation, but there are no perfect solutions.

Analyst Information Overload: This problem is only getting worse. As attackers devise various ways to exploit targets, TIS vendors try to identify and/or deny malicious activity. For example, Snort's signature base is rapidly approaching 10,000 rules. (It's important to realize Snort is not just a signature-based IDS/IPS. I'll explain why in a future *Snort Report*.) The information overload problem means **it's becoming increasingly difficult (if not already impossible) for security analysts to understand all of the attack types they might encounter while inspecting TIS alerts.** SIM/SEM/SIEM vendors try to mitigate this problem by correlating events, but at the end of the day **I want to know why a product is asking me to investigate an alert.** That requires drilling down to the individual alert level and understanding what is happening.

Lack of Supporting Details: **The vast majority of TIS continue to be alert-centric.** This is absolutely crippling for a security analyst. I am convinced that **the vast majority of TIS developers never use their products on operational networks supporting real clients with contemporary security problems.** If they did, developers would quickly realize their products do not provide the level of detail needed to figure out what is happening.

In brief, **we have TIS that don't/can't fully understand their environment, reporting more alerts than an analyst can understand, while providing not enough details to satisfy operational investigations. I did not even include usability as a critical aspect of this issue.**

161

How does this apply to MARS? It appears that MARS (like other SIM/SEM/SIEM) believes that the "more is better" approach is the way to address the lack of context. The idea is that collecting as many input sources as possible will result in a system that understands the environment. This works to a certain limited point, but what is really needed is comprehensive knowledge of a target's existence, operating system, applications, and configuration. That level of information is not available, so I was left with inspecting 209 "red" severity MARS alerts for the last 7 days (3099 yellow, 1672 green). Those numbers also indicate information overload to me. All I really want to know is which of those alerts represent intrusions? MARS (and honestly, most products) can't answer that question.

The way I am usually forced to determine if I should worry about TIS alerts is manual inspection. The open source project Sguil provides session and full content data -- independent of any alert -- that lets me know a lot about activity directly or indirectly related to an event of interest. With MARS and the like, I can basically query for other alerts. Theoretically NetFlow can be collected, but the default configuration is to collect NetFlow for statistical purposes while discarding the individual records.

If I want to see full content, the closest I can get is this sort of ASCII rendition of a packet excerpt. That is ridiculous; it was state-of-the-art in 1996 to take a binary protocol (say SMB -- not shown here but common) and display the packet excerpt in ASCII. That level of detail gives the analyst almost nothing useful as far as incident validation or escalation.

(Is there an alternative? Sure, with Sguil we extract the entire session from Libpcap and provide it in Ethereal/Wireshark, or display all of the content in ASCII if requested by the analyst.)

The bottom line is that I am at a loss regarding what I am going to tell my client. They spent a lot of money deploying a Cisco SDN but their investigative capabilities as provided by MARS are insufficient for incident analysis and escalation. I'm considering recommending augmentation with a separate product that collects full content and session data, then using MARS as a tip-off for investigation using those alternative data sources.

Are you stuck with similar products? How do you handle the situation? Several of you posted ideas earlier, and I appreciate hearing more.

https://taosecurity.blogspot.com/2007/01/operational-traffic-intelligence-system.html

Commentary

I bolded certain text that I thought was particularly relevant. We have many or all of the same detection problems in 2020. With the rise of so-called "artificial intelligence" (AI) and "machine learning" (ML) systems that produce their own form of alerts, my concerns have only intensified. If an analyst doesn't understand how or why a system created an alert, that analyst is likely to not trust the system. This is oddly one of the advantages of signatures -- because they are defined and generally human-readable, analysts can read, interpret, and potentially modify them. This is only true, of course, if the platform running the signatures provides access to its logic and the ability to implement user-defined changes.

TaoSecurity Enterprise Trust Pyramid

Saturday, January 27, 2007

My post *Monitor Your Routers* touched on the idea of trust. I'd like to talk about that for a moment, from the perspective of an operational security person. I'm not qualified to address trust in the same way an academic might, especially since trust is one of the core ideas of digital security. Trust can be described in extreme mathematical detail and in some cases even proven. I don't know how to do that. Instead, I'm going to describe how I decide what I trust when performing network incident response.

Imagine a pyramid with the following four tiers.

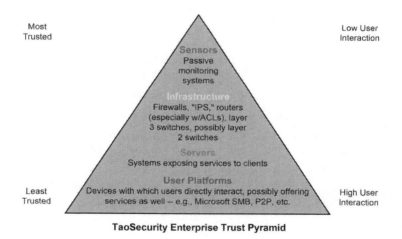

Figure 14. TaoSecurity Enterprise Trust Pyramid

At the very bottom of the pyramid would be an **end user platform, or client.** This could be a PC with a user browsing the Web, reading email, chatting on IM, swapping files on P2P, etc. (Administrative rights worsen the situation but are not necessary to make my point.) It could also be a smart phone or other powerful portable general computing device. Because of the extreme number and diversity of attacks against this victim pool and the relative vulnerability of the platform, **I hardly trust anything I see when interacting with a live victim system.** An image of a victim system hard drive is more trusted than the same system viewed via a potentially compromised operating system, but memory- or hardware-resident attacks confuse that situation too.

Above the level of end user platforms, imagine **servers. I trust servers more than clients because servers typically offer constrained means by which users access the server.** A properly designed and deployed server provides limited access to computing resources, although administrators typically interact directly with the platform. Sys admins are presumed to be more vigilant than regular users, but the level of exposure of services and the fallibility of human admins relegates the server to only one notch above client systems in my pyramid.

Next comes **infrastructure**. These are systems which carry user traffic, but users aren't expected to directly interact with them as they might with clients or servers. Again, admins will interact with the infrastructure, but most infrastructure is not a general computing platform with a very powerful shell. Note that users (and therefore attackers) can determine the existence of infrastructure when it interferes with traffic, as is the case when ACLs block communications. Infrastructure with directly addressable interfaces are more vulnerable to interaction and therefore less trusted than infrastructure with no directly addressable interfaces. For example, an unmanaged switch is potentially more trusted than a managed switch offering an administration interface. If properly designed, deployed, and managed -- all big "if's" -- **I trust infrastructure more than servers.**

At the top of the pyramid we find **sensors**. This being a Network Security Monitoring blog, you would expect that! **The reason I**

trust my network sensors so much is that, when properly designed and deployed, they are invisible to users. They do not act on traffic and therefore cannot be discovered. When remote connectivity is required, my sensors do need administrative interfaces. That is a potential weakness. Furthermore, like all devices with TCP/IP stacks, they are susceptible to high-end attacks against the stack itself or the inspection applications watching passing traffic. No devices (really, no devices) can be perfectly trustworthy, but they are leagues above the desktops at the bottom of the pyramid.

For a while I've held out hope that memory snapshots taken in some reliable manner might give valuable insights into the state of a victim system, thereby revealing useful evidence. I mentioned this last year. Now I read Joanna Rutkowska is demolishing this technique too. Back to the bottom of the trust heap goes the desktop!

https://taosecurity.blogspot.com/2007/01/taosecurity-pyramid-of-trust.html

Commentary

I could argue for and against the points I made in this post. In the "against" column, I might collect all devices except for sensors into the same level of trustworthiness. As evidence, I would cite the numerous vulnerabilities released in many infrastructure devices during the month of July 2020. Still, I tend to believe that the greater the interaction with users, the less trustworthy the platform. I am not blaming users by saying this. Rather, it's more a reflection of vulnerability surface area and general complexity.

The Self-Defeating Network

Sunday, January 28, 2007

At the risk of adding yet more fuel to the fire, I'd like to share a few more thoughts on NSM. Although the title of this post is *The Self-Defeating Network* (SdN), I don't intend it to be a slam of Cisco's Self-Defending Network (SDN). Rather, the post's title demonstrates a probably lame attempt at branding an otherwise potentially boring issue.

Thus far I've tried to explain NSM, and the related concept of *Defensible Network Architecture* (originated in my *Tao* book, expanded in *Extrusion*), from the view of best practices. I've tried to say "here's what you should do," because it gives you the best chance to survive on the mean streets of the Internet. In this post I'll take a different approach by describing the **Self-Defeating Network** -- what you should not do if you want to have a chance to defend your enterprise.

These are the characteristics of the Self-Defeating Network (SdN).

The SdN is *unknown*, meaning no one really understands how it works. There is no complete, current inventory of all infrastructure, hosts, services, applications, and data. No one knows what patterns of activity are normal, or which are suspicious or malicious. One cannot defend what one does not understand.

The SdN is *unmonitored*, which results in trust without verification. Those using the SdN trust the integrity, confidentiality, and availability of information resources but have no idea if their trust is well-placed. (Here's a hint: it's not.)

The SdN is *uncontrolled*, which means anything goes -- including suspicious and malicious traffic. Security is seen as an impediment and not a requirement, and as a result the enterprise is actually less capable of providing resources than one which is controlled. The uncontrolled environment also makes monitoring exceptionally difficult because no policy exists saying what is allowed and what is disallowed.

The SdN strives to be *unmanned* (i.e., to reduce headcount to zero), because products, not processes and people, are perceived as the "solution." Sadly enough one could argue this aspect of the SdN is shared by the SDN. For an explanation of why people are necessary, please read Hawke vs the Machine.

In addition to *(mis)placing trust* in an untrustworthy network, the users of the SdN also *(mis)trust their products to provide alert-centric warnings* when "bad things happen." If no alerts are sounded, SdN users assume everything is fine.

A friend described a case of this approach taken to the extreme, when a large company paid a MSSP for three years of service, during which **no alerts were ever raised**. After paying several hundred thousand dollars, the company realized the MSSP misconfigured the SPAN ports feeding the MSSP sensors. For three years no traffic was inspected so the MSSP reported nothing. The MSSP wrote a big refund check.

Hint on a future post: this is also the problem with log-centric detection methods. The absence of logs does not indicate an absence of problems. An absence of network traffic, however, does at least indicate an absence of remote connectivity with a suspected victim computer. Obviously an absence of network traffic does not preclude physical problems like stealing data via USB token.

Eventually I'll take all the notes I write in the wee hours of the night into blog posts. For now that's all!

Commentary

Cisco asked me to speak at one of their big annual events in the 2000s. I presented a version of this material. While I believe it resonated with some of the audience, I was never asked to return. I didn't receive reimbursement for my travel expenses, either. Eventually someone in the Cisco organization took pity on me, an independent contractor, and reimbursed me using their personal PayPal account!

Consider This Scenario

Friday, February 02, 2007

The other day I posted *I Am Not Anti-Log*. I alluded to the fact that I am not a big log fan but I do see the value of logs. This post will give you an indication as to why I prefer network data to logs.

Yesterday morning I installed OSSEC on the one system I expose to the Internet. OSSEC is really amazing in the sense that you can install it and immediately it starts parsing system logs for interesting activity.

The system on which I installed OSSEC only offers OpenSSH to the world. Therefore, you could say I was surprised when the following appeared in my Gmail inbox this morning:

OSSEC HIDS Notification.
2007 Feb 02 06:25:01

Received From: macmini->/var/log/auth.log
Rule: 40101 fired (level 12) -> "System user sucessfully logged to the system."
Portion of the log(s):

169

```
Feb  2 06:25:01 macmini su[14861]:
(pam_unix) session opened for user nobody by (uid=0)
```

I don't know what that means, but I don't feel good about it. At this
point I know what everyone is thinking -- SSH to host macmini and
look around! **Don't do it.** If my macmini box is owned, **the last
thing I want is for the intruder to know that *I know*. The only
defense when you suspect a box is compromised is to play dead
and stupid.** So where do I go to learn more about what's happened?

I do have one log-centric option. If I am running Syslog on macmini,
and sending the logs elsewhere via Syslog to a central collector, I
should check the collector for unusual logs from macmini. However,
if I check the Syslog server, and see nothing unusual, does that mean
anything? Not really! The lack of log messages may indicate whatever
the intruder did was not logged by the victim. Maybe the first act
involved killing remote logging! This is one of the reasons I am not a
big fan of logs. **The absence of logs does not confirm integrity.**
What can I do now?

My best option is to hop onto my NSM sensor and look for
suspicious connections to or from macmini around the time I got
this OSSEC alert. For example, my OSSEC event occurred at 1125
GMT. A search for inbound sessions shows only ICMP at the time
of the OSSEC event. A similar check for outbound sessions did not
reveal anything interesting. Therefore, the OSSEC event was
probably caused by some sort of daemon running on macmini, not
by a login from a remote unauthorized user.

Notice the difference between the data presented in network sessions
vs host logs. **The absence of suspicious session data means no
remote intruder interacted with the system during the time in
question.** In other words, a lack of a record showing an inbound
OpenSSH session **does mean** no OpenSSH sessions occurred at the
time in question. If you wonder if some sort of advanced covert

channel ICMP-fu is happening, I have the full content validating each of the ICMP "sessions" and could investigate them if I so desired.

Also keep in mind the **value of collecting session and full content independent of alerts**. If I waited for an alert before starting to log sessions and/or full content, I'd be in the same boat with the host-centric loggers. By doing **content-neutral logging** (i.e., grab everything, continuously) I can look for suspicious activity regardless of the presence or absence of alerts.

https://taosecurity.blogspot.com/2007/02/consider-this-scenario.html

Commentary

This post captures much of my network security monitoring philosophy. It assumes that you have a NSM sensor in place that is competently collecting traffic and generating reliable data. If your collection is poor, and your analysis is poor, then all the philosophy in the world can't help you. However, once you have those foundational elements in place, you can make the sorts of deductions that appear in this post.

Five Thoughts on Incident Response

Wednesday, March 14, 2007

Speaking of incidents, I thought it might be interesting to share a few brief observations based on incidents I've worked recently. Please remember this is a blog post. If you expect thorough explanations of these points with footnotes, historical references, arguments to the contrary expertly swept aside, etc., please wait for a future book! :)

Anti-Virus is not (or should not be) an incident response tool. I am baffled when I see machines compromised, and the owners think a magic signature from their AV vendor is going to save the day. In this day and age intruders who gain kernel level control of a host often disable AV and will not give up the fight so easily. My second point relates to this one.

Your default incident recovery strategy should be to rebuild from scratch. By scratch I mean reinstallation from original trusted media and re-installation of applications and data.

Today, in 2007, I am still comfortable saying that existing hardware can usually be trusted, without evidence to the contrary, as a platform for reinstallation. This is one year after I saw John Heasman discuss PCI rootkits (.pdf). I was lucky enough to spend a few hours chatting with John and fellow NGS Software guru David Litchfield after John's talk on firmware rootkits (.pdf). John's talks indicate that the day is coming when even hardware that hosted a compromised OS will eventually not be trustworthy.

One day I will advise clients to treat an incident zone as if a total physical loss has occurred and new platforms have to be available for hosting a reinstallation. If you doubt me now, wait for the post in a few years where I link back to this point. In brief, treat an incident like a disaster, not a nuisance. Otherwise, you will be perpetually compromised.

SPAN ports should not be the default traffic access option. I cannot tell you how much time, effort, and frustration has accompanied the use (or attempted use) of SPAN ports in incident response situations.

"The SPAN port is already used."

"The SPAN port can't do that." (although it probably can, the network engineer either doesn't know how to set it up or doesn't want it configured to help the security team) "Do you see anything? No? Try now. No? Try now. No?"

"You only see half the traffic? Wait, try this. Now you see double? Ok, try now."

For Pete's sake, buy a tap, put it in the proper place, and stand back while the packets are collected properly.

A Linux live CD is not a substitute for a real network security monitoring platform. Upon realizing that Cisco MARS is not an incident response solution, I was desperate to collect some form of useful network-centric data at one client site. In a last-ditch attempt to salvage a bad situation my on-site colleague deployed a Network Security Toolkit live CD on top of a box previously running Linux natively. I was able to SSH into it, mount the local filesystem, and start writing packets to the hard drive using Tshark's ring buffer. This is absolutely making the best out of a mess, which is standard incident response behavior.

I would ask anyone who turns to a live CD for their monitoring needs to avoid the temptation to think Snort on a live CD on spare, old hardware is anything like Snort on properly sized, configured, deployed hardware. Furthermore, **Snort != monitoring**. Live CDs are fine for assessment work but they are nearly worthless for packet capture. Needless to say I was able to talk my colleague through a FreeBSD installation and was soon collecting data in a somewhat better environment.

When you are compromised, you are probably not facing a zero-day exploit unique to you and not capable of being prevented. When you are compromised you're most likely suffering from some fairly modern variant of attack code that nevertheless contains exploits dating back to 2002. For some reason people seem to feel better if they think the incident is caused by some uber elite intruder who saved up his killer 0-day just for their enterprise. In reality someone probably connected an infected laptop physically to the network, or via VPN, and found a way to get a worm or other malware to the segment of the enterprise running "production" machines that never get patched.

Do you have any IR stories or lessons to share? Please post them as comments or write on your blog, then post a link here as a comment. Thank you.

https://taosecurity.blogspot.com/2007/03/five-thoughts-on-inciden t-response.html

Commentary

All of this is true today, with a couple improvements. No one really uses Linux distributions as live CDs, unless they are running something like Tails -- the "live CD" to access Tor. Also, anti-virus is slowly being replaced by endpoint detection and response (EDR) agents, which were built for incident response scenarios.

Incident Response Clarifications

Friday, March 16, 2007

Recently I posted *Five Thoughts on Incident Response*. Based on the comments and some blog responses I wanted to clarify what I originally posted. The first three items seemed to attract the most attention so I'll only address those.

Anti-Virus is not (or should not be) an incident response tool. **The emphasis here is on response.** I agree that AV is often an incident detection tool, and ideally an incident avoidance tool. However, if you think AV is going to help recover from a totally compromised system, you are probably going to be upset by the results.

Your default incident recovery strategy should be to rebuild from scratch. **The emphasis here is on recovery.** I am not saying your default incident response strategy should be to rebuild from scratch. **Your default response strategy should be to investigate to determine how the victim was compromised, what aspects of Confidentiality/Integrity/Availability were violated, and so on.** I agree that any response which begins with re-imaging the victim is a recipe for failure.

SPAN ports should not be the default traffic access option. I'm standing by this one. **The only time SPAN ports are superior to taps is the situation where intra-switch traffic needs to be seen.** Otherwise, spend a few dollars and get a product designed to grant reliable traffic access. I'm talking about professional ways to perform incident response here. Hardware is the easiest thing to gain budget for in any organization. It's easier to buy a piece of hardware than it is to send a person to training, or hire new help, or bring in outside consultants, or any other activity that could benefit a security shop.

I appreciate the other recommendations I've seen. These are only a few big thoughts which struck me based on recent engagements. I have over a dozen recommendations in my Network Security Operations class and I think I cover similar material in *Extrusion Detection*.

https://taosecurity.blogspot.com/2007/03/incident-response-clarifications.html

Commentary

There are indeed situations where only SPAN ports can offer the visibility one might need, at least when making a reasonable cost-benefit calculation. There are also much fancier products available on the market today that provide different capabilities. This has been a welcome innovation in the network visibility hardware market.

Nail in the TCP Options Coffin

Monday, March 19, 2007

I just listened to the relevant part of a recent SANS Webcast that mentioned my response to their conspiracy theory on SYN ACK and other packets with weird TCP options. At first all I wanted to do with this post was link to Michal Zalewski's *Museum of Broken Packets* and say that SANS ISC is wasting time on a non-issue. Then I started reading some of the MOBP entries. I nearly fell out of my chair when I read this.

Exhibit 7: DoS tool changes into DoS exploit

Internet Protocol Version: 4
Header length: 20 bytes
Differentiated Services Field: 0x00 (DSCP 0x00: Default; ECN: 0x00)
Total Length: 48
Identification: 0x6fbb
Flags: 0x04 (DF)
Fragment offset: 0
Time to live: 127
Protocol: TCP (0x06)
Header checksum: 0x63b6 (correct)
Source: 64.190.25.48 (64.190.25.48)
Destination: XXX.XXX.XXX.XXX (XXX.XXX.XXX.XXX)

Transmission Control Protocol, Src Port: 1113 (1113), Dst Port: 490 (490),
  Seq: 269484601, Ack: 0
Source port: 1113 (1113)
Destination port: 490 (490)
Sequence number: 269484601
Header length: 28 bytes
Flags: 0x0002 (SYN)
Window size: 16384
Checksum: 0x023b (correct)
Options: (8 bytes)

Maximum segment size: 1460 bytes
NOP
Maximum segment size (option length = 4 bytes says option goes past end of options)

```
0000 XX XX XX XX XX XX XX XX XX XX XX XX 08 00 45 00  ..............E.
0010 00 30 6f bb 40 00 7f 06 63 b6 40 be 19 30 XX XX  .0o.@...c.@.....
0020 XX XX 04 59 01 ea 10 10 02 39 00 00 00 00 70 02  ...Y.....9....p.
0030 40 00 02 3b 00 00 02 04 05 b4 01 02 04 03  .. .. @..;...........
```

Yes, those last eight bytes are exactly the same as the TCP options in the SANS packet on their slide.

Michal explains:

> This one comes from Andy Brown, who "does security" for a large web portal. It is a nice example of how a simple error in a DoS tool turned it into potential DoS exploit, and that a conspiracy theory is not always the best answer :). The packet you see above is generated by a DoS SYN tool called Juno-z. This tool was used against their site. As Andy describes, the fun is in the TCP options: 0x020405B4 MSS=1460, 0x01020403 NOP, MSS=0x03??

> Normally the NOP option (0x01) is used to pad options so they lie on 4-byte boundaries, causing the actual MSS value to lie conveniently on a 16-bit boundary. Here, it's not - this NOP causes MSS value to end past the end of this packet.

Might cause some dumb stack to have a bus/alignment fetch error because the MSS is shifted. Also, it could cause a dumb stack to read past the end of the packet causing a segmentation fault. Turns out, this was all unintentional - I talked to the author, and it was a coding glitch :-)

Here is juno-z (https://packetstormsecurity.com/DoS/juno-z.101f.c). Notice dre mentioned juno-z and bang.c as tools that produce malformed packets. Apparently the real victims in this DoS attack repeated the bad TCP options they saw.

So, between my previous post and this one, I've identified the real DoS victim (compton.ameri.ca), the botnet C&C ordering a related attack, (thanks to the ShadowServer project), and the actual tool used to conduct the attack.

I think it's time for SANS ISC to give up on this one. You are not seeing scanning, you are not seeing OS identification, you are not seeing another grand conspiracy whose secret lies in TCP options. You're seeing traffic caused by SYN floods.

https://taosecurity.blogspot.com/2007/03/nail-in-tcp-options-coffin.html

Commentary

In the first volume of this series I talked about disagreements I had with SANS. This is another unfortunate example. Years later, I better understand the psychology which encourages analysts to hold onto their initial assessments, even when contradictory evidence comes to light. This is a problem that affects far more than the security world.

Security Operations Fundamentals

Wednesday, March 28, 2007

Last year I last wrote:

> Marcus [Ranum] noted that the security industry is just like
> the diet industry. People who want to lose weight know they
> should eat less, eat good food, and exercise regularly. Instead,
> they constantly seek the latest dieting fad, pill, plan, or
> program -- and wonder why they don't get the results they
> want!

You might be wondering about the digital security equivalent to
eating less, eating good food, and exercising regularly. Addressing
that subject adequately would take more than this blog post, but I
want to share the steps I use as a consultant when encountering a
new client's enterprise.

You'll notice that these steps fit nicely within Mike Rothman's
Pragmatic CSO construct. These are a little more specific and
focused because I am not acting as a Chief Security Officer when I
work as a consultant.

1. Instrument sample ingress/egress points. What, monitor first?
That's exactly right. Start collecting NSM data immediately (at least
session, preferably alert, full content, session, and statistical). It's
going to take time to progress through the rest of the steps that
follow. While working on the next steps your network forensics
appliance can be capturing data to be analyzed later.

2. Understand business operations. Replace business with whatever term makes you more comfortable if you are a .gov, .mil, .edu, etc. You've got to know the purpose of the organization before you can understand the data it needs to do its job. This requires interviewing people who know this, preferably business owners and managers.

3. Identify and prioritize business data. Once you understand the purpose of the organization, you should determine the data it needs to function. Not all data is equal, so perform a relative ranking to determine the most important down to least important. This work must be done with the cooperation of the businesses; it cannot be security- or consultant-driven.

4. Identify and prioritize systems processing business data. By systems I mean an entire assemblage for processing data, not individual computers. Systems include payroll processing, engineering and development, finance projections, etc. Prioritize these systems as you did the data they carry. Hopefully these two sets of rankings will match, but perhaps not.

5. Identify and prioritize resources comprising systems. Here we start dealing with individual servers, clients, and infrastructure. For example, the database containing payroll data is probably more important than the Web server offering access to clients. Here tech people are more important than managers because tech people build and maintain these devices.

6. Define policy, profile resources, and identify violations. Steps 2-5 have gotten you to the point where you should have a good understanding of the business and its components. If you have a policy, review it to ensure it makes sense given the process thus far. If you haven't yet defined a policy for the use of your information resources, do so now.

Next, profile how those resources behave to determine if they are supporting business operations or if they are acting suspiciously or maliciously. I recommend taking a passive, traffic-centric approach. This method has near-zero business impact, and, if executed properly, can be done without alerting anyone inside or outside the company acting maliciously. Here you use the data you started collecting in step 1.

7. Implement short term incident containment, investigation, and remediation. I have yet to encounter an enterprise that doesn't immediately find a hot-button item in step 6. Put out those fires and score some early wins before moving on.

8. Plan and execute instrumentation improvements. Based on step 7, you'll realize you want visibility across the entire enterprise. Increase the number of sensors to cover all of the areas you want. This step encompasses improved host-centric logging and other visibility initiatives.

9. Plan and execute infrastructure improvements. You'll probably decide to implement components of my Defensible Network Architecture to take a more proactive stance towards defending the network. You may be able to reconfigure existing processes, products, and people to act in a more secure manner. You may need to design, buy, or train those elements.

10. Plan and execute server improvements. Here you decide what, if any, changes should be made to the resources offering business data to users, customers, partners, and the like. Maybe you want to encrypt data at rest as well as in motion. Maybe you decide to abandon an old Web framework for a new one... and so on.

11. Plan and execute user platform improvements. This step changes the gear users rely upon, so it's the last step. Users are most likely to resist that which they can immediately see, so tread carefully.

Improvements here involve OS upgrades or changes, moves to thin clients, removal or upgrades of software, and similar issues.

12. Measure results and return to step 1. I recommend using metrics like those I described here. Measure Days since last compromise of type X, System-days compromised, Time for a pen testing team of [low/high] skill with [internal/external] access to obtain unauthorized [unstealthy/stealthy] access to a specified asset using [public/custom] tools and [complete/zero] target knowledge, and so on.

You may notice steps 8-11 reflect my *TaoSecurity Pyramid of Trust.* That is no accident.

It is also important to realize that steps 8-11 are based on data collected in step 1 and analyzed in step 6. Enterprise security improvements should not be driven by the newest products or concepts. Improvements should be driven by understanding the enterprise and specifically the network. Otherwise, you are playing *soccer goal security* by making assumptions and not judgements.

Only when you understand what is happening in the enterprise should you consider changing it. Only when you realize existing processes, products, and/or people are deficient should you consider changes or additions. Think in terms of what problem am I trying to solve, not what new process, product, or person is now available.

https://taosecurity.blogspot.com/2007/03/security-operations-fund amentals.html

Commentary

This is still great advice for enterprise environments. In a holistic modern environment that encompasses mobile and cloud computing, security leaders must integrate those concerns into each step. I still agree with Bruce Schneier that the first step should be to **monitor first**. By gathering data on what is happening in your environment, you enable every other aspect of the security program. Furthermore, that initial monitoring does not need to be comprehensive, hence my use of the word "sample" in step 1. Start somewhere and make improvements as your situational awareness increases.

Asset-Centric vs Threat-Centric Digital Situational Awareness

Monday, July 02, 2007

As an Air Force officer I was taught the importance of situational awareness (SA). The surprisingly good (at least for now) Wikipedia entry describes SA as "knowing what is going on so you can figure out what to do" (Adam, 1993) and knowing "what you need to know not to be surprised" (Jeannot et al., 2003). Wikipedia also mentions fighter pilots who leveraged SA to win dogfights. When applied to information security, I like to use the term **digital situational awareness (DSA)**.

In 2005 I invented the term *pervasive network awareness* (PNA) for my book *Extrusion Detection* to describe one way to achieve a certain degree of SA:

> Pervasive network awareness is the ability to collect the network-based information -- from the viewpoint of any node on the network -- required to make decisions.

PNA is inherently an asset-centric means to improve SA. PNA involves watching assets for indications of violations of confidentiality, integrity, and/or availability (the CIA triad). An asset-centric approach is not the only means to detect incidents, however.

During the past few years several firms have offered services that report indications of security incidents using threat-centric means. These services are not traditional managed security service providers (MSSPs) because they are not watching assets, per se, under the control or operation of a client. In other words, these firms are not placing sensors on company networks and watching for breaches involving monitored systems.

Rather, these next-generation firms seek and investigate infrastructure used by threats to perpetrate their crimes. For example, **a threat-centric security firm will identify and analyze the command-and-control mechanisms used by malware or crimeware.** The reporting mechanism will be mined for indications of hosts currently under unauthorized control. An example of this is the ongoing Mpack activity I mentioned in *Web-Centric Short-Term Incident Containment.*

These services improve digital situation awareness by taking a threat-centric approach. **The ultimate threat-centric approach would be to monitor activities of the threats themselves, by instrumenting and observing their workplace, communications lines, and/or equipment.** Since that is out of the reach of everyone except law enforcement (and usually beyond their reach unless they are extraordinarily lucky and persistent), watching command-and-control channels is the next best bet.

Asset-centric and threat-centric DSA are not mutually exclusive. In fact, threat-centric DSA is a powerful complement to asset-centric DSA. If a company subscribes to a threat-centric DSA service, the service may report that a company system has been compromised and is leaking sensitive data. If confirmed to be true, and if not detected by asset-centric means, the event shows the following:

- Preventative measures failed (since the asset was compromised).
- Asset-centric monitoring failed (since it was not detected).
- Incident response must be initiated (since the compromised asset is not just vulnerable, but actually under the control of an unauthorized party).

With this new understanding, prevention and detection measures can hopefully be improved to reduce the chances of future incidents.

Please do not ask me for recommendations on any of these services; I am not trying to promote anyone. However, I have mentioned two such services before, namely *Support Intelligence* in *Month of Owned Corporations* and *Secure Science* in my review of *Phishing Exposed*.

https://taosecurity.blogspot.com/2007/07/asset-centric-vs-threat-centric-digital.html

Commentary

I'm sure many readers are wondering "what's the big deal?" Check the date on this post. Monitoring C2 channels as a service was a rare offering in 2007. There's probably a subset of readers saying "oh, my company was doing that, etc. etc." Feel free to post some proof, or better yet, point to a primary contemporary source.

I had also been monitoring C2 almost ten years earlier at the AFCERT, but that was the result of watching my compromised hosts being controlled by intruders. In this case, I'm talking about service providers running systems designed to be compromised, and then creating threat intelligence reports for customers based on what they learned about the intruders.

Some might say that this was normal honeypot activity, dating straight back to Bill Cheswick's 1991 paper *An Evening with Berferd*, or to subsequent work by pioneers like Lance Spitzner and his Honeynet Project. Like everything in security, each contributor builds on prior work.

Also note the secondary, albeit more effective, option discussed in this post: compromising the adversary's infrastructure and learning about his actions via direct observation. This can be a difficult proposition depending on the risk and legal tolerance of the security intelligence firm but there have been plenty of examples over the last twenty years. Remember that nation state intelligence agencies operate under a completely different set of rules.

More Engineering Disasters

Monday, July 09, 2007

I've written several times about engineering disasters.

Watching more man-made failures on The History Channel's "Engineering Disasters," I realized lessons learned the hard way by safety, mechanical, and structural engineers and operators can be applied to those practicing digital security.

1. In 1983, en route from Virginia to Massachusetts, the World War II-era bulk carrier SS Marine Electric sank in high seas. The almost forty year-old ship was ferrying 24,000 tons of coal and 34 Merchant Mariners, none of whom had survival suits to resist the February chill of the Atlantic. All but three died.

The owner of the ship, Marine Transport Lines (MTL), blamed the crew and one of the survivors, Chief Mate Bob Cusick, for the disaster. Investigations of the wreck and a trial revealed the Marine Electric's coal hatch covers were in disrepair, as reported by Cusick prior to the disaster. Apparently the American Bureau of Shipping (ABS), an inspection organization upon which the Coast Guard relied, but funded by ship operators like MTL, had faked reports on the Marine Electric's status. With gaping holes in the coal hatches, the ship's coal containers filled with water in high seas and doomed the crew.

In the wake of the disaster, the Coast Guard recognized that ABS could not be an impartial investigator because ship owners could essentially pay to have their vessels judged seaworthy. Widespread analysis of ship inspections revealed many similar ships and others were unsound, and they were removed from service. Unreliable Coast Guard inspectors were removed. Finally, the Coast Guard created its rescue swimmer team (dramatized by the recent movie "The Guardian") to act as a rapid response unit.

The lessons from the Marine Electric disaster are numerous.

First, **be prepared for incidents and have an incident response team equipped and trained for rapid and effective "rescue."**

Second, **be suspicious of reports done by parties with conflicts of interest.** Stories abound of vulnerability assessment companies who find all of their clients "above average." To rate them otherwise would be to potentially lose future business.

Third, **understand how to perform forensics to discover root causes of security incidents, and be willing to act decisively if those findings demonstrate problems applicable to other business assets.**

2. In 1931, a Fokker F-10 Trimotor carrying eight passengers and crew crashed near Kansas City, Kansas. All aboard died, including Notre Dame football coach Knute Rockne. At the time of the disaster, plane crashes were fairly common. Because commercial

passenger service had only become popular in the late 1920's, the public did not have much experience with flying. The death of Knute Rockne caused shock and outrage.

Despite the crude state of crash forensics in 1931, the Civil Aeronautics Authority (CAA) determined the plane crashed because its wood wing separated from its steel body during bad weather. TWA, operator of the doomed flight, removed all F-10s from service and burned them. Public pressure forced the CAA, forerunner of today's Federal Aviation Administration, to remove the veil of secrecy applied to its investigation and reporting processes. TWA turned to Donald Douglas for a replacement aircraft, and the very successful DC-3 was born.

The crash of TWA flight 599 provides several sad lessons for digital security.

First, **few seem to care about disasters involving new technologies until a celebrity dies.** While no one would like to see such an event occur, it's possible real change of opinion and technology will not happen until a modern Knute Rockne suffers at the hands of a security incident.

Second, **authorities often do not have a real incentive to fix processes and methods until a tragedy like this occurs.** Out of this incident came pressure to deploy flight data recorders and more robust aviation organizations.

Third, **real inspection regulations and technological innovation followed the crash, so such momentum may appear after digital wrecks.**

3. The final engineering disaster involves the Walt Disney Concert Hall in Los Angeles. This amazing, innovative structure, with a polished stainless steel skin, was completed in October 2003. When

finished, visitors immediately realized a problem with its construction. The sweeping curves of its roof act like a parabolic mirror, focusing the sun's rays like lasers on nearby buildings, intersections, and sections of the sidewalk. Temperatures exceeded 140 degrees Fahrenheit in some places, while drivers and passersby were temporarily blinded by the glare.

Investigators decided to model the entire facility in a computer simulation, then monitor for the highest levels of sunlight over the course of a year. Using this data, 2% of the building's skin was discovered to be causing the reflection problems. The remediation plan, implemented in March 2005, resulted in sanding problematic panels to remove their sheen. The six-week, $60,000 effort fixed the glare.

The lessons from the concert hall involve **complexity and unexpected consequences**. Architect Frank Geary wanted to push the envelope of architecture with his design. His innovation caused a building that no one, prior to its construction, really understood. Had the system been modeled before being built, it's possible problems could have been avoided. This situation is similar to those involving enterprise network and software architects who design systems that no single person truly understands. Worse, the system may expose services or functionality never expected by its creators. **Explicitly taking steps to simulate and test a new design prior to deployment is critical.**

Digital security engineers should not ignore the lessons their analog counterparts have to offer. A commitment to learn from the past is the best way to avoid disasters in the future.

https://taosecurity.blogspot.com/2007/07/more-engineering-disasters.html

Commentary

While I am a fan of learning from engineering disasters, make no mistake that there is a limit to their applicability. In each of the cases, the adversary was nature and/or physics. Making changes to procedures, designs, and constructs do not result in corresponding changes in nature. Mother Nature and her physical laws do not intelligently observe and adapt to human activity. Never forget that security is a discipline overshadowed by smart, initiative-taking and responsive counterparties pursuing their own agendas.

NORAD-Inspired Security Metrics

Tuesday, July 17, 2007

When I was a second degree cadet at USAFA (so long ago that, of my entire class, only myself and three friends had 486 PCs with Ethernet NICs) I visited NORAD. I remember thinking the *War Games* set was cooler, but I didn't give much thought to the security aspects of their mission.

Today I remembered NORAD and considered their mission with respect to my post last year titled *Control-Compliant vs Field-Assessed Security*. In case you can't tell from the pithy title, the central idea was that **it's more effective to measure security by assessing outcomes instead of inputs.** For example, **who cares if 100% of your systems have Windows XP SP2 if they are all 0wned by a custom exploit written just for your company?** Your security has failed. Inputs are important, but my experience with various organizations is that they tend to be the primary means of "measuring" security, regardless of how well they actually preserve the CIA triad.

Let's put this in terms of NORAD, whose front page states:

The North American Aerospace Defense Command (NORAD) is a bi-national United States and Canadian organization charged with the missions of aerospace warning and aerospace control for North America. Aerospace warning includes the monitoring of man-made objects in space, and the detection, validation, and warning of attack against North America whether by aircraft, missiles, or space vehicles, through mutual support arrangements with other commands. Aerospace control includes ensuring air sovereignty and air defense of the airspace of Canada and the United States...

To accomplish the aerospace warning mission, the commander of NORAD provides an integrated tactical warning and attack assessment to the governments of Canada and the United States. To accomplish the aerospace control mission, NORAD uses a network of satellites, ground-based radar, airborne radar and fighters to detect, intercept and, if necessary, engage any air-breathing threat to North America.

What are some control-compliant or input metrics for NORAD?

- Number of planes at the ready for intercepting rogue aircraft
- Average pilot rating (i.e., some sort of assessment of pilot skill)
- Radar uptime
- Radar coverage (e.g., percentage of North American territory monitored)

These are all interesting metrics. You might see some comparisons to metrics you might track, like the percentage of hosts with anti-virus.

Now consider: do any of those metrics tell you if NORAD is accomplishing its mission? In other words, **what is the outcome of all those inputs? What is the score of this game?**

Here are some field-assessed or **outcome-based metrics.**

- Number of rogue aircraft penetrating North American territory (indicates a failure to deter activity)
- Number of aircraft not detected by NORAD but discovered via other means to have penetrated North American territory (perhaps via intel sources; indicates a failure to detect activity)
- Number of aircraft not repelled by interceptors (hopefully this would never happen!)
- Time from first indication of rogue aircraft to launching interceptors (indicates effectiveness of pilot-to-plane-to-air process)

These metrics address the critical concern: accomplishing the mission.

Keep these in mind when you are devising metrics for your digital security program.

https://taosecurity.blogspot.com/2007/07/norad-inspired-security-metrics.html

Commentary

This post is still relevant today. I encourage anyone with a security leadership role to seriously consider if your metrics are measuring inputs or outputs. The closer you get to measuring outputs, the more likely your security program will be effective.

Lessons from the Military

Friday, August 31, 2007

Jay Heiser is a smart guy, but I don't know why he became so anti-military when he wrote *Military mindset no longer applicable in our line of work* last year. He wrote in part:

> The business world should stop looking to the defense community for direction on information security.

> I used to believe that the practice of information security owed a huge debt to the military. I couldn't have been more wrong...

> The business world doesn't need the defense community to help it develop secure technology, and, whenever it accepts military ideas, it winds up with the wrong agenda...

> It's time our profession stops playing war games and gets in touch with its business roots.

I found two responses, *Opinion: Military security legacy is one of innovation, integrity* and *Opinion: The importance of a military mindset*, countering Mr. Heiser. I also found poll results showing 77% of respondents answered "absolutely critical" or "somewhat important" when reading the question "How important is a military mindset when planning and executing an enterprise security strategy?"

Well, it's Friday night and you know what that means in the Bejtlich household. That's right, time to watch a new episode of *Dogfights*, a TV show about historical air-to-air fighter combat. I don't have any insights based on the episode I just watched, but it reminded me of training I received my first summer at Camp USAFA [United States Air Force Academy].

One of the exercises we ran involved Air Base Ground Defense (ABGD). We learned some basic principles and then acted first as attackers and then defenders. It occurred to me that ABGD is in some ways similar to defending digital assets, although we digital security people are not armed. This denies us the capability of truly deterring and incapacitating threats. Attribution is also easier when the enemy is physically present.

Still, I'd like to do my part showing Mr. Heiser what business can learn from the military. Much of corporate America (and Germany, and Japan) seems to be having its lunch eaten by the Chinese dragon, so it's time to take some lessons from people who do security for a living when lives are at stake.

I decided to take a look at DoD Joint Publications and found *Joint Tactics, Techniques, and Procedures for Base Defense*. Just skimming it I found several very interesting sections. For example, the executive summary includes this:

> The general characteristics of defensive operations are:
>
> 1. to understand the enemy;
> 2. see the battlefield;
> 3. use the defenders' advantages;
> 4. concentrate at critical times and places;
> 5. conduct counterreconnaissance and counterattacks;
> 6. coordinate critical defense assets;
> 7. balance base security with political and legal constraints;
> 8. and know the law of war and rules of engagement.

I think digital non-military, non-police forces can do all of these except the counterattack portion of number 5. For that we need the military and police to act, or to have them deputize us. Notice numbers 1 and 2 imply monitoring, and number 4 implies being able to recognize critical times and places via digital situational awareness.

The document continues:

> The primary mission of the base is to support joint force objectives.

In other words, the base does not exist to provide security. The base exists to perform "business functions."

> Essential actions of the defense force are to detect, warn, deny, destroy, and delay. Every intelligence and counterintelligence resource available to the base commander should be used to determine enemy capabilities and intentions. The base commander must make the best use of the terrain within the commander's AO [area of operation].

Again, we cannot destroy the enemy, but the police and military can.

A graphic in the document displays some physical perimeter defense measures. It shows principles like defense in depth. It includes an "intrusion detection" system (labeled "sensor") and a "network forensics" system (labeled "video camera"). Visibility is provided by lighting. If you're a *Jericho Forum* fan, imagine these defenses collapsed around the host or even data.

I plan to take a closer look at this document and the Air Force version, AFI 31-301, Air Base Defense.

https://taosecurity.blogspot.com/2007/08/lessons-from-military.html

Commentary

I agree that it is important to not let a military mindset consume security processes, people, or technologies. However, the military world is one of the few that includes intelligent, adaptive adversaries. Organized crime and certain aspects of corporate and diplomatic life also integrate this feature. While the military does not have the answer to all security problems, there are lessons to be learned if one is open to them.

Comment on NetWitness Article

Monday, September 10, 2007

About a year ago I wrote *Network Forensics with NetWitness*. Today NetWitness is an independent company (again, congratulations) and is launching a new product suite. I was already a fan of their product last year but I will be taking another look at it in the coming weeks. If you want to know why please see last year's post.

I'm writing this post in reaction to [a story titled] *Startup Led by Ex-DHS Cyberchief Rolls Out Forensics Tool*. Specifically, I take issue with this excerpt:

> [A] security and risk management analyst... says NetWitness's technology is basically immune from anti-forensic tools that attackers increasingly are using to deter investigations of breaches, for instance. "NetWitness allows organizations to investigate user activities at a level that neither attackers nor most users will be able to tamper with."

When I read that comment I immediately remembered *The Eavesdropper's Dilemma*, first mentioned in my blog post *Latest Plane Reading* from May 2007.

Network forensics can be attacked just like host forensics can be attacked. (If someone can please point me to the original citations for these, I would be grateful. I remember the terms but I can't remember who originally demonstrated the differences.)

- **Anti-forensics means attacking the evidence.** Encrypting network traffic is a simple network-based anti-forensic technique. Matt Blaze wrote a paper that describes anti-forensics. Chapter 18 of my first book describes ways to attack NSM as well.
- **Counter-forensics means attacking the tools.** All of the Wireshark security advisories describing remotely exploitable or denial of service conditions are examples of counter-forensics (e.g., *Ethereal 10.x AFP Protocol Dissector Remote Format String Exploit.*)

I am sure NetWitness suffers both types of problems just by the nature of its operation, like any other network forensics application.

Perhaps the comment was inspired by thoughts like *Hardware-Assisted Virtual Machine Rootkit* or *TaoSecurity Enterprise Trust Pyramid*, where I defend the notion that the network doesn't lie like a compromised host does. However, like I mentioned in Marcus Ranum Highlights from USENIX:

> At a certain point the complexity [of the firewall/filter] makes you just as likely to be insecure as the original application.

This is true for protocol-aware analysis tools as well as firewalls/filters.

Update: If you check the Dark Reading article again you'll see the word "resistant" replacing "immune". Please check the comments to see a post by the person who Dark Reading "quoted" to learn what can happen when you speak to reporters!

https://taosecurity.blogspot.com/2007/09/comment-on-netwitness-article.html

Commentary

I am a stickler for language, and **I like this distinction between anti-forensics (attacking the evidence) and counter-forensics (attacking the tools).** However, it is probably more important to simply be aware that adversaries can pursue either or both courses of action when trying to frustrate security teams.

Tactical Traffic Assessment

Friday, September 21, 2007

When I wrote *Extrusion Detection* in 2004-5 I used the term *Traffic Threat Assessment* to describe a means of inspecting network traffic for signs of malicious activity. I differentiated among various assessments using this terminology.

A vulnerability assessment identifies vulnerabilities and exposures in assets.

A penetration test identifies at least one way that an adversary could exploit vulnerabilities and exposures to compromise a target or satisfy a related objective.

A traffic threat assessment identifies traffic that indicates a network has already been compromised.

The goal of the customer determined which of the actions to perform.

I was not really comfortable with the term "traffic threat assessment," so I'm going to use **Tactical Traffic Assessment** starting now. That definition for TTA nicely differentiates between a short-term, focused, tactical effort and a long-term, enterprise-wide, strategic program like Network Security Monitoring.

Tactical Traffic Assessment removes the "threat assessment" part out of TTA, since **"threat assessment" is more about characterizing the capabilities and intentions of an adversary** and **not whether he has compromised the enterprise.**

Tactical Traffic Assessment also leaves room for finding non-security issues like misconfigured devices or other troubleshooting-related network problems.

https://taosecurity.blogspot.com/2007/09/tactical-traffic-assessment.html

Commentary

I wrote this post a few months after joining General Electric. I had performed assessments of this sort as a consultant for TaoSecurity LLC. I later learned that Mandiant was offering "compromise assessments," which was a great holistic term. I focused on the network aspect of this operation as I was not prepared to do host-based forensic investigations as a one-person security consultancy. Furthermore, the technology to more easily do that work didn't really exist in 2007.

Security Jersey Colors

Friday, September 21, 2007

I realized after my previous post that not everyone may be familiar with the "color" system used to designate various military security teams. I referenced a "red team" in my post NSA IAM and IEM Summary, for example.

I thought it might be helpful to post my understanding of these colors and to solicit feedback from anyone who could clarify these statements.

Red Team: **A Red Team is an adversary simulation team**. The Red Team attacks the asset to meet an objective. This activity is called penetration testing in the commercial world.

Blue Team: **A Blue Team is a security posture assessment and evaluation team.** The Blue Team determines the vulnerabilities and exposures of an enterprise. This activity is called vulnerability assessment in the commercial world.

White Team: **A White Team (or usually a "White Cell") controls the environment during an exercise.** The White Cell provides the framework in which the Red Team attacks friendly forces. (Note that in some situations the friendly forces are called the "Blue Team." This is not the same Blue Team that conducts vulnerability assessments and evaluations. Blue in this case is simply used to differentiate from Red.)

Green Team: **The Green Team is usually a training group that helps the asset owners.** Alternatively, the Green Team helps with long-term vulnerability and exposure remediation, as identified by the Blue Team. These descriptions are open for discussion because I haven't seen too many green team activities.

Did I miss any colors?

https://taosecurity.blogspot.com/2007/09/security-jersey-colors.html

Commentary

This is an example of the influence of military operations on civilian cyber security practices. The term "red team" was not as popular in 2007 among the commercial sector as it was in the military. You could potentially trace the terms back to the American War for Independence, or the Revolutionary War. In that conflict, the British were the "red coats" and the Americans wore blue. Similarly, in the Cold War, Americans represented friendly forces as "blue" and Soviet forces as "red." At the United States Air Force Weapons School, the adversary simulation team is called the "red team."

The Doomsday Clock

Wednesday, October 10, 2007

Tonight I finished watching a show called *The Doomsday Clock*, on the best TV channel (the History Channel, of course). I was vaguely aware of the clock, maintained by the Bulletin of the Atomic Scientists, but I didn't know the history of the project. According to *Minutes to Midnight*:

> The Bulletin of the Atomic Scientists' Doomsday Clock conveys how close humanity is to catastrophic destruction--the figurative midnight--and monitors the means humankind could use to obliterate itself. First and foremost, these include nuclear weapons, but they also

encompass climate-changing technologies and new developments in the life sciences and nanotechnology that could inflict irrevocable harm.

Interesting -- you know what this is? It's a risk assessment. In my first book **I defined risk as the probability of suffering harm or loss**. The Doomsday Clock supposedly displays how close we are to world-ending catastrophe.

I find two aspects of the clock appealing.

First, as depicted by Information Aesthetics, the clock rapidly and clearly communicates its message. If you see fewer and fewer minutes until midnight, you sense something bad is about to happen. It's language-neutral and concise.

Second, the act of moving the hands and then tracking hand position over time provides a sense of risk trending. You can get a historical reading of risk by watching the number of minutes to midnight rise and fall. The interval between the hand position changes is also significant.

The problem with the Doomsday Clock is the same problem found in many, if not most, risk assessments. It is more or less arbitrary. The creation of the clock and **the initial position of its hands was completely arbitrary**, in fact! The designer of the clock, artistic designer Martyl Langsdorf, invented the clock for the June 1947 issue of the Bulletin. **She positioned the hands to be aesthetically pleasing, not to show how close we were to destruction.** When you consider the amount of time she could have worked with (12 hours), **limiting herself to a fifteen minute window set a precedent for the next sixty years.** While the clock has moved outside this 15 minute window (for example, in 1991) the precedent was set too narrowly. What will the bulletin do when even greater threats exist -- move to second and then nano-second increments?

In response to the Soviet's 1949 detonation of their first atomic weapon, Bulletin founder and editor Eugene Rabinowitch told Langsdorf to move the hands from 7 minutes to midnight to 3 minutes to midnight. Again, this choice was basically to convey urgency. Only when the hands were moved on the magazine cover did readers start to appreciate the information conveyed by the clock.

From this point forward, the hands have moved back and forth as the Bulletin members and, more recently, outside parties have haggled about the position of the hands. I have a feeling these meetings would drive me crazy. It's a collection of people with opinions arguing about the location of hands on a clock created originally for artistic value. Still, as noted in my two "appealing" points, I think we can learn some lessons from the Doomsday Clock regarding the ability to quickly and powerfully communicate risk to others.

While researching this post I discovered that the ACLU jumped on the "clock bandwagon" with its Surveillance Society Clock. According to the ACLU, "It's six minutes before midnight as a surveillance society draws near within the United States." This is dumb for multiple reasons.

First, the ACLU chose a digital clock. I don't know about you, but for me a digital clock doesn't convey an amount of time as visually as an analog clock. It's like a speedometer; seeing it pegged to the right is more powerful than reading "101 MPH" or similar. Second, as Wired magazine astutely asked, how do we know when we're there? It's tough to ignore Armageddon; it's easy to ignore a "surveillance state." Third, the ACLU painted itself into the same corner as the Bulletin did when it chose to set its initial time so close to midnight. What's the ACLU going to do with the clock when remote mind-reading is in use?

https://taosecurity.blogspot.com/2007/10/doomsday-clock.html

Commentary

Since this post, I've commented about the overall silliness implied by the so-called "Doomsday Clock." In 2020, I wrote the following:

> "The Bulletin lost contact with reality in the early 2000s. No serious person would say we are at greater risk for a global apocalypse in 2020, with the clock 1 minute 40 seconds to midnight, than we were in 1963 (12 minutes) or 1984 (3 minutes). The incorporation of cyber elements does nothing to justify moving the clock hands to the current position."

I also Tweeted the following:

> "To show how irrelevant the @BulletinAtomic #DoomsdayClock is, they moved the hands because of 'information warfare,' yet the world faces a pandemic #coronavirus risk. Granted they did mention bio weapons in their bulletin, but never mind old-fashioned bugs from Chinese markets."

Counterintelligence and the Cyber Threat

Sunday, October 21, 2007

Friday I attended an open symposium hosted by the Office of the National Counterintelligence Executive (ONCIX). It was titled *Counterintelligence and the Cyber Threat* and featured speakers and panels from government, law enforcement, industry, legal, and academic organizations. I attended as a representative of my company because our CSO, Frank Taylor, participated in the industry panel.

If you're not familiar with the term counterintelligence, let me reproduce a section from the OCNIX Web site:

> **Counterintelligence** is the business of identifying and dealing with **foreign intelligence threats** to the United States. Its core concern is the **intelligence services of foreign states** and similar organizations of non-state actors, such as transnational terrorist groups. Counterintelligence has both a **defensive mission** — protecting the nation's secrets and assets **against foreign intelligence penetration** — and an **offensive mission** — **finding out what foreign intelligence organizations are planning to better defeat their aims.**

I also recommend reading the National Counterintelligence Strategy of the United States, 2007 (.pdf) which states:

> Our adversaries -- foreign intelligence services, terrorists, foreign criminal enterprises and cyber intruders -- use overt, covert, and clandestine activities to exploit and undermine US national security interests. Counterintelligence is one of several instruments of national power that can thwart such activities, but its effectiveness depends in many respects on coordination with other elements of government and with the private sector.

> During the Cold War, our nation's adversaries gained access to vital secrets of the most closely guarded institutions of our national security establishment and **penetrated virtually all organizations of the US intelligence and defense communities.** The resulting losses produced grave damage to our national security in terms of secrets

compromised, intelligence sources degraded, and lives lost, and would have been catastrophic had we been at war.

Minor note 1: if we were not at war during the "Cold War," then why is it called a "War"? I believe the people who died fighting would call it a war.

Minor note 2: foreign intelligence services, terrorists, and foreign criminal enterprises are all specific parties. "Cyber intruders" are more often one of those previous parties. Those who perform digital attacks but do not fall into one of those three categories are usually script kiddies or recreational hackers, and **should not be explicitly mentioned as counterintelligence targets.** My guess is the report considers cyber-instantiated threats to be serious enough to somehow mention explicitly, but **not enough intellectual rigor was applied to this sentence** (like the Cold War section).

Major note: does the section about penetrating virtually all organizations of the US intelligence and defense communities surprise you? When I attended Air Force intelligence school in 1996-1997, one of our first instructors said:

> "Most, if not all of the classified material you will see in your career has already been compromised. However, we have to act as if it's not."

I remembered thinking "What?!?" With hindsight, the more I hear about spies found inside government agencies, the more I understand that statement.

I found the symposium fascinating, so I'd like to share a few thoughts. Dr. Joel Brenner, the National Counterintelligence Executive, provided plenty of noteworthy comments. He said that **counterintelligence is not security.**

A security person sees a hole in a fence and wants to patch it.

A CI person sees a hole in a fence and wants to understand who created it, how it is being abused, and if it can be turned into an asset to use against the adversary.

Dr. Brenner said about 140 foreign intelligence surveillance organizations currently target the United States. Three strategic issues are at play:

Threats to sovereign (US) networks, especially in the cyber domain. Dr. Brenner said "there is growing acceptance that we face a cyber counterintelligence problem, not a security problem." I agree with this, and will have more to say about it in a future blog entry. He stressed the alteration attack (rather than the disclosure or destruction attacks) as being the major problem facing US networks.

Acquisition risk, i.e., supply chain risks. Dr. Brenner said we need technically literate lawyers and policymakers to address these risks.

Collaboration, or the lack thereof. Dr. Brenner notes that our current "cooperation model" is a function of our "classification model," resulting in an antiquated system that serves no one well.

One of the most interesting comments was this:

> **Industry talks risk management but they really do risk acceptance, not risk mitigation.**

How true that is!

Chris Inglis, Deputy Director of the NSA and a fellow USAFA grad, used a term I liked with regard to fighting the cyber adversary. He said **we need to outmaneuver the adversary, not solve security**

problems. I love this because it implies "security" can't be "solved," and it provides a reason to review maneuver warfare as a way to counter the adversary.

John McClurg, Vice President for security at Honeywell, described his "validated data" approach to obtaining business buy-in for security initiatives. He collects data to support a security program and presents it to managers as a means to justify his work. This sounds a lot like showing evidence that a business unit is owned or about to be owned. I like this idea and my work with NSM would help provide such data.

Scott O'Neal, Chief Computer Intrusion Section, Cyber Division, FBI, said "The adversary is clearly ahead of security. This is a fact we have to accept." This echoes statements I made earlier this year and at other times. The FBI addresses intrusions through three points of view: CT (counterterrorism), CI (counterintelligence) and criminal.

I'll have more to say on this subject in the months ahead.

https://taosecurity.blogspot.com/2007/10/counterintelligence-and-cyber-threat.html

Commentary

All of this is still true in 2020. However, all of the organizations mentioned in the post are providing more information to their corporate constituency, rather than keeping it in classified channels. This is helpful for everyone trying to defend their organizations, and embodies "defensive CI." Furthermore, there is public evidence that, especially beginning in 2018, US forces have done more work to penetrate and disrupt adversary intelligence organizations. This is a fulfilment of the "offensive" nature of CI.

Incident Severity Ratings

Much of digital security focuses on pre-compromise activities. Not as much attention is paid to what happens once your defenses fail. My friend Bamm brought this problem to my attention when he discussed the problem of rating the severity of an incident. He was having trouble explaining to his management the impact of an intrusion, so he asked if I had given any thought to the issue.

What follows is my attempt to apply a framework to the problem. If anyone wants to point me to existing work, please feel free. This is not an attempt to put a flag in the ground. We're trying to figure out how to talk about post-compromise activities in a world where scoring vulnerabilities receives far more attention.

This is a list of factors which influence the severity of an incident. It is written mainly from the intrusion standpoint. In other words, an unauthorized party is somehow interacting with your asset. I have ordered the options under each category such that the top items in each sub-list is considered worst, and the bottom is best. Since this is a work in progress I put question marks in many of the sub-lists.

1. Level of Control
   a. Domain or network-wide SYSTEM/Administrator/root
   b. Local SYSTEM/Administrator/root
   c. Privileged user (but not SYSTEM/Administrator/root
   d. User
   e. None?
2. Level of Interaction
   a. Shell
   b. API
   c. Application commands
   d. None?

3. Nature of Contact
   a. Persistent and continuous
   b. On-demand
   c. Re-exploitation required
   d. Misconfiguration required
   e. None?

4. Reach of Victim
   a. Entire enterprise
   b. Specific zones
   c. Local segment only
   d. Host only

5. Nature of Victim Data
   a. Exceptionally grave damage if destroyed/altered/disclosed
   b. Grave damage if destroyed/altered/disclosed
   c. Some damage if destroyed/altered/disclosed
   d. No damage if destroyed/altered/disclosed

6. Degree of Friendly External Control of Victim
   a. None; host has free Internet access inbound and outbound
   b. Some external control of access
   c. Comprehensive external control of access

7. Host Vulnerability (for purposes of future re-exploitation
   a. Numerous severe vulnerabilities
   b. Moderate vulnerability
   c. Little to no vulnerability

8. Friendly Visibility of Victim
   a. No monitoring of network traffic or host logs
   b. Only network or host logging (not both)
   c. Comprehensive network and host visibility

9. Threat Assessment
   a. Highly skilled and motivated, or structured threat
   b. Moderately skilled and motivated, or semi-structured threat
   c. Low skilled and motivated, or unstructured threat

10. Business Impact (from continuity of operations plan)
   a. High
   b. Medium
   c. Low

11. Onsite Support
   a. None
   b. First level technical support present
   c. Skilled operator onsite

Based on this framework, I would be most worried about the following -- stated very bluntly so you see all eleven categories: **I worry about an incident where the intruder has SYSTEM control, with a shell, that is persistent, on a host that can reach the entire enterprise, on a host with very valuable data, with unfettered Internet access, on a host with lots of serious holes, and I can't see the host's logs or traffic, and the intruder is a foreign intel service, and the host is a high biz impact system, and no one is on site to help me.**

What do you think?

https://taosecurity.blogspot.com/2007/12/incident-severity-ratings.html

Commentary

First, how did I create a framework that had 11 categories? I should have stopped at 10 or added a 12th.

Second, a post like this is meant to capture thoughts for the purpose of refining them and putting them into action in the enterprise. In that spirit, perhaps it has given you something to consider in your security role. It can't be adopted without modification into modern environments, as it is enterprise-centric and needs to integrate mobile and cloud concerns.

How Many Burning Homes

Saturday, March 15, 2008

I mentioned the idea of host integrity assessment in my post *Controls Are Not the Solution to Our Problem*. The idea is to sample live devices (laptops, desktops, servers, routers, switches -- anything that runs a network-enabled operating system) to see if they are trustworthy. (They may be **trusted**, but that does not make them **trustworthy**.)

I described how I might determine trustworthiness, or integrity, in *Three Capabilities, Three Companies*. I'd like to expand on these thoughts with five metrics. Before showing the security metrics, I'd like to introduce an analogy.

Imagine a city with an understaffed, under-resourced, and possibly unappreciated fire department. The FD would like to prevent fires, but it spends most of its time responding to fires. How should city leadership decide how to staff and resource the FD? (There is no way to eliminate fires, at least no way that could ever be financed using any foreseeable resources. Even if people lived in concrete cells with no furnishings, they would probably figure out a way to light each other or the ground on fire!)

In this situation, one might argue that one way to judge the peril of the situation is the ability of the FD to "manage the fires." In other words, perhaps there is some number of burning homes that can be maintained while the FD responds, contains, and extinguishes fires. If the FD is large enough the number of fires can be rapidly decreased such that the time to extinguish is very small. If the FD is too small, then eventually the whole city burns because the fires overwhelm the FD's ability to respond, contain, and extinguish.

The question becomes what is the "right" number? You could think in terms of the following metrics.

1. **Number of burning homes at any sampled time.** The higher this number, the more likely the fire will spread.
2. **Average length of time any home is burning.** Again, the higher this number, the more likely the fire will spread.
3. **Average time from detection to response.** This measures how fast the FD arrives on site.
4. **Average time from response to recovery.** This measures how effective the FD is fighting fires.
5. **Average property value of burning homes.** One would be less concerned if the burning homes are abandoned or condemned, and more concerned if they are inhabited.

I do not consider the number of arsonists here. That is relevant but it brings into question the role of the police to deter, investigate, apprehend, prosecute, and incarcerate threats. The FD cannot fight arsonists directly.

Now let's turn to digital security. While it's easy to spot a fire, identifying a "burning" (i.e., compromised) computer can be more difficult. If we could do that via host integrity assessment, we could imagine the following metrics.

1. **Number of compromised computers at any sampled time.** This is a statistically valid sample.
2. **Average length of time any computer is compromised.** Answering this question requires a forensic investigation to identify the point in time where the intrusion is most likely to have happened.
3. **Average time from detection to response.** This measures the effectiveness of the intrusion detection program.
4. **Average time from response to recovery.** This measures the effectiveness of the IRT and provisioning personnel.

5. **Average asset value of compromised computers.** Again, a lot of owned low-value assets might not be a big problem.

So what do you do with these numbers? First, I recommend just collecting them. Second, take them to business owners and ask if the situation is acceptable. For example:

- Is it acceptable to have 25% of a business' computers compromised? 50% 10%? 5%?
- Is it ok for them to be owned for 6 months? 1 day? 2 years?
- Is it ok for us to take 6 months to notice? 2 hours? 2 days?
- Is it ok for us to take 1 week to recover? 1 day? 1 month?
- Is it ok for us to be suffering compromise on development servers? Call center PCs? Human resources databases?

Note on arsonists: you should be able to tell that "arsonists" are intruders. Since most companies can't reduce threats directly, IRTs are in exactly the same position as the FD.

Note on prevention: you can extend the fire analogy to other areas. Fire resistance is like the time required for a red team to penetrate a target. Applying fire retardants is like blue teams taking countermeasures upon discovering vulnerabilities.

Finally, with these answers we can make decisions to change the metrics. For example, a firefighter could say "increase my staff by two people per shift, and buy this new fire engine, and I can change the metrics this way." In the digital realm, a security analyst could say "increase my staff by two people per shift, and buy this new sensor grid, and I can change the metrics this way."

You could also try to influence the prevention side by saying "change all antivirus software from vendor A to vendor B, and change all local users from administrators to unprivileged users" and then see if the metrics change.

The manager is now in a position where spending influences metrics, and the failure to spend could result in an unacceptable answer to the question "How many burning homes?"

https://taosecurity.blogspot.com/2008/03/how-many-burning-hom es.html

Commentary

I favor integrating lessons from the physical world, where appropriate, into digital security thinking. Metrics are most useful when they measure outputs, not inputs.

Ten Themes from Recent Conferences

Wednesday, March 19, 2008

I blogged recently about various conferences I've attended. I considered what I had seen and found ten themes to describe the state of affairs and some general strategies for digital defense. Your enterprise has to be of a certain size and complexity for these items to hold true. For example, I do not expect item one to hold true for my lab network since the user base, number of assets, and nature of the assets is so small. Furthermore, I heavily instrument the lab (that's the purpose of it) so I am less likely to suffer item one. Still, organizations that use their network for business purposes (i.e., the network is not an end unto itself) will probably find common ground in these themes.

Permanent compromise is the norm, so accept it. I used to think digital defense was a cycle involving *resist -> detect -> respond -> recover*. Between *recover* and the next attack there would be a period where the enterprise could be considered "clean." I've learned now that all enterprises remain "dirty" to some degree, unless massive and cost-prohibitive resources are directed at the problem.

We can not stop intruders, only raise their costs. Enterprises stay dirty because we can not stop intruders, but we can make their lives more difficult. I've heard of some organizations trying to raise the $ per MB that the adversary must spend in order to exfiltrate/degrade/deny information.

Anyone of sufficient size and asset value is being targeted. If you are sufficiently "interesting" but you don't think you are being attacked and compromised, you're not looking closely enough.

Less Enterprise Protection, more Enterprise Defense. We need to think less in terms of raising our arms to block our face while digitally boxing, and more in terms of side-stepping, ducking and weaving, counter-punching, and other dynamic defenses.

Less Prevention, more Detection, Response, Disruption. One of my laws from my books is **prevention eventually fails.** Your best bet is to identify intrusions and rapidly contain and frustrate the intruder. You have to balance information gathering against active responses, but most organizations cannot justify what are essentially intel gathering operations against the adversary.

Less Vulnerability Management, more System Integrity Analysis. Vulnerability management is still important, but it's an input metric. **We need more output metrics,** like SIA. Are all the defenses we institute doing anything useful? SIA can provide some answers.

Less Totality, more Sampling. In security, something is better than nothing. Instead of worrying about determining the trustworthiness of every machine in production, devise statistically valid sample sizes and conduct SIA, tactical traffic assessment, and other evaluation techniques and extrapolate to the general population.

Less Blacklisting, more Whitelisting. Organizations are waking up to the fact that there is no way to enumerate bad and allow everything else, but it is possible to enumerate good and deny everything else.

Use Infrequency/Rarity to our advantage. If your organization adopts something like the FDCC on your PCs and whitelists applications, the environment will be fairly homogenous. Many organizations are deciding to make the trade-off between diversity/survivability and homogeneity/susceptibility in favor of homogeneity. If you're going down that path, why not spend extra attention on anything that deviates from your core load? Chances are it's unauthorized and potentially malicious.

Use Blue and Red Teams to measure and validate. I've written about this a lot in my blog but I'm seeing other organizations adopt the same stance.

Have you adopted any themes based on your work or conference attendance?

https://taosecurity.blogspot.com/2008/03/ten-themes-from-recent-conferences.html

Commentary

These trends and suggestions are still applicable in 2020. I would change one point to say "less deny-only lists, and more allow-only lists."

Microsecurity vs Macrosecurity

Friday, August 15, 2008

I found the following insight by Ravila Helen White in *Information Security and Business Integration* to be fascinating:

> Economists figured out long ago that in order to understand the economy, they would have to employ a double-pronged approach. The first approach would look at the economy by gathering data from individuals and firms on a small scale. The second approach would tackle analysis of the economy as a whole. Thus was born micro and macro economics.

We can make information security more consumable by taking a page from economics. **If we divide information security in the same manner as economics (its analytical form), we get micro information security and macro information security.**

Micro information security is the nuts and bolts that support an organization's information security practice. It's the **technology, controls, countermeasures and tactical solutions that are employed day-to-day to defend against cyber threats.** It's a step-by-step examination of information security for educational purposes and to facilitate discussion with our peers.

Macro information security is the big picture and can be utilized to keep management in the loop. It's the **blueprint, framework, strategic plan, road map, governance and policies designed to influence and protect the enterprise.** It's the bottom line.

Macro information security also extends externally to support partners and customers as well as ensure compliance with regulations. Internal organization extension includes support of

218

convergence programs and includes alignment to business goals and objectives.

Macro information security enables security leaders to align themselves and the program(s) they oversee with the business. It bridges information security vernacular with traditional business acumen. When used correctly, macro information security can be the tool that equals success. And, success is being invited back to the table again and again.

I like this separation, although I am not as comfortable with the exact definitions. If you're fuzzy about the difference between microeconomics and macroeconomics, Wikipedia is helpful:

> Microeconomics is a branch of economics that studies how individuals, households and firms make decisions to allocate limited resources, typically in markets where goods or services are being bought and sold.

> Microeconomics examines how these decisions and behaviours affect the supply and demand for goods and services, which determines prices; and how prices, in turn, determine the supply and demand of goods and services.

> Macroeconomics is a branch of economics that deals with the performance, structure, and behavior of a national or regional economy as a whole... Macroeconomists study aggregated indicators such as GDP, unemployment rates, and price indices to understand how the whole economy functions. Macroeconomists develop models that explain the relationship between such factors as national income, output, consumption, unemployment, inflation, savings, investment, international trade and international finance.

The differences are striking and the distinction helpful. **I don't think anyone thinks of a microeconomist in a negative light because he or she doesn't dwell on the "big picture" macroeconomic view.** It's simply two different ways to contemplate and explain economic activity.

We have a separation of sorts in the security world. Macrosecurity types like to think about aggregate risk, capturing metrics, and enterprise-wide security postures. Microsecurity types prefer to focus on individual networks, hosts, applications, operating systems, and hardware, along with specific attack and defense options.

I think I prefer microsecurity issues but spend time on the macro side when I have to justify my work to management.

https://taosecurity.blogspot.com/2008/08/microsecurity-vs-macrosecurity.html

Commentary

This is one of those posts that I haven't thought about in the years since I wrote it, but which has some useful insights. This is an example of drawing upon other disciplines to extract lessons for the security world. I mean lessons, incidentally, not "learnings." I first heard that corporate-speak at General Electric and I hoped it would die there!

Managing Security in Economic Downturns

Friday, November 21, 2008

You don't need to read this blog for news on the global economic depression. However, several people have asked me what it means for security teams, especially when Schneier Agrees: *Security ROI is "Mostly Bunk"*. No one can generate cash by running a security team;

the best we can do is save money. If your security team generates cash, you're either a MSSP, a collection agency of some sort (these do exist, believe it or not!), in need of being spun-off, or not accounting for all of your true costs.

Putting the ROI debate aside, these are tough economic times. Assuming we can all stay employed, we might be able to work the situation to our advantage. Nothing motivates management like a financial argument. See if one or more of the following might work to your advantage, because of the downturn.

Promote centralization and consolidation. The more large organizations I've joined, consulted for, or met, the more I see that successful ones have centralized, consolidated security teams. There's simply not enough skilled security personnel to protect us, and spreading the talent across large organizations leaves too many gaps. Think of the pockets of talent distributed across your own company, and how their skills could be applied organization-wide if properly positioned. If head counts are threatened, make a play for creating a single central group that helps the whole company and brings the best talent into that team.

Convert business security leaders into local experts/consultants. If you work within a large company, your individual business leaders may not like seeing their local staff join a larger company-wide organization. However, those that remain in the business should now be free to focus on what is unique about their business, instead of the minutiae of managing anti-virus, firewalls, patches, and other "traditional" security measures that are absolutely vanilla functions which could be outsourced overseas in a heartbeat. What's more valuable, a security leader who can run an AV console, configure a firewall, and apply a patch, or one who can advise their business CEO on the risks, regulations, and realities of operating in their individual realm? Notice I said leader and not technician. Technicians do the routine tasks I mentioned and are ripe for outsourcing; don't cling to that role unless you want to be replaced by a Perl script.

Advocate standardization where it makes sense. For example, is it really necessary to have more than one "gold image" for your common desktop/laptop user? Why develop your own image when the Federal government is doing all the work for you with the Federal Desktop Core Configuration? Turn the team that creates your own image into a much smaller one that tweaks the FDCC, and redeploy the personnel where you need them.

Cut through bureaucracy and authority barriers with a financial knife. This one really bugs me. How many incident responders out there lose time, effectiveness, and data because 1) you don't know who owns a victim computer; 2) finding someone who owns the computer takes time; 3) getting permission to do something about the victim requires more time? You can probably make a case for reduced help desk costs, fewer support personnel, and faster/more accurate/cheaper incident response if you gain the authority to perform remote live response and/or forensics on any platform required, minus some accepted and reasonable exclusion list. This requires 1) good inventory management; 2) forensic agent pre-deployment or administrator credentials to deploy and agent or scripts as necessary; and 3) mature processes and trained people to execute.

Simplify and build visibility in. An example comes from my post *Feds Plan to Reduce, Then Monitor.* What's cheaper than 1) identifying all your gateways; 2) devising a plan to reduce that number; and 3) building visibility in? Step 1 takes some effort, step 2 might strain your network architects, and step 3 could require new monitoring platforms. However, when done, you're spending less money on gateways, less time scoping intrusions, and less resources on scrambling during incident response because you know all the ways in and out of your organization -- and you can see what is happening. This is a no-brainer.

Move data, not people. This is the principle I mentioned in *Green Security.* I'm sure your travel budget is being cut. **Why fly a security person around the world when, if you achieve the goals in step 4, you can move the data instead?** And, if you're building visibility in, you have more data available and don't need to scramble for it.

Wrap everything in metrics. This one is probably the most painful, but it's definitely necessary. If you can't justify your security spending, you're more likely to be cut in a downturn. This doesn't mean "security ROI." What it does mean is showing why your approach is better than the alternatives, with "better" usually meaning (but not always) "cheaper." It can be difficult to capture finances in our field, but I have some ideas. One is **intrusion debt.** If you've recently hired any outside consultants to assist with security work, their invoices provide a ton of metrics opportunities. (You have a tangible cost that you wish to avoid by taking steps X, Y, and Z in the future.) Metrics can also justify team growth, which is the next step out of the downturn. Be ready!

If you have any ideas, please post them here. I think this is an important topic. Thank you.

https://taosecurity.blogspot.com/2008/11/managing-security-in-eco nomic-downturns.html

Commentary

I wrote this post during the Great Recession of the 2000s, but it is even more appropriate in the time of Covid-19. The point about moving data and not people is even more important today. I learned this lesson at the AFCERT. We couldn't afford to fly our limited incident response team all over the world whenever someone suspected an intrusion in progress. Instead, we deployed sensors, collected and exported the data centrally to San Antonio, Texas, and analyzed it there. If necessary we flew the IRT somewhere, but that was kept to a minimum.

Don't Fight the Future

Friday, November 21, 2008

Digital security practitioners should fight today's battles while preparing for the future. I don't know what that future looks like, and neither does anyone else. However, I'd like to capture a few thoughts here. This is a mix of what I think will happen, plus what I would like to see happen. If I'm lucky (or good) the future will reflect these factors, for which I am planning.

A few caveats: I don't have an absolute time factor for these, and I'm not considering these my "predictions for 2009." This is not an endorsement of the Jericho Forum. I think it makes sense to plan for the environment I will describe next because it will be financially attractive, but not necessarily universally security-enhancing (or even smart).

Virtual Private Network (VPN) connections will disappear. For many readers this is nothing groundbreaking, but bring up the possibility with a networking team and they stare in bewilderment. Is there any reason why a remote system needs to have a simulated connection, using all available protocols, to a corporate network? Some of you might limit the type of connection to certain protocols, but why not just expose those protocols directly to the outside world and avoid the VPN altogether?

Intranets will disappear. This is the next step when you architect for situations where VPNs are no longer needed. What's the purpose of an Intranet if you expose all the corporate applications to the outside world? The Intranet essentially becomes a giant local ISP. That seems ripe for outsourcing. How many of you sit in a company office connected to someone else's network, perhaps using 3G, but still check your email or browse the Web? It's happening now.

Every device might be able to talk to every other device. This restores the dream of "end-to-end connectivity" destroyed by NAT, firewalls, and other "middleboxes." IPv6 seems to be making some ground, at least in mindshare in the Western world and definitely on the ground in the Far East. "End-to-end" is a core idea of IPv6, but scares me. Isolation is one of the few defensive measures that works in many intrusion scenarios.

Preferably, only authorized applications will talk to other authorized applications. This is one way to deal with the previous point. It's more complicated to implement, but will make me sleep better. I would like the ability to configure how my endpoint talks to the world, and how the world talks to it. For me, I would like to completely disable functionality, and abandon any kind of network-based filtering or blocking mechanism. It is a travesty that I have to use some aspects of Microsoft SMB for business functions, but generally allow any SMB traffic if I'm not willing to run a host-based layer 7 firewall (aka "IPS").

Every device must protect itself. This one really pains me, and I think it's the greatest risk. This one is going to happen no matter how much protests security people make. Again, it's already happening. Mobile devices are increasingly exposed to each other, with the owners completely at the mercy of the service provider. For me, this is an operational reality for which we must build in visibility and failure planning. We can't just assume everything will be ok, because prevention eventually fails. I'll say more on that later.

Devices will often have to report their own status, but preferably to a central location. Again, scary. It means that if an endpoint is exploited, the best you're likely to get from it is a last log event gasp as it reports something odd. After that a skilled intruder will make the endpoint appear as if nothing is wrong. At least if centralized logging is a core component you'll have that log as an indicator. However, past that point the endpoint cannot be trusted to report its state. This is happening more and more as mobile devices move from monitored connections (say a company network) to open ones (like wireless providers or personal broadband links).

As fast, high-bandwidth wireless becomes ubiquitous, smart organizations will design platforms to rely on centralized remote storage and protection of critical data. For certain types of data, we have to hope that our varied mobile devices act as little more than terminals to cloud-hosted, well-mannered information stores. The more data we keep centrally, the less persistent it needs to be on end devices, and therefore the less exposed it can be. Central data is easier to deduplicate, back up, archive, classify, inventory, e-discover, retain, destroy, and manage.

I called this post "don't fight the future" because I think these developments will transpire. The model they represent is financially more attractive to people who don't put security first, which is every decision maker I've met. This isn't necessarily a bad thing, but it does mean we security practitioners should be making plans for this new world.

https://taosecurity.blogspot.com/2008/11/dont-fight-future.html

Commentary

It's been 12 years (as of the time of writing this comment), and only some of this has come to pass, or is being discussed. Network segmentation, middleboxes, virtual private networks, and intranets enabled by network (port) address translation (NAT/NAPT) remain as common as ever. The main change I see is that so much of modern corporate work can be done using cloud resources that many of us never need to "connect" to a "corporate network" to accomplish work tasks.

Inputs vs Outputs, or Why Controls Are Not Sufficient

Friday, February 27, 2009

I have a feeling my post *Consensus Audit Guidelines Are Still Controls* is not going to be popular in certain circles. While tidying the house this evening I came across my 2007 edition of the *Economist's Pocket World in Figures*. Flipping through the pages I found many examples of inputs (think "control-compliant") vs outputs (think "field-assessed").

I'd like to share some of them with you in an attempt to better communicate the ideas in my last post.

1. Business creativity and research
    a. Input(s): Total expenditures on research and development, % of GDP
    b. Output(s): Number of patents granted (per X people)
2. Education
    a. Input(s): Education spending, % of GDP; school enrolment
    b. Output(s): Literacy rate
3. Life expectancy, health, and related categories
    a. Input(s): Health spending, % of GDP; population per doctor; number of hospital beds per citizen; (also add in air quality, drinking and smoking rates, etc.)

b.   Output(s): Death rates; infant mortality; and so on...
4.   Crime and punishment
a.   Input(s): Total police per X population
b.   Output(s): Crime rate

Is this making sense?

https://taosecurity.blogspot.com/2009/02/inputs-vs-outputs-or-why-controls-are.html

Commentary

Identifying whether a metric is measuring an input or an output should be the first step in any measurement exercise. Both have value but output metrics are the score of the game. They deserve more attention.

Recoverable Network Architecture

Friday, March 06, 2009

Last year I outlined my *Defensible Network Architecture 2.0*, consisting of 8 (originally 7, plus 1 great idea from a comment) characteristics of an enterprise that give it the best chance to resist an intrusion.

I'd like to step into the post-intrusion phase to discuss *Recoverable Network Architecture* (RNA, goes well with DNA, right?), a **set of characteristics for an enterprise that give it the best chance to recover from an intrusion**. This list is much rougher than the previous DNA list, and I appreciate feedback. The idea is that without these characteristics, you are not likely to be able to resume operations following an incident.

RNA does not mean your enterprise will be intruder-free, just as DNA didn't mean you would be intrusion free. Rather, **if you do not operate a Recoverable Network Architecture you have very little chance of returning at least the system of interest to a trustworthy state.** (Please remember the difference between trusted and trustworthy!)

The recoverable network must be defensible. Being defensible not only helps with resisting intrusions; it helps recovery too. For example, the network must already be:

Monitored: Monitoring helps determine incident scope before recovery and remediation effectiveness after recovery.

Inventoried: Inventories help incident responders understand the range of potential victims in an incident before recovery and help ensure no unrecognized victims are left behind after recovery.

Controlled: Control helps implement short term incident containment, if appropriate, before recovery, and enforces better resistance after recovery.

Claimed: Because an asset is claimed, incident responders know which asset owners to contact.

Minimized: Assets that retain security exposures following recovery are subject to easy compromise again.

Assessed: Assessment validates that monitoring works (can we see the assessment?), that inventories are accurate (is the system where it should be?), that controls work (did we need an exception to scan the target, or could we sail through?), and that minimization/keeping current worked (are easy holes present?)

Current: Assets that retain security vulnerabilities following recovery are subject to easy compromise again.

Measured: Measurement helps justify various recovery actions, e.g. showing that so-called "cleaning" is less effective and costs more than complete system rebuilds.

Assets in a recoverable network must be capable of being replaced -- fast. IT shops are slowly waking up to the fact that "cleaning" does not work, is too expensive, and should be standard for any disaster recovery/business process continuity activity anyway. Complete rebuilds are becoming the only semi-effective remedy. (I say semi-effective because even complete rebuilds can preserve BIOS-level and other persistent, extra-OS rootkits.)

Incident responders in a recoverable network must be authorized and empowered to collect evidence, analyze leads, escalate findings, and guide remediation. An IRT that is asked to assist with an incident, but that is not allowed or able to collect information from a victim, is basically helpless. An IRT that must wait for other parties to provide information is ineffective, and likely to find the "data" provided by the other party to be of decreasing value as time passes and asset owners trounce host-based evidence.

A recoverable network is supported by an organization that has planned for intrusions. The IR plan must engage a variety of parties, contain realistic scenarios, and actually be followed. IR plans help increase the likelihood of incident recovery because time is not wasted on phone calls asking "what do we do now?"

A recoverable network is supported by an organization that has exercised the IR plan. Drills find weaknesses in plans that will hamper recovery.

A recoverable network is supported by an IRT that is appropriately segmented. By that I mean that **the IRT's infrastructure is not hosted or maintained by the same infrastructure the IRT is trying to recover.** In other words, the IRT should not depend on equipment administered by the same people who suffered a loss of their credentials, or be part of the same Windows domain, and so on. If the IRT does share infrastructure with the victim, then the IRT can no longer trust its own systems and must first restore the trustworthiness of its own gear before turning to the organization.

A recoverable network is supported by an IRT that is also connected. The team can communicate in degraded situations, with itself and with outside parties. The IRT will definitely have requirements that exceed the end user community, and almost certainly even the IT shop.

What do you think of these requirements? I may try expanding on each of the DNA items with examples at some point. If that works well I will apply the same to RNA.

https://taosecurity.blogspot.com/2009/03/recoverable-network-architecture.html

Commentary

It seems my idea for a "recoverable network" was not the same as you might find in a business continuity plan (BCP). That would dictate data backups, system backups, and restoration as part of recovery. Those processes, people, and technology are definitely required, especially in the golden age of ransomware that we are currently enduring. The items in this post seem to deal more with incident responders and bringing compromised systems back to a trustworthy state for users and business purposes.

Requirements for Defensible Network Architecture: Monitored

Saturday, March 07, 2009

Last year I posted *Defensible Network Architecture 2.0*, consisting of 8 (originally 7, plus 1 great idea from a comment) characteristics of an enterprise that give it the best chance to resist an intrusion.

In this post I'd like to define some specifics for the first of the 8 characteristics: **monitored**. At some point in the future it would probably make sense to think of these characteristics in terms of a capability maturity model. Right now I'd like to capture some thoughts for use in later work. I will approach the requirements from a moderate point of view, meaning I will try to stay between what I would expect from a low-capability operation and a high-capability operation.

Like my related posts, this is a work in progress and I appreciate feedback.

A Defensible Network Architecture is an information architecture that is:

Monitored. Monitored can be described using the following categories, which collectively can be considered intrusion detection operations. (Add in Response or Resolution, depending on your IRT's mandate, and you have the CAER model for security operations.)

Collection. The following technical data is collected and available to the security operations team.

Network Security Monitoring (NSM) data from passive sensors; note the NSM data must depict true source IP and true destination IP (i.e., monitoring traffic between a NAT gateway and a proxy means seeing only the source IP of the NAT gateway and the destination IP of the proxy, radically decreasing the value of the observed traffic)

> **Alert data** from devices making judgements while inspecting network traffic

> **Statistical data** summarizing network traffic

> **Session data** describing conversations in network traffic

> **Full content data** providing traffic headers and payloads

Infrastructure Security Monitoring data from routers, firewalls, switches, so-called intrusion prevention systems, and other network infrastructure that actively manipulates network traffic, or provides fundamental network services; by "fundamental services" I mean services that, without which, nothing much else works, e.g., DHCP, DNS, BGP

> **Access Control logs** that report on allowed and denied traffic

> **Infrastructure logs** that report DHCP address assignments, DNS queries and responses, BGP routing tables, etc.

Platform Security Monitoring data from nodes (laptops, desktops, non-infrastructure servers, etc.)

Operating system security logs, like Windows Event Logs

Application logs, like Web server logs, Web application logs, etc.

Platform memory, preferably exposing memory segments as needed (think retrieving a live system registry) or the entire memory (think ManTech DD plus Volatility)

Analysis.

A dedicated **team** analyzes technical data collected in the previous stage.

The team has access to **subject matter experts** who can answer questions on the nature of threats, vulnerabilities, and assets in order to better understand the risk posed by monitored activity.

Analysis is understood and **supported by management** as a creative task that cannot be "automated away." If automation were possible for detecting intrusions, the same automation could be applied to preventing them. ("If you can detect it, why not prevent it?") Assuming everything detectable is preventable, by definition the analysis team is left to identify activity which is most likely not easily detectable, or at least not easily validated as being malicious.

Escalation.

The team has defined **categories** to identify the nature of intrusions and non-intrusions.

The team has defined **severity levels** describing the impact of various types of intrusions.

The team has an **escalation matrix** summarizing the steps to be taken given an intrusion of a specific category and severity.

You should **monitor at trust boundaries**, to the extent you perceive risk and have the technical and legal resources to do so. (For more on trust boundaries with respect to monitoring please see *NSM vs Encrypted Traffic, Plus Virtualization* and *NSM vs Encrypted Traffic Revisited*.

I will stop here, but continue with *Inventoried* when I have time.

https://taosecurity.blogspot.com/2009/03/requirements-for-defensible-network.html

Commentary

This was one attempt to provide more guidance for those who liked my Defensible Network Architecture. These days, I characterize NSM data as transaction logs, extracted content, alert data, and full content data. I consider statistical data a derived data type which can apply to all of the first-order NSM data types.

Lessons from CDX

Wednesday, May 06, 2009

In my post *Thoughts on 2009 CDX* I described my initial reaction to the Cyber Defense Exercise from the point of view of seeing the white and red cells in action. Thanks to this press release I learned the outcome of the event:

The National Security Agency/Central Security Service (NSA/CSS) is pleased to announce that the United States Military Academy at West Point has won the 2009 Cyber Defense Exercise (CDX) trophy for the third year in a row.

I found more detail here:

The USMA team won the exercise for the third year in a row—–West Point's fifth win since the competition began in 2001. That means they successfully fended off the NSA hackers better than the U.S. Naval Academy, U.S. Air Force Academy, U.S. Coast Guard Academy, U.S. Merchant Marine Academy, the Naval Postgraduate School, the Air Force Institute of Technology and Royal Military College of Canada...

"We had large attacks against our e-mail and Web server from multiple (Internet protocol) addresses (all NSA Red Team), Firstie Josh Ewing, cadet public affairs officer for the team, said. "We were able to withstand their attacks and blocked over 200 IPs that they were using to attack the network."

All the while, the cadets were tasked with extra projects such as network forensics. The cadets' scores from these extra tasks contributed to their win, Adams said.

Based on my discussions with people from the exercise, it is clear that West Point takes the CDX very seriously. As in previous years, **West Point dedicated 30-40 cadets to the event. They appear to use the CDX as a capstone exercise for a computer security class.** Based on manpower alone they dwarf the other participants; for example, the Coast Guard had a team of less than 10 (6-7?) from what I heard.

Thinking about this exercise caused me to try classifying the **various stages through which a security team might evolve.**

Ignorance. "Security problem? What security problem?" No one at the organization realizes there is even an issue to worry about.

Denial. "I hear others have security problems, but we don't." The organization thinks they are special enough that they don't share the vulnerabilities and exploitation suffered by others.

Incompetence. "We have to do something!" The organization accepts there is a problem but is not equipped to do what is required. They may or may not realize they are not equipped to handle the problem.

Heroics. "Stand back! I'll fix it!" The organization develops or hires staff who can make a difference for the first time. This is a dangerous phase, because the situation can improve but it is not sustainable.

Capitalization. "Now I have some resources to address this problem." The heroes receive some funds to advance their cause, but funding alone is not sufficient.

Institutionalization. "Our organization is integrating our security measures into the overall business operations." This is real progress. The organization is taking the security problems seriously and it's not just the security team's problem anymore.

Specialization. "We're leveraging our unique expertise in X and Y to defend ourselves and contribute back to the security community." The organization has matured enough that it can take advantage of its own environment to defend itself, as well as bring lessons to others in the community.

Based on what I know of the West Point team, they seem to be at the Institutionalization phase. Contrast their approach and success with a team that might only be at the Heroics phase. Heroics can produce a win here and there, but Institutionalization will produce the sort of sustainable advantage we're seeing in the West Point team.

You may find these labels apply to your security teams too.

https://taosecurity.blogspot.com/2009/05/lessons-from-cdx.html

Commentary

From the beginning of "cyber" in the military, I could see that the Air Force relied on heroics and the Army built institutions. We had some amazing heroes at various points in Air Force history, and we vaulted to an early lead thanks to their drive and skill. The Army, however, went "rolling along," throwing resources and people at the challenge, to the point where they became regular winners in exercises like CDX. I do not know how the various services compare in 2020, but I hope they can at least learn what works and what doesn't by studying their respective programs.

Cheap IT Is Ultimately Expensive

Thursday, May 21, 2009

I'm positive many of you are familiar with the idea that there are benefits to detecting software security defects early.

In other words, **it is ultimately cheaper to design, code, sell, and support a more secure software product than a more insecure software product.** Achieving this goal requires recognizing this advantage, investing in developers and processes that work, and dealing with exceptions (defects) as soon as possible through detection and response capabilities, even including customer-facing organizations (like PSIRTs).

I'm not aware of any studies supporting the following assertion, but I would be interested in feedback if you know any. I think it should be obvious that **it's also cheaper to design, build, run, and support more secure computing assets than more insecure computing assets.** In other words:

It is not cheaper to run legacy platforms, operating systems, and applications because "updates break things."

It is not cheaper to delay patching because of "business impact."

It is not cheaper to leave compromised systems operating within the enterprise because of the "productivity hit" taken when a system must be interrupted to enable security analysis.

It is not cheaper to try to manually identify and remove individual elements of malware and other persistence mechanisms, rather than rebuild from the ground up (and apply proper updates and configuration improvements to resist future compromise).

It is not cheaper to watch intellectual property escape the enterprise in order to prove that intruders are serious about stealing an organization's data.

Security doesn't make money; security is a loss prevention exercise. It's tough to justify security spending. However -- and these are the killers:

It's easy to show cost savings when experienced, professional system administrators are replaced by outsourced providers who are the lowest bidders.

It's easy to show the financial benefit of continuous availability of a revenue-producing system, or, conversely, easy to show the financial cost of downtime of a revenue-producing system.

Unfortunately, being seduced by those arguments ignores **intrusion debt.** One day the intrusion debt of poorly-run systems will be claimed by the intruders already inside the enterprise or those who are unleashed like an earthquake. Worse for you and me, the costs of dealing with the disaster are likely to be borne by the security team!

I thought of this vicious cycle when reading about the Sichuan earthquake in last week's Economist magazine:

> In the days after the earthquake, senior officials vowed to investigate whether shoddy construction was to blame for the destruction of more than 7,000 classrooms in the disaster. But the issue was soon played down...

> Mr Ai [investigating the disaster] says the refusal of central leaders to admit policy failures has exacerbated parents' frustration. In the 1990s, he says, shoddy school buildings were erected across China because of the government's drive to provide enough classrooms for all children to undergo nine years of compulsory education. Building costs were supposed to be shared by central and local authorities, but the latter often failed to chip in. This led to quality problems.

Ultimately, **security is an IT problem, not a "security" problem.** The faster asset owners realize this and be held responsible for the security of their systems, the less intrusion debt will mount and the greater the chance that enterprise assets will survive digital earthquakes. Cheap IT is ultimately expensive -- more expensive than proper investment in IT in the first place.

Commentary

We have been seeing the consequences of "cheap IT" play out for the last few years due to the rash of ransomware incidents crippling companies worldwide. Regularly the press reports that companies are willing to pay 8-figure ransoms to decrypt their data. This is not ultimately a better strategy than investing in proper information technology and security programs. These payouts will only encourage other criminals to attack victims again, extorting more money from them.

Information Security Incident [Intrusion] Rating [Classification]

Sunday, May 31, 2009

I've been trying to describe to management how close various individual information assets (primarily computers -- desktops, laptops, etc.) are to the doomsday scenario of **sensitive data exfiltrated by unauthorized parties**. This isn't the only type of incident that worries me, but it's the one I decided to tackle first. I view this situation as a continuum, rather than a "risk" rating. I'm trying to summarize the state of affairs for an individual asset rather than "model risk."

Here is the text version of this chart, in the form of Classification: Description.

Vuln 3: Intruder must apply substantial effort to compromise asset and exfiltrate sensitive data

241

Vuln 2: Intruder must apply moderate effort to compromise asset and exfiltrate sensitive data

Vuln 1: Intruder must apply little effort to compromise asset and exfiltrate sensitive data

Cat 6: Intruder is conducting reconnaissance against asset with access to sensitive data

Cat 3: Intruder is attempting to exploit asset with access to sensitive data

Cat 2: Intruder has compromised asset with access to sensitive data but requires privilege escalation

Cat 1: Intruder has compromised asset with ready access to sensitive data

Breach 3: Intruder has established command and control channel from asset with ready access to sensitive data

Breach 2: Intruder has exfiltrated nonsensitive data or data that will facilitate access to sensitive data

Breach 1: Intruder has exfiltrated sensitive data or is suspected of exfiltrating sensitive data based on volume, etc.

The first three rows bear "Vuln" ratings. I list these because some of my constituents consider the discovery of a vulnerability in an asset to be an "incident" by itself. Traditional incident detectors and responders don't think this way, but I wanted to include this aspect of our problem set.

For these first three rows, I consider these assets to exist without any discoverable or measurable adversary activity. In other words, assets of various levels of vulnerability are present, but no intruder is taking interest in them (as far as we can tell).

The next four rows (Cat 6, 3, 2, 1) should be familiar to those of you with military CIRT background. About 7 or 8 years ago I wrote a *Category Descriptions* document for Sguil. You'll remember Cat 6 as Reconnaissance, Cat 3 as Attempted Intrusion, Cat 2 as User Intrusion, and Cat 1 as Root/Admin Intrusion. I've mapped those "true incidents" here.

These incidents indicate an intruder is taking interest in a system, to the degree that the intruder gains user or root level control of it. In the event the intruder doesn't need to gain control of the asset in order to steal data, you can simply jump to the appropriate description of the event in the final three rows.

The final three rows (Breach 3, 2, 1) are what you might consider "post exploitation" activities, or direct exploitation activities if no control of the asset is required in order to accomplish the adversary's data exfiltration mission. They loosely map to the reinforcement, consolidation, and pillage phases of compromise I outlined years ago. I've used the term "Breach" here to emphasize the seriousness of this aspect of an intrusion. (Gunter's recent post *Botnet C&C Participation is a Corporate Data Breach* reinforced my decision to use the term "breach" in situations like this.) Clearly Breach 3 is a severe problem. You might still be able to avoid catastrophe if you can contain the incident at this phase. However, intruders are likely to quickly move to Breach 2 and 1 phases, when it's Game Over.

If there has to be an "impact 0" rating, I would consider that to be the absence of an information asset, i.e., it doesn't exist. Any asset whatsoever has value, so I don't see a 0 value for any existing systems.

At the other end of the spectrum, if we have to "crank it to 11," I would consider an 11 to be publication of incident details in a widely-read public forum like a major newspaper or online news site.

[I originally published an "impact" score for each item.] I used the term "impact" in this sense: what is the negative impact of having the individual asset in the state described? In other words, the negative impact of having an asset with impact 1 is very low. We would all like to have assets that require an intruder to apply substantial effort to compromise the asset and exfiltrate sensitive data. At the other end of the spectrum we have the "game over" impact -- the intruder has exfiltrated sensitive data or is suspected of exfiltrating sensitive data based on volume, etc. Even if you can't tell exactly what an intruder exfiltrated, if you see several GBs of data leaving a system that houses or access sensitive data, you can be fairly confident the intruder grabbed it.

What do you think of this rating system? I am curious to hear how others explain the seriousness of an incident to management.

Update: Since writing this post, I've realized it is more important to think of these events as **intrusions**. The word "incident" applies to a broader set of events, including DDoS, lost or stolen devices, and the like. My use of the word "intruder" throughout the post indicates my real intention.

https://taosecurity.blogspot.com/2009/05/information-security-inc ident-rating.html

Commentary

This is one of the most frequently referenced posts from my blog. I've had numerous requests for a high resolution image of the chart, which I've produced here in simple text. (Sorry, I don't have a high resolution version. It's easy enough to copy and paste to create your own.) Looking back at the comments, I noticed some people complained that this rating system was too complicated. I don't think they understood the overall point.

Because I modified the chart in the following post, I simply included the modified version in this one. It would be confusing and redundant to include both versions.

At the AFCERT we had incident categories, 4 of which (Cats 6, 3, 2, and 1) I adopted, as they make sense compared to those I left out. This was sufficient for my purposes for many years. When I joined General Electric, I encountered two factors which drove changes to our incident management system. The first involved the vulnerability management team. Once our incident management system became popular, they felt that it would be helpful to treat vulnerabilities in a similar manner. They were also influenced by the Information Technology Infrastructure Library (ITIL) tendency to call everything an "incident," so I added three different "Vuln" ratings.

The second factor which changed how I managed incidents was the need to speak in more nuanced terms to business leaders. In the Air Force, a Cat 1 incident was not questioned. If we identified a compromised asset, service leaders perceived it as a serious problem. The AFCERT sought immediate short term incident containment, followed by proper escalation and remediation.

In the corporate world, upon being notified of a Cat 6 intrusion, business leaders asked "well, has anything bad happened yet?" This mindset forced me to show that intruders moved through a spectrum of stages, which ended with command-and-control, and then exfiltration of limited or nonsensitive data, and finally exfiltration of sensitive data. With this level of granularity, however, we could show how fast action kept Cat 1s from becoming Breach 3s, or 2s, or even 1s.

Information Security Incident Classification

Friday, June 05, 2009

Thank you to those who commented on my previous post on this subject. I've had a few people ask to use this chart, but I wanted to clarify a few items now that there has been some good public and private discussion about it.

My intention with this chart is to help **classify an incident involving compromise of an individual system.** There are plenty of other sorts of information security incidents, but at the moment this is the biggest problem I deal with on a daily basis. I need a way to talk about the state of an individual compromised asset. I found the traditional DoD Category system wasn't sufficient, especially in the post-Cat 1 world. I still like those Categories but I needed to go further (post-exploitation) and for one of my constituents, backwards (to when a system is just vulnerable, but no one is yet interested in it -- as far as we can tell).

I decided to call this updated chart a "classification" rather than a "rating," and to remove the label "impact." The words rating and impact imply "risk" and asset value to some degree, and I'm not talking about either here. This is a little bit like assigning a CVE number; it says nothing about the seriousness of the vulnerability, but at least we can all reference the same vulnerability. With my chart I can now build service expectation timelines around the incident type. **I can also quickly understand where we are with any incident when one of our team says "we have a Cat 1, but our perimeter defenses appear to have contained the incident so it has not reached Breach 3 status."**

I think it is important to keep in mind that having anything remotely approaching a valid understanding of "risk" requires a great deal of understanding about the assets in question. Not only must you understand the nature of the compromised asset (its function, normal usage patterns, its inputs, its processes, its outputs), but you must understand the means by which the asset interacts with the network, any trust relationships, and many other factors. In most cases the only way to gain a real appreciation of these real-world conditions is to either 1) observe the intruder in action, seeing what he can do or get, or 2) red-team the system yourself to see what you can do or get. Modern systems and enterprises are far too complex for anyone to sit back like Mycroft Holmes and truly understand the "risk" of a compromise.

I should also say that I would never expect to tell a manager that we have discovered a Breach 2 and then walk away. The natural next question involves the issues of the previous paragraph, and answering them takes far longer than the process of detecting and validating the incident. If you doubt me, try talking to the office in the DoD that does nothing but computer incident damage assessment all day long.

Incidentally, please feel free to use this diagram, providing you cite the source. I am encouraged when others seek to adopt this sort of language for their own programs, because it moves us closer to having common ways to discuss operational problems. Thank you.

https://taosecurity.blogspot.com/2009/06/information-security-incident.html

Commentary

The highlighted portion is probably the most useful aspect of this post. By differentiating between a Cat 1 and a Breach 3, for example, we could explicitly describe, to the best of our understanding, the current state of an intrusion. Of course that requires a high level of collection and analysis, but by the time of this post (mid-2009) GE-CIRT was well on its way.

Incident Phases of Compromise

Saturday, June 06, 2009

This is the first in a series of "mindset" posts where I'd like to outline how I've been thinking of various aspects of incident detection and response. My primary focus for these discussions will be intrusions.

First I'd like to discuss phases of compromise, again primarily designed for intrusions. They can be extended to other scenarios, but as with other recent posts I'm focusing on advanced persistent threats who operate beyond the norms of regular intruders. I've listed the phases elsewhere but they are relevant here; I've also expanded the last phase. I list the information security incident classification for each where appropriate.

Reconnaissance. Identify target assets and vulnerabilities, indirectly or directly. Cat 6.

Exploitation. Abuse, subvert, or break a system by attacking vulnerabilities or exposures. If the intruder does not seek to maintain persistence, then this could be the end of the compromise. Cat 2 or 1.

Reinforcement. The intruder deploys his persistence and stealth techniques to the target. Still Cat 2 or 1, leading to Breach 3.

Consolidation. The intruder ensures continued access to the target by establishing remote command-and-control. Breach 3.

Pillage. The intruder executes his mission. Here we assume data theft and persistence are the goals.

Propagation. Intruders usually expand their influence before stealing data, but this is not strictly necessary. At this point the incident classifications should be applied to the new victims.

Exfiltration. The intruder steals data. Depending on the type of data, Breach 2 or 1.

Maintenance. The intruder ensures continued access to the victim until deciding to execute another mission.

With these phases of compromise outlined I'll have them ready for later reference.

https://taosecurity.blogspot.com/2009/06/incident-phases-of-compromise.html

Commentary

This 2009 post was based on the phases of compromise I included in my 2004 book *The Tao of Network Security Monitoring: Beyond Intrusion Detection*. This was my version of a "kill chain." I was partly inspired by a previous book, the original *Hacking Exposed*, published in 1999. It included a "kill chain" of its own, called "An Anatomy of a Hack." That list consisted of footprinting, scanning, enumeration, gaining access, escalating privilege, pilfering, covering tracks, creating back doors, and, oddly, but perhaps for completeness, denial of service.

In 2010 Mandiant published their first *M-Trends* report. It included their Exploitation Life Cycle, which consisted of reconnaissance, initial intrusion, establish a backdoor, obtain user credentials, install various utilities, privilege escalation / lateral movement / data exfiltration, and maintain persistence.

This "chain" approach became famous, however, with the publication of the 2011 paper *Intelligence-Driven Computer Network Defense: Informed by Analysis of Adversary Campaigns and Intrusion Kill Chains* by Eric M. Hutchins, Michael J. Cloppert, and Rohan M. Amin. Their intrusion kill chain, later renamed and trademarked by their employer, contains the following steps: reconnaissance, weaponization, delivery, exploitation, installation, command and control, and actions on objective.

Shortly thereafter, MITRE created their ATT&CK framework, with its own list, including the following: initial access, execution, persistence, privilege escalation, defense evasion, credentialed access, discovery, lateral movement, collection, command and control, exfiltration, and impact. MITRE ATT&CK is currently the most popular characterization of these steps in use.

Incident Detection Paradigms

Saturday, June 06, 2009
This is the second in a series of "mindset" posts where I'd like to outline how I've been thinking of various aspects of incident detection and response. My primary focus for these discussions will be intrusions.

I'd like to discuss incident detection paradigms. These are ways that security people tend to think when they are trying to identify intrusions. I'm going to list the **three attitudes** I've encountered.

1. Detection is futile. This school of thought says that some intruders are so crafty that it is not possible to detect them. I consider this paradigm short-sighted and defeatist. If you read the intruder's dilemma you'll know that it is generally not possible for intruders to hide themselves perfectly, continuously, perpetually. True, as the intruder's persistence time decreases, and as the amount of data exfiltrated decreases, it becomes more difficult to detect the intruder. However, both conditions are good for the defense. The question for the intruder is how persistent and successful he can be without alerting the defender to his presence.

2. Sufficient knowledge. This school of thought says that it is possible for a defender to know so much about an intruder's actions that one can apply that understanding to automated systems to detect the intruder. This is essentially the opposite of the futility school. Unfortunately, this paradigm is unrealistic too. As I mentioned in Security Event Correlation: Looking Back, Part 3, the natural question to ask if one believes the sufficient knowledge paradigm is this: if you can detect it, why can't you prevent it?

As I explained in *Why is the Snort IDS still alive and thriving?*, that question supposedly made "IDS dead" at the expense of IPS. Users and vendors who believe the sufficient knowledge school expect security people to be satisfied when they receive an alert that something bad happened, but the analyst is not given sufficient evidence to validate that claim.

3. Indicators plus retrospective security analysis. In good debating style I save the best approach for last. I wish I had a better name but this phrase captures the essence of this paradigm. Here the analyst recognizes that any alert or other input one collects and analyzes is simply an indicator. Indicators may have various levels of confidence associated with them, but the importance of an indicator is that it should signal the start of the analysis process. **Validating the indicator to produce a warning that can be escalated to perform incident response is accomplished by analyzing sufficient evidence.** This evidence can be network traffic or data about network traffic, system logs, host information, and so on.

As I discussed in *Black Hat Briefings Justify Retrospective Security Analysis*, once an analyst has learned of new indicators to detect advanced intruders, he can apply them to stored evidence.

251

Retrospective security analyst finds the crafty intruders missed by traditional approaches, but it requires sufficient digital situational awareness to know how to proceed.

I'll discuss different digital situational awareness paradigms in a later post.

https://taosecurity.blogspot.com/2009/06/incident-detection-paradigms.html

Commentary

These days people would call mindset 3 "hunting." Once again I showed that my marketing skills are not up to par! I'm a strong proponent of the third mindset. Occasionally proponents of the first and second mindset appear in the security scene. Given the history of this field over the last three decades or more, I don't see how they believe it's just impossible to detect intruders, or that it's possible to detect all intruders automatically.

Digital Situational Awareness Methods

Saturday, June 06, 2009

I've written about digital situational awareness before, but I wanted to expand on the topic as I continue my series of posts on various aspects of incident detection and response.

Here I would like to describe ways that an enterprise can achieve digital situational awareness, or a better understanding of their security posture. What is interesting about these methods is that they do not exclude each other. In fact, a mature enterprise should pursue all of them, to the extent possible allowed by technical and legal factors.

External notification is the most primitive means of learning the state of the enterprise's security posture. If all you do is wait until law enforcement or the military knock at your door, you're basically neglecting your responsibilities to your organization and customers.

Vulnerability assessment identifies vulnerabilities and exposures in assets. This is necessary but not sufficient, because VA (done by a blue team) typically cannot unearth the complicated linkages and relationships among assets and their protection mechanisms. You have to do it however, and knowing your vulnerabilities and exposures is better than waiting for a knock on the door.

Adversary simulation or penetration testing identifies at least one way that an adversary could exploit vulnerabilities and exposures to compromise a target or satisfy a related objective. AS (done by a red team) shows what can be done, moving beyond the theoretical aspects of VA. Many times this is the only way to really understand the enterprise and prove to management that there is a problem.

Incident detection and response shows that real intruders have compromised the enterprise. If you think it's bad to see your red team exfiltrate data, it's worse when a real bad guy does it. Knowing that intruders are actively exploiting you is almost the best way to achieve digital situational awareness, and it's usually the highest form an enterprise can practice since it's closest to the ground truth of the state of the enterprise.

Counterintelligence operations are the ultimate way to achieve digital situational awareness. As I wrote in *The Best Cyber Defense*, this means finding out what the enemy knows about you. I covered this extensively in the referenced post, but now you can see where counterintelligence fits in the overall digital situational awareness hierarchy.

Commentary

Remember that counterintelligence means activities that *counter*
adversary *intelligence* teams. Perhaps "counteradversary" would be
more appropriate for activities that counter adversaries who are more
generally not intelligence operatives? We do need a term that
distinguishes between actions against intelligence agencies and
actions against adversaries of a general nature.

Crisis 0: Game Over

Sunday, June 07, 2009

A veteran security pro just sent me an email on my post *Extending
the Information Security Incident Classification with Crisis Levels.* He
suggested a Crisis beyond Crisis 1 -- "organization collapses." That is
a real Game Over -- Crisis 0. In other words, the cost of dealing with
the crisis bankrupts the victim organization, or the organization is
ordered to shut down, or any other consequence that removes the
organization as a "going concern," to use some accountant-speak.

I guess the hunt is on now to discover example organizations which
have ceased to exist as a result of information security breaches. The
rough part of that exercise is connecting all the dots. Who can say
that, as a result of stealing intellectual property, a competitor gained
persistent economic advantage over the victim and drove it to
bankruptcy? These are the sorts of consequences whose timeline is
likely to evade just about everyone.

Putting on my historian's hat, I remember the many spies who stole
the manufacturing methods developed by the pioneers of the
Industrial Revolution in Great Britain, resulting in technology

transfers to developing countries. Great Britain's influence faded in the following century.

I'm sure some savvy reader knows of some corporate espionage case that ended badly for the victim, i.e., bankruptcy or the like?

Incidentally, I should remind everyone (and myself) that my classification system was intended to be applied to a single system. It is possible to imagine a scenario where one system is so key to the enterprise that a breach of its data does result in Crisis 3, 2, 1, or 0, but that's probably a stretch for the worst Crisis levels. Getting to such a severe state probably requires a more comprehensive breach. So, let's not get too carried away by extending the classification too far.

https://taosecurity.blogspot.com/2009/06/crisis-0-game-over.html

Commentary

Unfortunately, due to the rise of ransomware during the last few years, we now have publicly documented cases of organizations shutting down due to information security incidents. For example, in early January 2020, accomplished reporter Catalin Cimpanu posted *Company shuts down because of ransomware, leaves 300 without jobs just before holidays.*

https://www.zdnet.com/article/company-shuts-down-because-of-ra nsomware-leaves-300-without-jobs-just-before-holidays/

Counterintelligence [Counter-Criminal Operator] Options for Digital Security

Monday, June 08, 2009

As a follow-up to my post *Digital Situational Awareness Methods*, I wanted to expand on the idea of conducting counterintelligence operations, strictly within the digital security realm. I focus [here] almost exclusively on counter-criminal operations, as opposed to actions against nation-states or individuals.

Those of you who provide security intelligence services (SIS), or subscribe to those services, may recognize some or all of these. By SIS I am not talking about vulnerability notices repackaged from other sources.

Note that **some of these approaches can really only be accomplished by law enforcement, or by collaboration with law enforcement.** Even taking a step into the underground can be considered suspicious. Therefore, I warn blog readers to not try implementing these approaches unless you are an experienced professional with the proper associations. The idea behind this post is to explain what could be done to determine what one sort of adversary (primarily the criminal underground) knows about your organization. It obviously could be extended elsewhere but that is not the focus of this post.

See who is selling or offering to sell your information or access to your information. This approach is similar to identifying places where credit cards or personally identifiable information are sold. Stepping into the underground and seeing where your company is mentioned is one way to estimate how prevalent your data might be outside your control. This is a passive approach.

Solicit the underground for your organization's data or for access to your organization. By taking this step you ask if anyone would be able to provide stolen data or access to the organization. This is a dangerous step because it may motivate the underground to go looking for data. On the other hand, if your data is freely available you're simply unearthing it. This is the first of the active approaches.

Penetrate adversary infrastructure. By this step I mean gaining entry or control of command-and-control channels or other mechanisms the adversary uses to exploit victim organizations. Security intelligence services do this all the time, but gaining access to a server owned by another organization is fairly aggressive.

Infiltrate the adversary group. An underground organization usually functions as a team. It might be possible to infiltrate that group to learn what it knows about your organization. Acting with law enforcement would be the only real way to more or less "safely" accomplish this task.

Pose as an individual underground member. In this capacity, other criminals with access to your organization's data might come to you. This is exceptionally dangerous too and would only be done in collaboration with law enforcement.

None of these steps are new; you can review success stories posted by the FBI and other organizations to know they work. However, I post them here to reinforce that asset-centric mindset and not just the vulnerability-centric mindset in digital security.

https://taosecurity.blogspot.com/2009/06/counterintelligence-options-for-digital.html

While the main points of this post are sound, I unfortunately did not apply the right title to this post. None of these are *counterintelligence* activities. Because they are directed against a criminal group, they should be called something like "counter-criminal operator" activities. Counterintelligence is conducted mainly against adversary intelligence agencies. Note also that pursuing the sort of work outlined in this post poses significant risk for the participants. I have avoided it throughout my career and left it to the people with the skill and legal cover to conduct it successfully.

Black Hat Budgeting

Saturday, June 27, 2009

Earlier this month I wondered How much to spend on digital security. I'd like to put that question in a different light by imagining what a black hat could do with a $1 million budget.

The ideas in this post are rough approximations. They certainly aren't a black hat business plan. I don't recommend anyone follow through on this, although I am sure there are shops out there who do this work already.

Let's start by defining the mission of this organization, called Project Intrusion (PI). PI is in "business" to steal intellectual property from organizations and sell it to the highest bidders. In the course of accomplishing that mission, PI may develop tools and techniques that it could sell down the food chain, once PI determines their utility to PI has sufficiently decreased.

With $1 million in funding, let's allocate some resources.

Staff. Without people, this business goes nowhere. We allocate **$750,000 of our budget to salaries and benefits** to hire the following people.

The **team leader** should have experience as a vulnerability researcher, exploit developer, penetration tester, enterprise defender, and preferably an intelligence operative. The leader can be very skilled in at least one speciality (say Web apps or Windows services) but should be familiar with all of the team's roles. The team leader needs a vision for the team while delivering value to clients. **$120,000.**

The team needs at least one **attack tool and technique developer for each target platform** or technology that PI intends to exploit. PI hires three. One focuses on Windows OS and client apps, one on Web apps, and one on Unix and network infrastructure. **$330,000.**

The team hires **two penetration operators** who execute the team leader's mission directives by using the attack tools and techniques supplied by the developers. The operators penetrate the target and establish the persistence required to acquire the desired intellectual property. **$180,000.**

The team hires **one intelligence operative** to direct the penetration operators' attention toward information of value, and then assess the value of exfiltrated data. The intel operative interfaces with clients to make deals. **$120,000.**

Technology. The team will need the following, for a total of **$200,000.**

Lab computers running the software that is likely to be attacked during operations.

Operations computers from which the penetration operators run attacks.

Network connectivity and hosting for the lab computers and operations computers, dispersed around the world.

Software required by the team, since many good attack tools are commercial. MSDN licenses are needed too. There's no need to steal these; we have the budget!

Miscellaneous. The last **$50,000** could be spent on incidentals, bribes, team awards, travel, or whatever else the group might require in start-up mode.

If the attack developers manage to make enough extra money by selling original exploits, I would direct the funds to additional penetration operators. It would take about six of them to support a sustainable 24x7 operation. With only two they would need to be careful and operate within certain time windows.

So what is the point of this exercise? **I submit that for $1 million per year an adversary could fund a Western-salaried black hat team that could penetrate and persist in roughly any target it chose to attack.** This team has the structure and expertise to develop its own attack methods, execute them, and sell the results of its efforts to the highest bidders.

This should be a fairly scary concept to my readers. Why? **Think about what $1 million buys in your security organization.** If your company is small, $1 million could go a long way. However, when you factor in all of the defensive technology you buy, and the salaries of your staff, and the scope of your responsibilities, and so on, quickly you realize you are probably out-gunned by Project Intrusion. PI has the in-house expertise to develop its own exploits, keep intruders on station, and assess and sell the information it steals.

Worse, **PI can reap economies of scale by attacking multiple targets for that same $1 million.** Why? Everyone runs Windows. Everyone uses the same client software. Everyone's enterprise tends to have the same misconfigurations, missing patches, overworked staff, and other problems. The tools and techniques that penetrate company A are likely to work against company B.

This is why I've always considered it folly to praise the Air Force for standardizing its Windows deployment with supposedly secure configurations. If PI looks at its targets and sees Windows, Windows, some other OS that might be Linux or BSD or who knows what, Windows, Windows, who do you think PI will avoid?

It's all about cost, on the part of the attacker or defender. **Unfortunately for defenders, it's only intruders who can achieve "return on investment" when it comes to exploiting digital security.**

https://taosecurity.blogspot.com/2009/06/black-hat-budgeting.html

Commentary

This is one of my more popular posts. There is plenty of room to critique it. Of course the costs of everything would be more now due to 11 years of inflation, and/or higher demand for security expertise. However, in some lesser parts of the world, you might hire people for the same cost, or even less. Observe that I allocated ¾ of the budget for personnel, ⅕ for technology, and the remainder for miscellaneous expenses, all on an annual basis.

Whatever your level of agreement or disagreement with the specific allocations, the main point remains true: it is far cheaper to work as an offensive team, especially when one multiplexes campaigns against many targets. This is the root of the asymmetry inherent in information security and I do not see it changing anytime soon, or ever.

Some claim that the defense is stronger, or at times at least, has been stronger, in the physical world. They assume that a similar dynamic will eventually prevail in the digital world. The problem with that logic is that it ignores how defense works on the battlefield.

Defense in the age of the firearm does not generally mean hunkering down in a bunker and surviving assault, although that happened on multiple occasions during the Gulf Wars. Rather, defense in the age of the firearm means *mowing down attackers as they charge your trenches.*

Modern physical defense is **lethal** to the attacker. Modern digital defense is an obstacle to be circumvented, all the while leaving the attacker alive and maneuverable. There is no comparison between the two worlds.

White Hat Budgeting

Tuesday, July 14, 2009

After publishing *Black Hat Budgeting* last month, several readers asked me how to spend the same $1 million on defense. This is a more difficult question. As I wrote in the previous post, **for $1 million per year an adversary could fund a Western-salaried black hat team that could penetrate and persist in roughly any target it chose to attack.** That does not hold true for defense, i.e., **for $1 million per year a defender could not fund a Western-salaried white hat team that could plan, resist, detect, and respond to any $1 million black hat team.**

So, if you had $1 million to spend on defense, how could you spend it? I turned to my 2008 post *Defensible Network Architecture 2.0* as a guide. One interesting aspect of the eight DNA 2.0 tenets is that half of them are IT responsibilities (or at least I would strongly argue they are): **inventoried, claimed, minimized, current.** All of that is just "good IT." Security can provide inputs, but IT should own those aspects. That leaves **monitored, controlled, assessed, and measured.**

With that's, let's allocate the funding. With such a small team we would expect people to move among the roles so they don't burn out, and so they can grow their capabilities.

Staff. Without people, this operation goes nowhere. We allocate **$850,000** of our budget to salaries and benefits to hire the following people.

The **team leader** should have experience as an enterprise defender as a minimum. The leader can be very skilled in at least one speciality but should be familiar with all of the team's roles. The team leader needs a vision for the team while preserving business value. Because this team is so small the leader has to do strategic thinking and overall management, including the "measured" aspect of DNA 2.0. **$120,000.**

The **incident response team** is responsible for detecting and responding to intrusions. They perform the "monitor" aspect of DNA 2.0. We hire **three people,** one with Windows expertise, one with Unix expertise, and one with infrastructure expertise. **$330,000.**

The **security operator** is responsible for the "controlled" aspect of DNA 2.0. He or she seeks to minimize intrusions by deploying and operating countermeasures. This person is also a utility player who can learn other roles and consult as necessary. **$80,000.**

The **threat operator** performs an advanced security intelligence and analysis role. He or she should be able to reverse engineer malware while also paying attention to underground activities and applying that knowledge to all aspects of the team's work. **$120,000.**

The **Red-Blue Team** performs adversary simulation/penetration testing (red) and collaborative vulnerability assessment (blue) activities. With a team this size there is only room for **two technicians**. Red-Blue handles the "assessed" aspect of DNA 2.0. **$80,000 for the blue, $120,000 for the red.**

Technology. At this point we only have $150,000 left. **We can spend $100,000 on technology**. It should be clear that $100,000 isn't going to buy much of any commercial tools. In fact, the $1 million security operation is going to have to rely on several realities.

Built-in capabilities. This team is going to have to rely on capabilities built into the products deployed by other IT teams, like the computer and networking groups. This actually makes a good amount of sense. Is it really necessary to deploy another host firewall on Windows if you can use IPsec policies and/or Windows firewall? With a budget that small, these are the uncomfortable choices to be made.

Open source software. The $1 million security team should deploy a lot of open source software. Sguil could be the NSM suite of choice, for example. By spending money on staff who know their way around open source tools, you can go very far using what can be downloaded for free. Let the staff contribute back to the community and it's a win-win situation.

Commodity hardware. You can't buy hardware for free, and those NSM sensors and other open source packages need to run on something. A decent amount of the budget will be spent on hardware.

Cloud hosting. The Cloud becomes an attractive place to store logs, do processing, and other activities that don't scale well or work well on commodity hardware. Security concerns are lessened when the alternative is no security services.

Miscellaneous. The last **$50,000** could be spent on incidentals, training, team awards, travel, or whatever else the group might require to attract and retain talent.

Note I did not advocate outsourcing here. You spend too much money and probably won't receive value for it.

With such a small team, there is no concept of 24x7 support. 8x5 is the best you can get. The ability of the team to detect and respond to intrusions in a timely manner is going to decrease as the enterprise grows. **A team of 8 security defenders will be strained once the company size exceeds 10,000 people, at the largest.**

I am much less comfortable building out this team, compared to the *Black Hat Budgeting* exercise. There are way too many variables involved in defending any enterprise. Most companies really are unique. However, this is a good point to stop to see if anyone has comments on this approach.

https://taosecurity.blogspot.com/2009/07/white-hat-budgeting.html

Commentary

If I were to reallocate funds today, I would cut the Red-Blue Team to save $200,000. I would hire a policy expert for at least $100,000, and use some of the remaining $100,000 to fund adversary simulation exercises by outside consultants, which may be required by the company anyway. I would use the remaining funds to beef up the technology spending and reduce reliance on open source software. Running a lot of open source software means hiring extra people to manage it. This is one of the reasons why my company, Corelight, has made a lot of progress putting Zeek, Suricata, and more in the hands of enterprise defenders. It became uneconomical for many customers to continue funding detection platform administrators, as they were hard to find and expensive to retain.

Technical Visibility Levels

Wednesday, October 07, 2009

It's no secret that I think technical visibility is the key to trustworthy technology. Via Twitter I wrote **The trustworthiness of a digital asset is limited by the owner's capability to detect incidents compromising the integrity of that asset.** This topic has consumed me recently as relatively closed but IP-enabled systems proliferate. This ranges from handheld computers (iPhone, Blackberry, etc.) all the way to systems hosted in the cloud. How are we supposed to trust any of them?

One of the first problems we should address is how to describe the level of technical visibility afforded by these technologies. The following is very rough and subject to modification, but I'm thinking in these terms right now.

Level 0. System status available only by observing explicit failure.

Level 1. Anecdotal status reporting or limited status reporting.

Level 2. Basic status reporting via portal or other non-programmatic interface.

Level 3. Basic logging of system state, performance, and related metrics via defined programmatic interface.

Level 4. Debug-level logging (extremely granular, revealing inner workings) via defined programmatic interface.

Level 5. Direct inspection of system state and related information possible via one or more means.

Let me try to provide some examples.

Level 0. I pick up my POTS [Plain Old Telephone Service] line and there is no dial tone.

Level 1. https://status.twitterstat.us/ or Gmail Last account activity.

Level 2. https://www.google.com/appsstatus or https://status.aws.amazon.com

Level 3. Pick an app that writes to /var/log/messages on Unix. Cisco IOS logging. Amazon S3 Server Access Logging.

Level 4. Pick an app that writes debug-level messages to /var/log/messages on Unix. Cisco IOS debug logging.

Level 5. Tcpdump of network traffic. Memory capture and analysis.

There must be dozens of other examples here. Keep in mind this is more of a half-thought than a finished thought, but I've been sitting on it for too long. Hopefully out in the open someone might comment on it. Thank you.

https://taosecurity.blogspot.com/2009/10/technical-visibility-levels.html

Commentary

Many times when I write a post I'm trying to compare and contrast aspects of a problem. The goal of this article was to show differing levels of visibility and how they manifest in various circumstances and technologies.

Control "Monitoring" is Not Threat Monitoring

Monday, November 23, 2009

As I write this post I'm reminded of General Hayden's advice:

> "Cyber" is difficult to understand, so be charitable with those who don't understand it, as well as those who claim "expertise."

It's important to remember that plenty of people are trying to act in a positive manner to defend important assets, so in that spirit I offer the following commentary.

Thanks to John Bambanek's SANS post I read *NIST Drafts Cybersecurity Guidance* by InformationWeek's J. Nicholas Hoover.

The article discusses the latest draft of *SP 800-37 Rev. 1: DRAFT Guide for Applying the Risk Management Framework to Federal Information Systems: A Security Life Cycle Approach.*

I suspected this to be problematic given NIST's historical bias towards "controls," which I've criticized in *Controls Are Not the Solution to Our Problem* and *Consensus Audit Guidelines Are Still Controls.* The subtext for the article was:

The National Institute for Standards and Technology is urging the government to continuously monitor its own cybersecurity efforts.

As soon as I read that, I knew that NIST's definition of "monitor" and the article's definition of "monitor" did not mean the real sort of monitoring, threat monitoring, that would make a difference against modern adversaries.

The article continues:

> Special Publication 800-37 fleshes out six steps federal agencies should take to tackle cybersecurity: categorization, selection of controls, implementation, assessment, authorization, and continuous monitoring...
>
> Finally, and perhaps most significantly, the document advises federal agencies to put continuous monitoring in place. Software, firmware, hardware, operations, and threats change constantly. Within that flux, security needs to be managed in a structured way, Ross says.
>
> "We need to recognize that we work in a very dynamic operational environment," Ross says. "That allows us to have an ongoing and continuing acceptance and understanding of risk, and that ongoing determination may change our thinking on whether current controls are sufficient."
>
> The continuous risk management step might include use of automated configuration scanning tools, vulnerability scanning, and intrusion detection systems, as well as putting in place processes to monitor and update security guidance and assessments of system security requirements.

Note that the preceding text mentions "intrusion detection systems," but the rest of the text has nothing to do with real monitoring, i.e., detecting and responding to intrusions. I'm not just talking about network-centric approaches, by the way -- infrastructure, host, log, and other sources are all real monitoring, but this is not what NIST means by "monitoring."

To understand NIST's view of monitoring, try reading the new draft. I'll insert my comments.

APPENDIX G

CONTINUOUS MONITORING

MANAGING AND TRACKING THE SECURITY STATE OF INFORMATION SYSTEMS

A critical aspect of managing risk from information systems involves the continuous monitoring of the security controls employed within or inherited by the system. 65

[65 A continuous monitoring program within an organization involves a different set of activities than Security Incident Monitoring or Security Event Monitoring programs.]

So, it sounds like activities that involve actually watching systems are not within scope for "continuous monitoring."

Conducting a thorough point-in-time assessment of the deployed security controls is a necessary but not sufficient condition to demonstrate security due diligence. An effective organizational information security program also includes a rigorous continuous monitoring program integrated into the system development life cycle. The objective of the continuous monitoring program is to determine if the set of deployed security controls continue to be effective over time in light of the inevitable changes that occur.

That sounds ok so far. I like the idea of evaluations to determine if controls are effective over time. In the next section below we get to the heart of the problem, and why I wrote this post.

An effective organization-wide continuous monitoring program includes:

• Configuration management and control processes for organizational information systems;

• Security impact analyses on actual or proposed changes to organizational information systems and environments of operation;67

• Assessment of selected security controls (including system-specific, hybrid, and common controls) based on the organization-defined continuous monitoring strategy;68

• Security status reporting to appropriate organizational officials;69 and

• Active involvement by authorizing officials in the ongoing management of information system-related security risks.

Ok, where is threat monitoring? I see configuration management, "control processes," reporting status to "officials," "active involvement by authorizing officials," and so on.

The next section tells me what NIST really considers to be "monitoring":

Priority for security control monitoring is given to the controls that have the greatest volatility and the controls that have been identified in the organization's plan of action and milestones...

[S]ecurity policies and procedures in a particular organization may not be likely to change from one year to the next...

Security controls identified in the plan of action and milestones are also a priority in the continuous monitoring process, due to the fact that these controls have been deemed to be ineffective to some degree.

Organizations also consider specific threat information including known attack vectors (i.e., specific vulnerabilities exploited by threat sources) when selecting the set of security controls to monitor and the frequency of such monitoring...

Have you broken the code yet? **Security control monitoring is a compliance activity.** Granted, this is an improvement from the typical certification and accreditation debacle, where "security" is assessed via paperwork exercises every three years. **Instead, .gov compliance teams will perform so-called "continuous monitoring," meaning more regular checks to see if systems are in compliance.**

Is this really an improvement?

I don't think so. **NIST is missing the point.** Their approach advocates *Control-compliant security, not field-assessed security*. **Their "scoreboard" is the result of a compliance audit, not the** number of systems under adversary control or the amount of data exfiltrated or degraded by the adversary.

I don't care how well your defensive "controls" are informed by offense. If you don't have a Computer Incident Response Team performing continuous threat monitoring for detection and response, you don't know if your controls are working. The NIST document has a few hints about the right approach, at best, but **the majority of the so-called "monitoring" guidance is another compliance activity.**

https://taosecurity.blogspot.com/2009/11/control-monitoring-is-not-threat.html

Commentary

This is another example of the running philosophical battle I had with elements of the government information security world. They were so wedded to their implementation of controls, despite, at that point, having intruders roaming Federal networks for the last decade. Controls are necessary but not sufficient.

Let a Hundred Flowers Blossom

Thursday, December 03, 2009

I know many of us work in large, diverse organizations. The larger or more complex the organization, the more difficult it is to enforce uniform security countermeasures. The larger the population to be "secure," the more likely exceptions will bloom. Any standard tends to devolve to the least common denominator. There are some exceptions, such as FDCC, but I do not know how widespread that standard configuration is inside the government.

Beyond the difficulty of applying a uniform, worthwhile standard, we run into the diversity vs monoculture argument from 2005. I tend to side with the diversity point of view, because diversity tends to increase the cost borne by an intruder. In other words, it's cheaper to develop exploitation methods for a target who 1) has broadly similar, if not identical, systems and 2) publishes that standard so the intruder can test attacks prior to "game day."

At the end of the day, the focus on uniform standards is a manifestation of the battle between two schools of thought: **Control-Compliant vs Field-Assessed Security. The control-compliant team believes that developing the "best standard," and then applying that standard everywhere, is the most important aspect of security. The field-assessed team (where I devote my effort) believes the result is more important than how you get there.**

I am not opposed to developing standards, but I do think that the control-compliant school of thought is only half the battle -- and that controls occupy far more time and effort than they are worth. If the standard withers in the face of battle, i.e., once field-assessed it is found to be lacking, then the standard is a failure. Compliance with a failed standard is worthless at that point.

However, I'd like to propose a variation of my original argument. **What if you abandon uniform standards completely?** What if you make the focus of the activity field-assessed instead of control-compliant, by conducting assessments of systems? In other words, let a hundred flowers blossom.

(If you don't appreciate the irony, do a little research and remember the sorts of threats that occupy much of the time of many of this blog's readers!)

So what do I mean? **Rather than making compliance with controls the focus of security activity, make assessment of the results the priority.** Conduct blue and red team assessments of information assets to determine if they meet various resistance and (maybe) "survivability" metrics. In other words, **we don't care how you manage to keep an intruder from exploiting your system, as long as it takes longer for a blue or red assessor with time X and skill level Y and initial access level Z** (or something to that effect).

In such a world, there's plenty of room for the person who wants to run Plan 9 without anti-virus, the person who runs FreeBSD with no graphical display or Web browser, the person who runs another "nonstandard" platform or system -- as long as their system defies the field assessment conducted by the blue and red teams. (Please note the one "standard" I would apply to all assets is that they 1) do no harm to other assets and 2) do not break any laws by running illegal or unlicensed software.)

If a "hundred flowers" is too radical, maybe consider 10. Too tough to manage all that? Guess what -- you are likely managing it already. So-called "unmanaged" assets are everywhere. **You probably already have 1000 variations, never mind 100. Maybe it's time to make the system's inability to survive against blue and red teams the measure of failure, not whether the system is "compliant" with a standard, the measure of failure?**

Now, I'm sure there is likely to be a high degree of correlation between "unmanaged" and vulnerable in many organizations. There's probably also a moderate degree of correlation between "exceptional" (as in, this box is too "special" to be considered "managed") and vulnerable. In other instances, the exceptional systems may be impervious to all but the most dedicated intruders. In any case, **accepting that diversity is a fact of life on modern networks, and deciding to test the resistance level of those assets, might**

be more productive than seeking to develop and apply uniform standards.

What do you think?

https://taosecurity.blogspot.com/2009/12/let-hundred-flowers-blossom.html

Commentary

Diversity has a quality all its own. What's easier for an intruder to exploit: a Windows domain that controls all of its endpoints, or endpoints not connected to a Windows domain, *ceteris paribus*?

Attribution Using 20 Characteristics

Friday, January 22, 2010

My post *Attribution Is Not Just Malware Analysis* raised some questions that I will try to address here. I'd like to cite Mike Cloppert as inspiration for some of this post.

Attribution means identifying the threat, meaning the party perpetrating the attack. Attribution is not just malware analysis. There are multiple factors that can be evaluated to try to attribute an attack.

Timing. What is the timing of the attack, i.e., fast, slow, in groups, isolated, etc.?

Victims or targets. Who is being attacked?

Attack source. What is the technical source of the attack, i.e., source IP addresses, etc.?

Delivery mechanism. How is the attack delivered?

Vulnerability or exposure. What service, application, or other aspect of business is attacked?

Exploit or payload. What exploit is used to attack the vulnerability or exposure?

Weaponization technique. How was the exploit created?

Post-exploitation activity. What does the intruder do next?

Command and control method. How does the intruder establish command and control?

Command and control servers. To what systems does the intruder connect to conduct command and control?

Tools. What tools does the intruder use post-exploitation?

Persistence mechanism. How does the intruder maintain persistence?

Propagation method. How does the intruder expand control?

Data target. What data does the intruder target?

Data packaging. How does the intruder package data for exfiltration?

Exfiltration method. How does the intruder exfiltrate data?

External attribution. Did an external agency share attribution data based on their own capabilities?

Professionalism. How professional is the execution, e.g., does keystroke monitoring show frequent mistakes, is scripting used, etc.?

Variety of techniques. Does the intruder have many ways to accomplish its goals, or are they limited?

Scope. What is the scope of the attack? Does it affect only a few systems, many systems?

As you can see, there are many characteristics that can be assessed in order to determine if an incident is likely caused by a certain party. Mature security shops use profiles like this to make their own intelligence assessments, often confidentially collaborating with others sharing the same problems.

https://taosecurity.blogspot.com/2010/01/attribution-using-20-characteristics.html

Commentary

This list is still valid today. It's unfortunate that the proliferation of post exploitation software tools (PESTs) mean that intruders can dispense with investing in research and development of their own technologies to abuse targets. Instead they can download code from GitHub written by "security researchers." Even worse, they can then abuse protocols advertised as "enhancing privacy," and use those protocols to mask their activities. Catalin Cimpanu provided an example of this in August 2020 when he wrote about Iranian threat group APT34.

https://www.zdnet.com/article/iranian-hacker-group-becomes-first-known-apt-to-weaponize-dns-over-https-doh/

This team switched from using custom, in-house command-and-control tools to DNSExfiltrator, available from

278

GitHub. Then they transitioned from using routine DNS traffic to DNS over HTTPS (DoH).

I understand that because the code is public on GitHub, defenders can download it to see how it works. They can then (possibly) deploy detection methods. I'm asking for policymakers, especially, to weigh the costs and benefits of situations like this. I estimate the costs to the 99% of organizations victimized by this state of affairs far outweigh the benefits that accrue to the 1% who can better defend themselves.

Time and Cost to Defend the Town

Friday, March 19, 2010

Recently I guest-blogged on the importance of learning how another person thinks. This week I had a chance to apply this lesson with a new decision maker. I learned that I need to develop a way for this executive to think about our security program. I discussed the situation with my wife and she suggested focusing on cost. I thought about this a little more and realized that was the right way to approach the problem.

Consider the following scenario. You're the mayor of a town. You need to decide how much of your budget to allocate to the fire department. To apply the most simplistic analysis to the problem, consider this scene. As mayor you give the fire chief a simple goal: "protect us from fires!" **The fire chief asks you: "Mayor, on average, how fast do you want the fire department to respond to a fire?"**

I am not an expert on fighting real fires, but let's think about a range of some possible answers.

Option 1. **Instantly.** Literally as soon as a fire is detected, fire fighters are on site. Assume this level of response produces the maximum level of containment and preservation of property value, on average.

Option 2. **Within 15 minutes.** Assume this level of response produces 75% containment and preservation of property value, on average.

Option 3. **Within 30 minutes.** 50% containment and preservation of property value, on average.

Option 4. **Within 45 minutes.** 25% containment and preservation of property value, on average.

Option 5. **Within 60 minutes.** It's too late. With this timing, the property value is destroyed.

As mayor you're likely to first reach for option 1. After all, you want to preserve property value. However, the fire chief says "maybe you should consider the following data."

Option 1 costs $64 million. Fire fighters are deployed at 16 locations.

Option 2 costs $32 million. Fire fighters are deployed at 8 locations.

Option 3 costs $16 million. Fire fighters are deployed at 4 locations.

Option 4 costs $8 million. Fire fighters are deployed at 2 locations.

Option 5 costs $4 million. Fire fighters are deployed at 1 location.

At this point you're starting to sweat. There has to be a way out of this situation! You decide that you can't afford option 1, or 2, or probably even 3. The recession is hitting your town hard. You ask the fire chief if there's a way to reduce the number of fires expected to occur, so that a smaller fire fighting force can react more quickly to fewer fires.

The fire chief switches from his fire fighter role to that of fire marshall. He says that is certainly possible, if the mayor wants to pick from one or more of the following options.

- Rebuild dwellings using fire-resistant materials.
- Inspect and rewire electrical systems, including aggressive, persistent monitoring for faults.
- Deploy advanced fire, smoke, and related alarms everywhere.
- Remove flammable materials from dwellings.
- Educate citizens on fire hazards.
- Ensure all citizens know how to contact the fire department, and have the means to do so efficiently and effectively.
- Plus a dozen more options...

You are probably getting the hang of this scenario. At this point the mayor needs to know the cost of each of the fire resistant methods outlined above. Let's not forget one other element: **the fire chief asks the police chief to inform the mayor of the arsonist threat, and describes how dedicating counter-threat activities can deter and detain adversaries who set dwellings ablaze.**

At the end of the day, the fire chief is presenting options to the mayor, and it's up to the mayor to decide how fast do we want to be able to respond to the **fires that will happen**, for how much cost.

(I underline the "fires that will happen" because that is the reality of life. Disasters happen, so you have to plan for them.)

For me, this is the best way to approach this executive. **The fire chief doesn't get to decide how much money to spend on the problem. That's the mayor's decision.** The mayor needs to make a budget choice, preferably with the fire chief's input, and then let the fire chief make the best resource allocation to meet the time goals requested by the mayor.

For me, **time and cost are the best levers we can move in digital security.** I can measure detection and response time for the incidents we handle. I can track how much money I am spending to meet those time requirements. If the mayor wants faster response time, the mayor can try to reduce the number of fires via fire marshall programs and/or apply more resources to the fire fighters.

Beyond measuring incident detection and response for real intrusions, you can use red teaming/adversary simulation to create metrics. You can say **"for the money currently spent on our security resistance program, it takes a Red Team X number of minutes to accomplish Goal X. Is that acceptable?"** If X minutes is unacceptable, you can again present cost-benefit analysis in order to derive a decision.

If you think you've heard this line of reasoning before (outside this blog), please check whether the other advocates have emphasized outcomes as I do here and elsewhere. **I'm not saying "spend $10 million to achieve 95% patch compliance." That's an input metric. I'm talking about output metrics against real intrusion activity and adversary simulations.**

https://taosecurity.blogspot.com/2010/03/time-and-cost-to-defend-town.html

Commentary

I did not say in this post the following: if the mayor chooses option 5, and you, as the fire chief, cannot abide by the decision, then you should resign. You should also go to the press so that the townspeople know that they are being put at risk of fire loss due to their mayor's decisions. Thankfully, I have not been put in this situation. I have, however, resigned for other reasons. Security team members who complain about their situation due to poor management choices or mindsets might want to keep resignation in their tool kit.

More on Black Hat Costs

Monday, May 24, 2010

About a year ago I wrote *Black Hat Budgeting*, explaining how an offensive security team might spend $1 million. I said

"I submit that for $1 million per year an adversary could fund a Western-salaried black hat team that could penetrate and persist in roughly any target it chose to attack."

Tonight Jeremiah Grossman asked via Twitter:

> regarding black hat budgeting, does defense-in-depth exacerbate the value cost inequity for defenders http://is.gd/cnGW9

I was tempted to squeeze some sort of reply into less than 140 characters, but decided to answer here instead.

First, vulnerability research is not free. Funny enough the No More Free Bugs movement is about one year old now. Charlie, Dino, and Alex are right -- it costs real resources to find vulnerabilities in software, with the level depending on the target.

Second, exploit development is not free. It is not trivial to devise a reliable, multi-target, stealthy-if-necessary exploit for a discovered vulnerability. Projects like Metasploit have made it a little easier since the days of one-off code for every proof of concept. Still, professional exploit writers still spend a lot of time on Metasploit, commercial alternatives, or their own mechanisms.

Third, victim management is not free. Everyone likes to talk about "risk management." Let's flip that notion around and think from the intruder's perspective. **One of the features separating amateurs from professionals is the degree to which the intruder can manage his or her presence in the victim enterprise.** The greater the persistence of the intruder the more professional the intruder, almost by definition. It takes a decent amount of work to stay present and/or undetected in an enterprise, depending on the defender's capabilities.

So, black hats have a lot of costs to manage, beyond those in my original post. I can pretty confidently argue, however, that **intruder costs are dwarfed by defender costs**. To the extent that "defense in depth" (DiD) applies additional costs yet does not meaningfully reduce exposure and vulnerability, DiD does indeed "exacerbate the value cost inequity for defenders."

Aside: a quick way to identify ineffective DiD is to review network diagrams showing "firewall stacks." I mean, seriously, in 2010, who needs more than one "traditional" firewall on a network segment? 10 or more years ago I remember network security people thinking you needed multiple different firewalls so they would each "catch something different" or cover for errors. These days everyone lets [TCP ports] 80 and 443 traverse the firewall so malicious traffic just uses those services. How much money is wasted on these "traditional" designs?

https://taosecurity.blogspot.com/2010/05/more-on-black-hat-costs.html

The No More Free Bugs movement, as described by Dino Dai Zovi in his March 2009 blog post, included the following concepts:

> Vulnerabilities place users and customers at risk. Otherwise, vendors wouldn't bother to fix them. Internet malware and worms spread via security vulnerabilities and place home users' and enterprises' sensitive data at risk.

> Vulnerabilities have legitimate value. Software vendors pay their own employees and consultants to find them and help them fix them in their products during development.

> Reporting vulnerabilities can be legally and professionally risky. When a researcher discloses the vulnerability to the vendor, there is no "whistle blower" protection and independent security researchers may be unable to legally defend themselves.

> It is unfair to paying customers. Professional bug hunting is a specialized and expensive business. Software vendors that "freeload" on the security research community place their customers at risk by not putting forth resources to discover vulnerabilities in and fix their products.

> Therefore, reporting vulnerabilities for free without any legal agreements in place is risky volunteer work... There just need to be more legal and transparent options for monetizing security research. This would provide a fair market value for a researcher's findings and incentivize more researchers to find and report vulnerabilities to these organizations. All of this would help make security research a more widespread and legitimate profession.

I include this for reference, not to endorse or critique the movement.

Forget Pre-Incident Cost, How Much Did Your Last Incident Cost?

Monday, May 24, 2010

I just read this great post by Rich Mogull titled *FireStarter: The Only Value/Loss Metric That Matters.*

His basic argument, or at least the idea that I derived from it, is the following (all in my own words).

So-called "risk managers" spend a lot of time imagining they can determine "annualized loss expectancy" by predicting how much an incident will cost. Forget all that nonsense. Before imaging what a future incident will cost, figure out how much your last incident cost.

This is brilliant because it is so simple yet drives straight at the heart of the problem. We work incidents all the time and I can't tell you how much they cost. Think about all the factors to consider:

- Value of professional time of everyone who detected and responded to the incident
- Value of computing resources affected by the incident
- Value of data affected by the incident, whether disclosed, degraded, or denied
- Value of brand, reputation, and other "goodwill" items

What else can you imagine?

So, think about answering these questions for a really good recent interest before wasting time imagining costs of future incidents. I think what you will find is that this can be a really difficult exercise. However, if you can derive some general guidelines, it's worth it.

https://taosecurity.blogspot.com/2010/05/forget-pre-incident-cost-how-much-did.html

Commentary

In 2010, many readers might have responded by saying "I don't have any past incidents from which I can derive costs!" Ten years later, everyone has been compromised and had to work through the incident response exercise.

Five Reasons "dot-secure" Will Fail

Saturday, September 25, 2010

Thom Shanker reported in *Cyberwar Chief Calls for Secure Computer Network* the following this week:

> The new commander of the military's cyberwarfare operations is advocating the creation of a separate, secure computer network to protect civilian government agencies and critical industries like the nation's power grid against attacks mounted over the Internet.

> The officer, Gen. Keith B. Alexander, suggested that such a heavily restricted network would allow the government to impose greater protections for the nation's vital, official on-line operations. General Alexander labeled the new network "a secure zone, a protected zone." Others have nicknamed it "dot-secure."

It would provide to essential networks like those that tie together the banking, aviation, and public utility systems the kind of protection that the military has built around secret military and diplomatic communications networks — although even these are not completely invulnerable.

I'd like to share five reasons why I think this approach will fail.

1. "dot-secure" becomes new target number one. I can't think of an easier way to help an adversary target the most critical information and capabilities on industry computers. If you're going to attack a company with hundreds of thousands of users and computers, it can be tough to decide where to focus attention. Multiply that target set across dozens or hundreds of companies and the adversary's problems also multiply. Now, suppose those companies put their most sensitive, important data on "dot-secure." Now all the adversary has to do is penetrate that network and take everything.

2. "Separation" is a fool's goal. Didn't we just read about Operation Buckshot Yankee, where malware jumped between networks of different classification levels? I guarantee users will want and need to transfer information between their normal company Internet-connected computers and "dot-secure." As long as those vectors exist, there is no "separation."

3. The network will be too big to keep "secure." Organizations build networks because there is value in exchanging information. In fact, the larger the network, the more valuable it becomes. So, what organizations will be allowed to connect to "dot-secure"? It will surely be more than the small handful that have a prayer of successfully defending themselves from APT and similar threats. That means weaker organizations will participate, and they will be compromised. As the network grows, it will get weaker and weaker.

4. How can "dot-secure" be any more successful than SIPRNet? I don't expect "dot-secure" to be as well-protected as SIPRNet. (And calling SIPRNet "well-protected" is probably causing some people to laugh.) Trying to get a SIPRNet terminal deployed is very expensive, and I don't expect DoD to make the same demands upon organizations as those required to host SIPRNet terminals. Many people consider SIPRNet compromised (I'm repeating public rumors, not confirming -- I have no direct knowledge), so why would "dot-secure" be any more successful?

5. "dot-secure" is another technical "solution" to a non-technical problem. I am dismayed to see DoD, of all places, taking a vulnerability-centric approach to an inherently threat-centric problem. It's clear that DoD is much more proficient in offense and that the "defense" part of the Department's name is increasingly misplaced. (I prefer the original "Department of War" anyway. Let's not fool ourselves!) How many hundreds of millions, or billions of dollars of taxpayer money could be wasted on "dot-secure," only to see DoD report to the Secretary or the President in 5 or 8 years that the network is also thoroughly compromised. Oops!

I think it would be far cheaper, and more effective, to engage the diplomatic and economic instruments of power to convince threats that they should keep their military and state hands out of American private enterprise.

https://taosecurity.blogspot.com/2010/09/five-reasons-dot-secure-will-fail.html

Commentary

The "dot-secure" program went nowhere in 2010. In 2020, however, the National Security Agency created a pilot program to offer DNS services to defense contractors, as reported by Cyberscoop reporter Shannon Vavran in June 2020:

> In an effort to better protect the U.S. defense industrial base from malware-based threats, the National Security Agency has launched a pilot program on securing Domain Name System use for U.S. defense contractors.
>
> The NSA's cybersecurity directorate has been working on the pilot, called secure DNS, for six weeks, the directorate's chief, Anne Neuberger, said during a virtual event Thursday...
>
> The NSA pilot also comes amid a broader push from the U.S. government to bolster government defenses against threat actors' efforts to exploit DNS. DHS's cybersecurity agency also recently announced that it is working to rollout a DNS resolver service to interfere with threat actors' malware, ransomware, or botnet campaigns against U.S. government agencies.
>
> The NSA's secure DNS pilot is targeted at providing secure services to small- and medium-sized companies working on Department of Defense weapons technologies, according to Neuberger.
>
> "This is a model that can help kind of jumpstart that security particularly for smaller- and medium- sized companies that may not have the ability to invest the resources or [have] the right skilled personnel," Neuberger said. "We know they're targets because they're building weapons technology for the department."

Neuberger said ideally the pilot will help the NSA establish a baseline for other companies to offer secure DNS services to defense contractors in the future.

https://www.cyberscoop.com/nsa-secure-dns-service-pilot-defense-industrial-base/

This is a great idea. There are plenty of such services already available, so the general approach is sound. The value, in my opinion, is two-fold. First, assuming NSA asserts the right to monitor the DNS requests from its constituents, it gains insight into attack activity affecting the cleared defense base. I'm sure some readers are complaining about a lack of privacy, but defense contractors do not have any expectation of privacy when using work networks. Second, the NSA is likely able to resist intrusion attempts from threat actors who want to compromise the DNS service itself.

For these two reasons, I disagree with the idea that NSA should pilot this service and then let commercial actors step in. Cleared defense contractors would do well to use the NSA provided DNS services. DoD might want to make it a requirement for future contracts.

TaoSecurity Security Effectiveness Model

Monday, August 29, 2011

After my last few Tweets as @taosecurity on threat-centric vs vulnerability-centric security, I sketched this diagram to help explain my thinking.

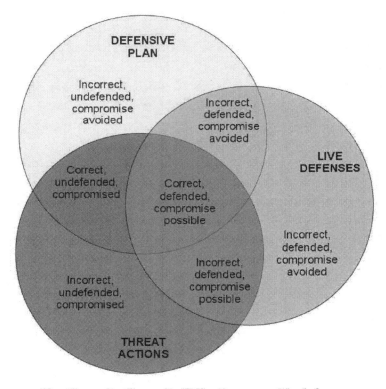

TaoSecurity Security Effectiveness Model

Figure 15. TaoSecurity Security Effectiveness Model

Security consists of three areas of interest: 1) What defenders think should be defended, whether or not it matters to the adversary or whether it is in reality defended, what I label "**Defensive Plan**"; 2) What the adversary thinks matters and really should be defended, but might not be, what I label as **"Threat Actions"**; and 3) What is in reality defended in the enterprise, whether or not defenders or the adversary cares, what I label **"Live Defenses"**.

I call the Defensive Plan **"Correct"** when it overlaps with the Adversary Actions, because the defenders correctly assessed the threat's interests. I call it **"Incorrect"** when Live Defenses are applied to areas outside the interest of the security team or outside the interest of the adversary.

I call the area covered by the Live Defenses as **"Defended,"** but I don't assume the defenses are actually sufficient. Some threats will escalate to whatever level is necessary to achieve their mission. In other words, the only way to not be compromised is to not be targeted! So, I call areas that aren't defended at all **"Compromised"** if the adversary targets them. Areas not targeted by the adversary are **"Compromise Avoided."** Areas targeted by the adversary but also covered by Live Defense are **"Compromise Possible."**

The various intersections produce some interesting effects. For example:

If you're in the lower center area titled **"Incorrect, defended, compromise possible,"** and your defenses hold, you're just plain lucky. You didn't anticipate the adversary attacking you, but somehow you had a live defense covering it.

If you're near the left middle area titled **"Correct, undefended, compromised,"** this means you knew what to expect but you couldn't execute. You didn't have any live defenses in place.

If you're in the area just below the previous space, titled **"Incorrect, undefended, compromised,"** you totally missed the boat. You didn't expect the adversary to target that resource, and you didn't happen to have any live defenses protecting it.

If you're in the very center, called "**Correct, defended, compromise possible**," congratulations -- this is where you expected your security program to operate, you deployed defenses that were live, but the result depends on how much effort the adversary applies to compromising you. This is supposed to be "security Nirvana" but your success depends more on the threat than on your defenses.

The top-most part titled "**Incorrect, undefended, compromise avoided**" shows a waste of planning effort, but not wasted live defenses. That's a mental worry region only.

The right-most part titled "**Incorrect, defended, compromise avoided**" shows a waste of defensive effort, which you didn't even plan. You could probably retire all the security programs and tools in that area.

The area near the top titled "**Incorrect, defended, compromise avoided**" shows you were able to execute on your vision but the adversary didn't bother attacking those resources. That's also waste, but less so since you at least planned for it.

What do you think of this model? Obviously you want to make all three circles overlap as much as possible, such that you plan and defend what the threat intends to attack. That's the idea of threat-centric security in a nutshell -- or maybe a Venn diagram.

https://taosecurity.blogspot.com/2011/08/taosecurity-security-effectiveness.html

Commentary

For these TaoSecurity Blog volumes, I tried to avoid, or at least limit, the inclusion of diagrams. However, I made an exception for this one, as it best conveys the main idea. I hope you internalize the concept that it's the threat actor's capabilities and intentions that are the governing dynamic in security. If you are targeted by a capable and willing threat actor, you are in a heap of trouble. The only situations in which you completely avoid compromise, per the diagram, are those in which the threat does not target you. There are three situations where one avoids compromise, two where compromise is guaranteed, and two where compromise is possible. This is why prevention eventually fails.

The Limits of Tool- and Tactics-Centric Thinking

Saturday, February 22, 2014

Earlier today I read a post by Dave Aitel to his mailing list titled *Drinking the Kool-aid*. Basically Dave lists several gross categories of defensive digital security technology and tools, then lists what he perceives as deficiencies and benefits of each. Embedded in these pluses and minuses are several tactical elements as well. I had three reactions to this post.

First, I recognized that it's written by someone who is not responsible for defending any network of scale or significance. **Network defense is more than tools and tactics. It's more often about people and processes.** My initial response is unsatisfying and simplistic, however, even though I agree broadly with his critiques of anti-virus, firewalls, WAFs, and some traditional security technology.

Second, staying within the realm of tools and tactics, Dave is just wrong on several counts:
He emphasizes the role of encryption to defeat many defensive tools, but ignores that security and information technology architects regularly make deployment decisions to provide visibility in the presence of encryption.

He ignores or is ignorant of technology to defeat obfuscation and encryption used by intruders.

He says "archiving large amounts of traffic is insanely expensive and requires massive analytics to process," which is wrong on both counts. On a shoestring budget my team deployed hundreds of open source NSM sensors across my previous employer to capture data on gateways of up to multi-Gbps bandwidth. Had we used commercial packet capture platforms we would have needed a much bigger budget, but open source software like Security Onion has put NSM in everyone's hands, cheaply. Regarding "massive analytics," it's easier all the time to get what you need for solid log technology. You can even buy awesome commercial technology to get the job done in ways you never imagined.

I could make other arguments regarding tactics and tools, but you get the idea from the three I listed.

Third, and this is really my biggest issue with Dave's post, is that **he demonstrates the all-too-common tendency for security professionals to constrain their thinking to the levels of tactics and tools.** What do I mean? Consider this outline from my O'Reilly Webinar on my newest book:

A "Strategic Security" program consists of the following:

- Program Goals
- Strategies
- Operations and Campaigns
- Tactics
- Tools

A strategic security program doesn't start with tools and tactics. Instead, it starts with one or more overall program goals. The strategy-minded CISO gets executive buy-in to those goals; this works at a level understood by technicians and non-technicians alike. Next the CISO develops strategies to implement those goals, organizes and runs campaigns and operations to support the strategies, helps his team use tactics to realize the campaigns and operations, and procures tools and technology to equip his team.

Here is an example of one strategic security approach to minimize loss due to intrusions, using a strategy of rapid detection, response, and containment, and NSM-inspired operations/campaigns, tactics, and tools.

A sample "Strategic Security" program might consists of the following:

- Program Goals: minimize loss due to intrusions
- Strategies: rapid detection, response, and containment
- Operations and Campaigns: match and hunt for intruders using NSM
- Tactics: collect, analyze, escalate, and resolve incidents using NSM data
- Tools: NSM software

Now I don't want to seem too harsh, because tool- and tactics-centric thinking is not just endemic to the digital security world. I read how it played out during the planning and execution of the air campaign during the first Gulf War.

I read the wonderful *John Warden and the Renaissance of American Air Power* and learned how the US Air Force at the time suffered the same problems. **The Air Force was very tactics- and technology-focused. They cared about how to defeat other aircraft in aerial combat and sought to keep the Army happy by making close air support their main contribution to the "joint" fight.** The Air Force managed to quickly deploy planes to

Saudi Arabia but had little idea how to use those forces in a campaign, let alone to achieve strategic or policy goals. It took visionaries like John Warden and David Deptula to make the air campaign a reality, and forever change the nature of air warfare.

I was a cadet when this all happened and remember my instructors exhibiting the contemporary obsession with tactics and tech we've seen in the security world for decades. Only later in my Air Force career did I see the strategic viewpoint gain acceptance.

Expect to hear more from me about the need for strategic thinking in digital security. I intend to apply to a PhD program this spring and begin research in the fall. I want to apply strategic thinking to private sector digital defense, because that is where a lot of the action is and where the need is greatest.

https://taosecurity.blogspot.com/2014/02/the-limits-of-tool-and-tactics-centric.html

Commentary

Dave Aitel is a very smart guy, and he applies that thought to cyber security policy in addition to his day job. However, this fixation on tool- and tactics-centric thinking was a blind spot he demonstrated in 2014. There are many others who still demonstrate it.

I continue to use this "strategic security" model today. I recorded a webinar on the topic for O'Reilly Media in 2014, from a Brookings Institution conference room! The recording is online here:

https://www.youtube.com/watch?v=MPY_oh404OI

Alternatively, search for "Network Security Monitoring to Win Against a Variety of Intruders - O'Reilly Webcast."

Five Reasons Attribution Matters

Tuesday, December 30, 2014

Attribution is the hottest word in digital security. The term refers to identifying responsibility for an incident. What does it matter, though? Here are five reasons, derived from the five levels of strategic thought. I've covered those before, namely in *The Limits of Tool- and Tactics-Centric Thinking*.

Note that the reasons I outline here are not the same as performing attribution based on these characteristics. Rather, I'm explaining how attribution can assist responsible actors, from defenders through policymakers.

1. Starting from the bottom, at the **Tools** level, **attribution matters because identifying an adversary may tell defenders what software they can expect to encounter during an intrusion or campaign.** It's helpful to know if the adversary uses simple tools that traditional defenses can counter, or if they can write custom code and exploits to evade most any programmatic countermeasures.

Vendors and software engineers tend to focus on this level because they may need to code different defenses based on attacker tools.

2. The benefits of attribution are similar at the Tactics level. Tactics describes how an adversary acts within an engagement or "battle." It describes how the foe might use tools or techniques to accomplish a goal within an individual encounter.

For example, some intruders may abandon a system as soon as they detect the presence of an administrator or the pushback of a security team. Others might react differently by proliferating elsewhere, or fighting for control of a compromised asset.

Security and incident response teams tend to focus on this level because they have direct contact with the adversary on a daily basis. They must make defensive choices and prioritize security personnel attention in order to win engagements.

3. The level of Operations or Campaigns describes activities over long periods of time, from days to months, and perhaps years, over a wider theater of operations, from a department or network segment to an entire organization's environment.

Defenders who can perform attribution will better know their foe's longer-term patterns of behavior. Does the adversary prefer to conduct operations around holidays, or certain hours of the day or days of the week? Do they pause between tactical engagements, and for how long? Do they vary intrusion methods? Attribution helps defenders answer these and related questions, perhaps avoiding intrusion fatigue.

CISOs should focus on this level and some advanced IR teams incorporate this tier into their work. This is also the level where outside law enforcement and intelligence teams organize their thinking, using terms like "intrusion sets." All of these groups are trying to cope with long-term engagement with the adversary, and must balance hiring, organization, training, and other factors over budget and business cycles.

4. At the level of Strategy, attribution matters to an organization's management and leadership, as well as policymakers. These individuals must decide if they should adjust how they conduct business, based on who is attacking and damaging them. Although they might direct technical responses, they are more likely to utilize other business methods to deal with problems. For example, strategic decisions could involve legal maneuvering, acquiring or invoking insurance, starting or stopping business lines, public relations, hiring and firing, partnerships and alliances, lobbying, and other moves.

Strategy is different from planning, because strategy is a dynamic discipline derived from recognizing the interplay with intelligent, adaptive foes. One cannot think strategically without recognizing and understanding the adversary.

5. Finally, the level of Policy, or "program goals," is the supreme goal of government officials and top organizational management, such as CEOs and their corporate boards. These individuals generally do not fixate on technical solutions. **Policymakers can apply many government tools to problems, such as law enforcement, legislation, diplomacy, sanctions, and so forth. All of these require attribution.** Policymakers may choose to fund programs to reduce vulnerabilities, which in some sense is an "attribution free" approach. However, addressing the threat in a comprehensive manner demands knowing the threat. Attribution is key to any policy decision where one expects other parties to act or react to one's own moves.

Remember the five levels of strategic thought and their associated parties and responsibilities when you hear anyone (especially a techie) claim "attribution doesn't matter" or "don't do attribution."

Also, check out *Attributing Cyber Attacks* by my KCL [King's College London] professor Thomas Rid, and fellow PhD student Ben Buchanan.

https://taosecurity.blogspot.com/2014/12/five-reasons-attribution-matters.html

Attribution has mattered, at all levels of conflict, since humans first attacked each other. If you think that you don't care who's firing at you, and that you just need to hunker down or fire back, wouldn't you like to know if you're suffering a friendly fire accident?

Five Ways That Good Guys Share More Than Bad Guys

Tuesday, October 18, 2016

It takes a lot for me to write a cybersecurity blog post these days. I spend most of my writing time working on my PhD. Articles like *Nothing Brings Banks Together Like A Good Hack* drive me up the wall, however, and a Tweet rant is insufficient. What fired me up, you might ask? Please read the following excerpt:

> [Troels] Oerting, with no small dose of grudging admiration, says his adversaries excel at something that can't be addressed with deep pockets or killer software: They're superb networkers. "The organized crime groups in cyber are sharing much better than we are at the moment," says Oerting, a Dane with a square jaw and the watchful eyes of a cop who's investigated the underworld for 35 years. "They are sharing methodologies, knowledge, tools, practices—what works and what doesn't."

Statements like these are regularly submitted without evidence. In response, I provide **five sources of evidence why organized crime groups do not share more than defenders.**

1. Solution providers share. Both commercial and not-for-profit solution providers share enormous amounts of information on the security landscape. Some of it is free, and some of it is sold as products or consulting. Thousands of security companies and not-for-profit providers compete for your attention, producing white papers, Webinars, and other resources. You might argue that all of them claim to be the answer to your problem. However, this situation is infinitely better than the 1980s and early 1990s. Back then, hardly any solutions, or even security companies and organizations, existed at all.

Criminal solution providers share, but they do so by selling their wares. This is true for the open world as well, but the volume of the open world is orders of magnitude greater.

2. Government agencies share. My fellow Americans, has your organization been visited by the FBI? Federal agents notified more than 3,000 U.S. companies [in 2013] that their computer systems had been hacked.

https://www.washingtonpost.com/world/national-security/2014/03/24/74aff686-aed9-11e3-96dc-d6ea14c099f9_story.html

The agents didn't just walk in, drop a letter, and leave. If a relationship did not exist previously, it will now be developed.

Beyond third party breach notifications, agencies such as NIST, DHS, and others regularly share information with organizations. They may not share as much as we would like, but again, historical perspective reveals great progress.

3. Books, articles, and social media share. The amount of readable material on security is astounding. Again, in the late 1980s and early 1990s hardly any books or articles were available. Now, thousands of resources exist, with new material from publishers like No Starch arriving monthly. Where are the books written by the underground?

4. Security conferences share. You could spend every week of the year at a security conference. If you happen to miss a talk, it's likely the incomparable Iron Geek recorded it. Does the underground offer similar opportunities?

5. Private groups and limited information exchange groups share. A final category of defender sharing takes place in more controlled settings. These involve well-established Information Sharing and Analysis Centers (ISACs), developing Information Sharing and Analysis Organizations (ISAOs), and private mailing lists and forums with limited membership. These could possibly be the closest analogue to the much-esteemed underground. Even if you disregard points 1-4 above, the quality of information shared in this final category absolutely equals, if not exceeds, anything you would find in the criminal world.

If you disagree with this analysis, and continue to lament that bad guys share more than the good guys, what evidence can you provide?

https://taosecurity.blogspot.com/2016/10/five-ways-that-good-guys-share-more.html

Commentary

When you read someone complain that "defenders don't share," you're reading that they don't share what the complainant wants, or in the way the complainant wants. There's a limit to sharing, and sometimes that limit butts against the desires of law enforcement, the intelligence community, or other parties, usually in some position of authority.

Why Do SOCs Look Like This?

Thursday, June 28, 2018

When you hear the word "SOC," or the phrase "security operations center," what image comes to mind? Do you think of analysts sitting at desks, all facing forward, towards giant screens? Why is this?

The outstanding movie Apollo 13 is a docudrama about the challenged 1970 mission to the moon. In the movie, you see mission control in Houston, Texas. Mission control looks remarkably like a SOC, doesn't it? When builders of computer security operations centers imagined what their "mission control" rooms would look like, perhaps they had Houston in mind?

Or perhaps they thought of the 1983 movie War Games? Do you remember what NORAD was supposed to look like? Reality was way more boring however. I visited NORAD under Cheyenne Mountain in 1989, I believe, when visiting the Air Force Academy as a high school senior. I can confirm it did not look like the movie depiction!

Let's return to mission control. Consider the resources available to personnel manning the mission control room. The big screens depict two main forms of data: telemetry and video of the rocket. What about the individual screens, where people sit? They are largely customized. Each station presents data or buttons specific to the role of the person sitting there. Remember when Ed Harris' character called out the stations: booster, retro, vital, etc.?

This is one of the key differences between mission control and any modern computerized operations center. In the 1960s and 1970s, workstations (literally, places where people worked) had to be customized. They lacked the technology to have generic workstations where customization was done via screen, keyboard, and mouse.

They also lacked the ability to display video on demand, and relied on large television screens. Personnel with specific functions sat at specific locations, because that was literally the only way they could perform their jobs.

With the advent of modern computing, every workstation is instantly customizable. There is no need to specialize. Anyone can sit anywhere, assuming computers allow one's workspace to follow their logon. In fact, modern computing allows a user to sit in spaces outside of their office. A modern mission control could be distributed.

With that in mind, what does the current version of mission control look like? The modern Johnson Space Center's mission control room looks similar to the 1960s-1970s version, except it's dominated by screens, keyboards, and mice.

What strikes me about every image of a "SOC" that I've ever seen is that no one is looking at the big screens. They are almost always deployed for an audience. No one in an operational role looks at them.

There are exceptions. Consider the Arizona Department of Transportation operations center. Their "big screen" is a composite of 24 smaller screens showing traffic and roadways. No one is looking at the screen, but that sort of display is perfect for the human eye.

It's a variant of Edward Tufte's "small multiple" idea. There is no text. The eye can discern if there is a lot of traffic, or little traffic, or an accident pretty easily. It's likely more for the benefit of an audience, but it works decently well.

Compare those screens to what one is likely to encounter in a cyber SOC. In addition to a "pew pew" map and a "spinning globe of doom," it will likely include a slew of big screens. However the big screens are a waste of time. No one is standing near them. No one sitting at their workstations can read what the screens show. They are purely for an audience, who can't discern what they show either.

The bottom line for this post is that if you're going to build a "SOC," don't build it based on what you've seen in the movies, or in other industries, or what a consultancy recommends. Spend some time determining your SOC's purpose, and let the workflow drive the physical setting. You may determine you don't even need a "SOC," either physically or logically, based on maturing understandings of a SOC's mission. That's a topic for a future post!

https://taosecurity.blogspot.com/2018/06/why-do-socs-look-like-th is.html

Commentary

I considered removing this post from the collection, because the original version referenced images and screen captures. I could not reproduce them here. If you want to see them, please visit the online version. However, I think it still conveys my main point. When I wrote this story, my then-employer wanted to build a security operations center (SOC), more as a showpiece than anything else. Unfortunately they asked me to work with parties who were wedded to the traditional "desks-forward" model seen at Mission Control and other locations. This post tried to capture my thoughts on why this should not be the default model. One might still choose that model, but I suggest a process to determine why that configuration best meets your business needs.

Defining Counterintelligence

Sunday, July 22, 2018

I've written about counterintelligence (CI) before, but I realized today that some of my writing, and the writing of others, may be confused as to exactly what CI means.

The authoritative place to find an American definition for CI is the United States National Counterintelligence and Security Center. I am more familiar with the old name of this organization, the Office of the National Counterintelligence Executive (ONCIX).

The 2016 National Counterintelligence Strategy cites Executive Order 12333 (as amended) for its definition of CI:

> Counterintelligence – Information gathered and activities conducted to identify, deceive,
> exploit, disrupt, or protect against **espionage, other intelligence activities, sabotage, or assassinations** conducted for or on behalf of foreign powers, organizations, or persons, or their agents, or international terrorist organizations or activities.

The strict interpretation of this definition is **countering foreign nation state intelligence activities,** such as those conducted by China's Ministry of State Security (MSS), the Foreign Intelligence Service of the Russian Federation (SVR RF), Iran's Ministry of Intelligence, or the military intelligence services of those countries and others.

In other words, **counterintelligence is countering foreign intelligence.** The focus is on the party doing the bad things, and less on what the bad thing is.

The definition, however, is loose enough to encompass others; "organizations," "persons," and "international terrorist organizations" are in scope, according to the definition. This is just about everyone, although criminals are explicitly not mentioned.

The definition is also slightly unbounded by moving beyond "espionage, or other intelligence activities," to include "sabotage, or assassinations." In those cases, **the assumption is that foreign intelligence agencies and their proxies are the parties likely to be conducting sabotage or assassinations.** In the course of their CI work, paying attention to foreign intelligence agents, the CI team may encounter plans for activities beyond collection.

The bottom line for this post is a cautionary message. It's not appropriate to call all intelligence activities "counterintelligence." **It's more appropriate to call countering adversary intelligence activities counterintelligence.**

You may use similar or the same approaches as counterintelligence agents when performing your cyber threat intelligence function. For example, you may recruit a source inside a carding forum, or you may plant your own source in a carding forum. This is similar to turning a foreign intelligence agent, or inserting your own agent in a foreign intelligence service. However, activities directed against a carding forum are not counterintelligence. Activities directing against a foreign intelligence service are counterintelligence.

The nature and target of your intelligence activities are what determine if it is counterintelligence, not necessarily the methods you use. Again, this is in keeping with the stricter definition, and not becoming a victim of scope creep.

https://taosecurity.blogspot.com/2018/07/defining-counterintellige nce.html

Commentary

I was inspired to write this post by the ending of the FX television series *The Americans*, which ended in the spring of 2018. I recommend watching it, although it's not suitable for younger audiences.

More on Threat Hunting

Friday, November 23, 2018

Earlier this week hellor00t asked via Twitter:

> Where would you place your security researchers/hunt team?

I replied:

> **For me, "hunt" is just a form of detection. I don't see the need to build a "hunt" team. IR teams detect intruders using two major modes: matching and hunting. Junior people spend more time matching. Senior people spend more time hunting. Both can and should do both functions.**

This inspired Rob Lee to blog a response, from which I extract his core argument:

> [Hunting] really isn't, to me, about detecting threats...

> Hunting is a hypothesis-led approach to testing your environment for threats. The purpose, to me, is not in finding threats but in determining what gaps you have in your ability to detect and respond to them...

In short, hunting, to me, is a way to assess your security (people, process, and technology) against threats while extending your automation footprint to better be prepared in the future. Or simply stated, it's incident response without the incident that's done with a purpose and contributes something.

As background for my answer, I recommend my March 2017 post *The Origin of Threat Hunting*, which cites my article *Become a Hunter*, published in the July-August 2011 issue of *Information Security Magazine*. I wrote it in the spring of 2011, when I was director of incident response for GE-CIRT.

For the term "hunting," I give credit to briefers from the Air Force and NSA who, in the mid-2000s briefed "hunter-killer" missions to the Red Team/Blue Team Symposium at the Johns Hopkins University Applied Physics Lab in Laurel, MD.

As a comment to that post, Tony Sager, who ran NSA VAO at the time I was briefed at ReBl, described hunting thus:

> [Hunting] was an active and sustained search for Attackers...
>
> For us, "Hunt" meant a very planned and sustained search, taking advantage of the existing infrastructure of Red/Blue Teams and COMSEC Monitoring, as well as intelligence information to guide the search.

For the practice of hunting, as I experienced it, I give credit to our GE-CIRT incident handlers -- David Bianco, Ken Bradley, Tim Crothers, Tyler Hudak, Bamm Visscher, and Aaron Wade -- who took junior analysts on "hunting trips," starting in 2008-2009.

It is very clear, to me, that hunting has always been associated with detecting an adversary, not "determining what gaps you have in your ability to detect and respond to them," as characterized by Rob.

For me, Rob is describing the job of an enterprise visibility architect, which I described in a 2007 post:

> [W]e are stuck with numerous platforms, operating systems, applications, and data (POAD) for which we have zero visibility.
>
> I suggest that enterprises consider hiring or assigning a new role -- Enterprise Visibility Architect. The role of the EVA is to identify visibility deficiencies in existing and future POAD and design solutions to instrument these resources.
>
> A primary reason to hire an enterprise visibility architect is to build visibility in, which I described in several posts, including this one from 2009 titled Build Visibility In. As a proponent of the "monitor first" school, I will always agree that it is important to identify and address visibility gaps.

So where do we go from here?

Tony Sager, as one of my wise men, offers sage advice at the conclusion of his comment:

> "Hunt" emerged as part of a unifying mission model for my Group in the Information Assurance Directorate at NSA (the defensive mission) in the mid-late 2000's. But it was also a way to unify the relationship between IA and the SIGINT mission - intelligence as the driver for Hunting. The marketplace, of course, has now brought its own meaning to the term, but I just wanted to share some history.

In my younger days I might have expressed much more energy and emotion when encountering a different viewpoint. At this point in my career, I'm more comfortable with other points of view, so long as they do not result in harm, or a waste of my taxpayer dollars, or other clearly negative consequences. I also appreciate the kind words Rob offered toward my point of view.

tl;dr I believe the definition and practice of hunting has always been tied to adversaries, and that Rob describes the work of an enterprise visibility architect when he focuses on visibility gaps rather than adversary activity.

Update 1: If in the course of conducting a hunt you identify a visibility or resistance deficiency, that is indeed beneficial. The benefit, however, is derivative. You hunt to find adversaries. Identifying gaps is secondary although welcome.

The same would be true of hunting and discovering misconfigured systems, or previously unidentified assets, or unpatched software, or any of the other myriad facts on the ground that manifest when one applies Clausewitz's directed telescope towards their computing environment.

https://taosecurity.blogspot.com/2018/11/more-on-threat-hunting.html

Commentary

As this was a two-part post, please see the next post for commentary.

Even More on Threat Hunting

Saturday, November 24, 2018

In response to my post More on Threat Hunting, Rob Lee asked:

> [D]o you consider detection through ID'ing/"matching" TTPs not hunting?

To answer this question, we must begin by clarifying "TTPs." Most readers know TTPs to mean tactics, techniques and procedures, defined by David Bianco in his Pyramid of Pain post as:

> How the adversary goes about accomplishing their mission, from reconnaissance all the way through data exfiltration and at every step in between.

In case you've forgotten David's pyramid, it looks like this.

- TTPs [Tactics, Techniques, and Procedures]: Tough!
- Tools: Challenging
- Network/Host Artifacts: Annoying
- Domain Names: Simple
- IP Addresses: Easy
- Hash Values: Trivial

It's important to recognize that **the pyramid consists of indicators of compromise (IOCs)**. David uses the term "indicator" in his original 2014 post, but his follow-up post from his time at Sqrrl makes this clear:

> **There are a wide variety of IoCs ranging from basic file hashes to hacking Tactics, Techniques and Procedures (TTPs).** Sqrrl Security Architect, David Bianco, uses a concept called the Pyramid of Pain to categorize IoCs.

You can read his 2014 post here:

https://detect-respond.blogspot.com/2014/03/use-of-term-intellige
nce-at-rsa.html

At this point it should be clear that **I consider TTPs to be one
form of IOC.**

In *The Practice of Network Security Monitoring (2013)*, I included
the following workflow:

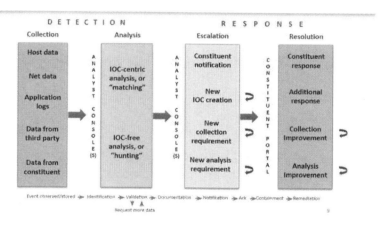

Figure 16. Incident Detection and Response Workflow

You can see in the second column that I define hunting as "IOC-free
analysis." On page 193 of the book I wrote:

> Analysis is the process of identifying and validating normal,
> suspicious, and malicious activity. IOCs expedite this
> process. Formally, **IOCs are manifestations of observable
> or discernible adversary actions.** Informally, IOCs are
> ways to codify adversary activity so that technical systems
> can find intruders in digital evidence...

315

I refer to relying on IOCs to find intruders as IOC-centric analysis, or matching. Analysts match IOCs to evidence to identify suspicious or malicious activity, and then validate their findings.

Matching is not the only way to find intruders. More advanced NSM operations also pursue **IOC-free analysis, or hunting.** In the mid-2000s, the US Air Force popularized the term hunter-killer in the digital world. Security experts performed friendly force projection on their networks, examining data and sometimes occupying the systems themselves in order to find advanced threats.

Today, NSM professionals like David Bianco and Aaron Wade promote network "hunting trips," during which a senior investigator with a novel way to detect intruders guides junior analysts through data and systems looking for signs of the adversary.

Upon validating the technique (and responding to any enemy actions), the hunters incorporate the new detection method into a CIRT's IOC-centric operations. (emphasis added)

Let's consider Chris Sanders' blog post titled *Threat Hunting for HTTP User Agents* as an example of my definition of hunting.

I will build a "hunting profile" via excerpts (in italics) from his post:

Assumption: *"Attackers frequently use HTTP to facilitate malicious network communication."*

Hypothesis: If I find an unusual user agent string in HTTP traffic, I may have discovered an attacker.

Question: *"Did any system on my network communicate over HTTP using a suspicious or unknown user agent?"*

Method: *"This question can be answered with a simple aggregation wherein the user agent field in all HTTP traffic for a set time is analyzed. I've done this using Sqrrl Query Language here:*

SELECT COUNT(*),user_agent FROM HTTPProxy GROUP BY user_agent ORDER BY COUNT(*) ASC LIMIT 20

This query selects the user_agent field from the HTTPProxy data source and groups and counts all unique entries for that field. The results are sorted by the count, with the least frequent occurrences at the top."

Results: Chris offers advice on how to interpret the various user agent strings produced by the query.

This is the critical part: Chris did not say "look for *this user agent*. He offered the reader an assumption, a hypothesis, a question, and a method. It is up to the defender to investigate the results. This, for me, is true hunting.

If Chris had instead referred users to this list of malware user agents (for example) and said look for "Mazilla/4.0", then I consider that manual (human) matching. If I created a Snort or Suricata rule to look for that user agent, then I consider that automated (machine) matching.

This is where my threat hunting definition likely diverges from modern practice. Analyst Z sees the results of Chris' hunt and thinks "Chris found user agent XXXX to be malicious, so I should go look for it." Analyst Z queries his or her data and does or does not find evidence of user agent XXXX.

I do not consider analyst Z's actions to be hunting. I consider it matching. There is nothing wrong with this. In fact, one of the purposes of hunting is to provide new inputs to the matching process, so that future hunting trips can explore new assumptions, hypotheses, questions, and methods, and let the machines do the matching on IOCs already found to be suggestive of adversary activity. This is why I wrote in my 2013 book "Upon validating the technique (and responding to any enemy actions), the hunters incorporate the new detection method into a CIRT's IOC-centric operations."

The term "hunting" is a victim of its own success, with emotional baggage. We defenders have finally found a way to make "blue team" work appealing to the wider security community. Vendors love this new way to market their products. "If you're not hunting, are you doing anything useful?" one might ask.

Compared to "I'm threat hunting!" (insert chest beating), the alternative, "I'm matching!" (womp womp), seems sad.

Nevertheless, we must remember that threat **hunting methodologies were invented to find adversary activity for which there were no IOCs. Hunting was IOC-free analysis because we didn't know what to look for.** Once you know what to look for, you are matching. Both forms of detection require analysis to validate adversary activity, of course. Let's not forget that.

I'm also very thankful, however it's defined or packaged, that people are excited to search for adversary activity in their environment, whether via matching or hunting. It's a big step from the mindset of 10 years ago, which had a "prevention works" milieu.

tl;dr Because TTPs are a form of IOC, then detection via matching IOCs is a form of matching, and not hunting.

https://taosecurity.blogspot.com/2018/11/even-more-on-threat-hunting.html

Commentary

This post demonstrated the value of documenting a thought process. The term "hunting" in the cyber security sphere wasn't widely used when I wrote my 2011 article for Information Security Magazine. I wrote it based on the hunt activity conducted by GE-CIRT in 2009-2010. Hunting as an idea existed before then, as demonstrated in this volume and elsewhere, but it did not acquire that name until the late 2000s.

Thoughts on Cloud Security

Wednesday, March 13, 2019

Recently I've been reading about cloud security and security with respect to DevOps. I'll say more about the excellent book I'm reading, but I had a moment of déjà vu during one section.

The book described how cloud security is a big change from enterprise security because it relies less on IP-address-centric controls and more on users and groups. The book talked about creating security groups, and adding users to those groups in order to control their access and capabilities.

As I read that passage, it reminded me of a time long ago, in the late 1990s, when I was studying for the MCSE, then called the Microsoft Certified Systems Engineer. I read a book titled *Windows NT Security Handbook*, published in 1996 by Tom Sheldon. It described the exact same security process of creating security groups and adding users. This was core to the new NT 4 role based access control (RBAC) implementation.

Now, fast forward a few years, or all the way to today, and consider the security challenges facing the majority of legacy enterprises: securing Windows assets and the data they store and access. How could this wonderful security model, based on decades of experience (from the 1960s and 1970s no less), have failed to work in operational environments?

There are many reasons one could cite, but I think the following are at least worthy of mention.

The systems enforcing the security model are exposed to intruders.

Furthermore:

Intruders are generally able to gain code execution on systems participating in the security model.

Finally:

Intruders have access to the network traffic which partially contains elements of the security model.

From these weaknesses, a large portion of the security countermeasures of the last two decades have been derived as compensating controls and visibility requirements.

The question then becomes:

Does this change with the cloud?

In brief, I believe the answer is largely "yes," thankfully. **Generally, the systems upon which the security model is being enforced are not able to access the enforcement mechanism, thanks to the wonders of virtualization.**

Should an intruder find a way to escape from their restricted cloud platform and gain hypervisor or management network access, then they find themselves in a situation similar to the average Windows domain network.

This realization puts a heavy burden on the cloud infrastructure operators. The major players are likely able to acquire and apply the expertise and resources to make their infrastructure far more resilient and survivable than their enterprise counterparts.

The weakness will likely be their personnel.

Once the compute and network components are sufficiently robust from externally sourced compromise, then internal threats become the next most cost-effective and return-producing vectors for dedicated intruders.

Is there anything users can do as they hand their compute and data assets to cloud operators?

I suggest four moves.

First, small- to mid-sized cloud infrastructure users will likely have to piggyback or free-ride on the initiatives and influence of the largest cloud customers, who have the clout and hopefully the expertise to hold the cloud operators responsible for the security of everyone's data.

Second, lawmakers may also need improved whistleblower protection for cloud employees who feel threatened by revealing material weaknesses they encounter while doing their jobs.

Third, government regulators will have to ensure no cloud provider assumes a monopoly, or no two providers assume a duopoly. We may end up with the three major players and a smattering of smaller ones, as is the case with many mature industries.

Fourth, users should use every means at their disposal to select cloud operators not only on their compute features, but on their security and visibility features. The more logging and visibility exposed by the cloud provider, the better. I am excited by new features like the Azure network tap and hope to see equivalent features in other cloud infrastructure.

Remember that **security has two main functions: planning/resistance, to try to stop bad things from happening, and detection/response, to handle the failures that inevitably happen.** "Prevention eventually fails" is one of my long-time mantras. **We don't want prevention to fail silently in the cloud.** We need ways to know that failure is happening so that we can plan and implement new resistance mechanisms, and then validate their effectiveness via detection and response.

Update: I forgot to mention that the material above assumed that the cloud users and operators made no unintentional configuration mistakes. If users or operators introduce exposures or vulnerabilities, then those will be the weaknesses that intruders exploit. We've already seen a lot of this happening and it appears to be the most common problem. Procedures and tools which constantly assess cloud configurations for exposures and vulnerabilities due to misconfiguration or poor practices are a fifth move which all involved should make.

A corollary is that complexity can drive problems. When the cloud infrastructure offers too many knobs to turn, then it's likely the users and operators will believe they are taking one action when in reality they are implementing another.

https://taosecurity.blogspot.com/2019/03/thoughts-on-cloud-security.html

Commentary

This post focused mainly on cloud providers who offer infrastructure as a service, software as a service (SaaS), platform as a service (PaaS), and serverless offering. It did not consider cloud-based services like social media companies such as Twitter. However, 2020 witnessed the massive breach of high profile Twitter user accounts.

https://blog.twitter.com/en_us/topics/company/2020/an-update-on-our-security-incident.html

I wrote in this post that "the weakness will likely be their personnel."

This appears to be the case in the Twitter compromise. However, technology and process likely failed, when one sees a breach of this magnitude.

Conclusion

This chapter was longer than I expected, but it balanced out the shorter nature of chapter 2. I hope the concepts of black and white hat budgeting, attribution, counterintelligence, and incident response resonated with you. In the final chapter, I turn to the topics of China and the advanced persistent threat.

Chapter 4. China and the Advanced Persistent Threat

Introduction

This chapter is about China, the original advanced persistent threat (APT). A single individual, a then-Air Force colonel, invented the term APT in 2007 as an unclassified means to talk about Chinese threat actors exploiting commercial, primarily defense industrial base (DIB), targets. Only later did APT become watered down as a generic term for any nation state actor attacking any target.

Chinese hacking was taking place well before 2007. One of the first threat actors I ever encountered in the Air Force in 1998 was Chinese. This chapter will discuss Chinese intrusion activity in the pre- and post-APT era, although the first post here dates from 2006.

I named this chapter "China and the Advanced Persistent Threat," although it would be more accurate to the original meaning of the term APT to name it "China, the Advanced Persistent Threat." The designated title is my attempt at a compromise with the evolution of the term, away from its original meaning.

More Real Threat Reporting

Friday, August 18, 2006

Harlan Carvey sent me a link to the following: *Chinese seek military ID info*. From the article:

Maj. Gen. William Lord, director of information, services and integration in the Secretary of the Air Force Office of Warfighting Integration and Chief Information Officer, today told an audience of civilian Air Force personnel attending the Air Force IT Conference that **"China has downloaded 10 to 20 terabytes of data from the NIPRNet [Non-secure or Non-classified Internet Protocol Router Network]. They're looking for your identity, so they can get into the network as you...**

We don't think they've gotten into the SIPRNet [Secret Internet Protocol Router Network] yet," [the classified Global Information Grid network], he said, "though we know they have [penetrated] the NIPRNet. There is a nation-state threat by the Chinese."

10 to 20 TB? Details, please. That's a lot of data.

https://taosecurity.blogspot.com/2006/08/more-real-threat-reporting.html

Commentary

This was an unusually blunt statement on Chinese attacks on military infrastructure. It would be rare to read unclassified reporting like that in the years to follow. I wonder if the 10-20 TB was an aggregation of data exfiltration over a long period, or during a single campaign, or during a single incident? This points to one of the problems we have with military intrusions. Absent admissions like these, the details generally remain classified forever. I imagine a Freedom of Information Act request might be possible, if researchers wished to try to learn more.

Germany v China

Tuesday, August 28, 2007

Thanks to the Dark Reading story *China's Premier 'Gravely Concerned' by Hack on Germany* I learned of recent digital economic espionage conducted by China against Germany. I found the most authoritative reference on the event to be published by the magazine that broke the story, which is currently running an article titled *Merkel's China Visit Marred by Hacking Allegations*:

> German Chancellor Angela Merkel was all smiles after meeting Chinese Premier Wen Jiabao on Monday, praising relations between the two countries as open and constructive.
>
> But her visit has been marred by a report in SPIEGEL that a large number of computers in the German chancellery as well as the foreign, economy and research ministries had been infected with Chinese spy software. Germany's domestic intelligence service, the Office for the Protection of the Constitution, discovered the hacking operation in May, the magazine reported in its new edition, published Monday...
>
> The so-called "Trojan" espionage programs were concealed in Microsoft Word documents and PowerPoint files which infected IT installations when opened, SPIEGEL reported. Information was taken from German computers in this way on a daily basis by hackers based in the north-western province of Lanzhou, Canton province and Beijing. German officials believe the hackers were being directed by the People's Liberation Army and that the programs were

redirected via computers in South Korea to disguise their origin.

German security officials managed to stop the theft of 160 gigabytes of data which were in the process of being siphoned off German government computers. "But no one knows how much has leaked out," a top official told SPIEGEL.

The hacking operation has triggered fears in Germany that China may also have infiltrated the computer systems of leading German companies, to steal technology secrets and thereby speed up its inexorable economic growth. The domestic intelligence service plans to help businesses hunt for spy programs in their computers.

China's Foreign Ministry spokesperson had this official comment:

Q: German media reported that German government computers were attacked by Chinese hackers. What's your comment?

A: The Chinese Government has always opposed to and forbidden any criminal acts undermining computer systems including hacking. We have explicit laws and regulations in this regard.

Hacking is an international issue and China is also a frequent victim. China has established a sound mechanism of cooperation with many countries in jointly countering internet crimes. China is willing to cooperate with Germany in this regard.

I find it interesting that the Germans are willing to directly confront this problem in public.

Commentary

This post began a series of "Country v China" posts during the second half of 2007, 2 ½ years before the flood gates opened with the revelation of Google's intrusion in late 2009 / early 2010. I will reserve further comments for the last of the series.

Japan v China

Friday, August 31, 2007

I couldn't make this up. Thanks to SANS Newsbites for catching the article *Japan Military Homes, Ship Raided Over Data Leak.*

> The homes of several serving members of Japan's Maritime Self Defense Force (JMSDF) and a destroyer were raided as part of an investigation into a leak of sensitive military data from a computer, Japan's Kyodo News reported Tuesday.

> Officers from the Kanagawa prefectural police force and the JMSDF's own criminal investigations unit are investigating the leak of information related to the Aegis missile defense system, the sea-based Standard Missile-3 interceptor system and the reconnaissance satellite data exchange Link 16 system.

> The Aegis leak first came to light in March this year when police were conducting an immigration-related investigation into the Chinese wife of a JMSDF officer. During the search they came across the data, which included the radar and transmission frequencies of the Aegis system. The officer

wasn't authorized to be in possession of the data so the investigation was begun.

He apparently came into possession of the data while swapping pornography with another JMSDF officer, according to a previous report in the Yomiuri Shimbun newspaper.

Any guesses which will be the next country to reveal its fight against Chinese intelligence services?

https://taosecurity.blogspot.com/2007/08/japan-v-china.html

United Kingdom v China

Wednesday, September 05, 2007

In Japan v China I asked "Any guesses which will be the next country to reveal its fight against Chinese intelligence services?" Thanks to *China targets UK with high-tech spy ring* and *China v the West: an ongoing digital struggle* we have the answer. From the first article:

> Several recent attempts to hack into British Government computer networks have been traced to China, Whitehall sources said today.

> The attacks are part of a pattern in which China and Russia are switching from "old-fashioned espionage" techniques to electronic hacking into government computers to gain Britain's military secrets, the sources added.

> The growing threat from hacking was underlined yesterday when President Bush said he might raise the sensitive issue with Beijing when he meets President Hu Jintao, the

Chinese leader, in Sydney tomorrow for an Asia-Pacific Economic Cooperation (Apec) summit.

Asked to respond to allegations that China's People's Liberation Army had hacked into a computer system in the office of Robert Gates, the US Defence Secretary, Mr Bush said: "I'm very aware that a lot of our systems are vulnerable to cyber attack from a variety of places."

He acknowledged he did not have the intelligence "at my fingertips" on the latest hacking allegations, but he said: "In terms of whether or not I'll bring this up to countries ... from which there may have been an attack, I may."

From the second article:

Mr Preatoni, who founded Zone-h.org, which monitors digital attacks, said that he was told three years ago of an attack on the European Parliament's computer network that originated from hackers based in the Jiangsu Province of China. The attack appeared too sophisticated to be the work of script kiddies and cyber gangsters. To Mr Preatoni's thinking, it was the first clear indication of a state-sponsored Chinese hack.

Like those who attacked the Pentagon, the hackers who targeted the European Parliament picked as their weapon of choice a Trojan – a program, often attached to an e-mail, that attempts to take control of part of a computer network after being downloaded. This particular Trojan was programmed to look for Microsoft Excel and PowerPoint files, along with e-mails and ".doc" files on the Parliament web servers, Mr Preatoni said...

What worries Mr Preatoni are the attacks that go undetected. "We think that governments have the most sophisticated cyber defences on the planet," he said. "This is the wrong assumption. In my work with governments, I see they face the same problems as the business world in securing their networks. There's a lack of expertise. The machines aren't properly administered. There are budget cuts. They face the same problems as the corporate world. They are hit by the same vulnerabilities."

Now who is next?

https://taosecurity.blogspot.com/2007/09/united-kingdom-v-china.html

France v China

Saturday, September 08, 2007

In *United Kingdom v China* I asked who would be the next country to announce it's been 0wned by China. Thanks to Benny Ketelslegers I hear it's France. He cites Maarten Van Horenbeeck who read the original French to say the following:

> Agence France Presse has reported that France is the most recent nation to be targeted by what are probably cyber attacks of Chinese origin. The news came from Mr Francis Delon, secretary general of the Secrétariat général de la défense nationale (SGDN). He notes: Chinese origin, not necessarily indicating involvement of the Chinese military.

It's a veritable "who's who" of the industrialized world -- US, Germany, UK, Japan, and now France. When will we hear from Canada, Italy... anyone else?

New Zealand v China

Thursday, September 13, 2007

According to *NZ's Clark won't identify hackers*, New Zealand is the latest victim of the someone's cyber brigades:

> New Zealand Prime Minister Helen Clark says she knows which countries tried to hack into her government's computers but is refusing to name names.
>
> Clark on Tuesday confirmed foreign spies had tried to hack into government computers, but they failed to gain access to any classified information.
>
> She said she knew which governments were involved but refused to name them, saying: "That's not the way intelligence matters are handled".

That's interesting. Everyone else likes to point the finger! More on that in a future post. So is China involved? According to *New Zealand: China's Spying On Us, Too* the answer is yes:

> China is once again being blamed for cyberattacks on a foreign country, with New Zealand secret service officials saying the Chinese were behind an attack on its systems...
>
> However, like the US case, a government official identified the source of the hack through the media. In an interview with The Dominion Post, Security Intelligence Service director Warren Tucker hinted that the Communist country was behind it.

333

We've almost got all of the "five eyes" now -- US, UK, New Zealand...
what about Canada and Australia?

https://taosecurity.blogspot.com/2007/09/new-zealand-v-china.ht
ml

Canada v China

Thursday, September 13, 2007

Just as I posted my last story on New Zealand I noticed the following
in *Editorial: The spy business is alive and well*:

> SIS head Warren Tucker said government computer systems
> had been hacked into by foreign states. Information had
> been stolen and hard-to-detect software installed that could
> be used to take control of computer systems, he said.

> Mr Tucker would not name the culprits. But he did refer to
> recent comments by Canada's security service about
> Chinese spying. Canada's spy-meister, Jim Judd, has said
> that almost half his security intelligence efforts were focused
> on that country's spies.

Canada, eh? Next I found *China is top espionage risk to Canada:
CSIS*:

> Almost half the effort the country's spy-watchers put into
> monitoring suspicious foreign activity in Canada is devoted
> to Chinese operatives... Jim Judd, director of the Canadian
> Security Intelligence Service, said... 15 countries account for
> most of the concern when it comes to foreign
> intelligence-gathering or interference in Canadian affairs.

He wouldn't identify all those countries, but did tell senators that China tops the list...

Prime Minister Stephen Harper, when he was still Opposition leader, claimed there were up to 1,000 Chinese agents in Canada.

He quoted a CSIS official as saying that Chinese spies stole $1 billion worth of technological secrets every month.

Last year, Foreign Affairs Minister Peter MacKay said he wanted a crackdown on Chinese espionage. MacKay is currently on a China visit.

In a 2004 report, CSIS said Chinese economic espionage targeted information including contract details, supplier lists, planning documents, research and development data, technical drawings and computer databases.

Foreign students and scientists, business delegations and immigrants were among those recruited as informants, the spy agency said.

Only Australia needs to be mentioned now.

https://taosecurity.blogspot.com/2007/09/canada-v-china.html

Australia v China

Thursday, September 13, 2007

My blog readers are quick. No sooner do I ask about Australia do I get a link to *China 'hacked Australian government computers'*:

CHINA has allegedly tried to hack into highly classified government computer networks in Australia and New Zealand as part of a broader international operation to glean military secrets from Western nations.

The Howard Government yesterday would neither confirm nor deny that its agencies, including the Defence Department, had been subject to cyber attack from China, but government sources acknowledge that thwarting such assaults is a continuous challenge.

"It's a serious problem, it's ongoing and it's real," one senior government source said...

Australian Attorney-General Philip Ruddock is sufficiently concerned about cyber attacks to be spending more than $70 million to improve the e-security of government and private computer networks.

https://taosecurity.blogspot.com/2007/09/australia-v-china.html

Commentary

This was an amazing few weeks in the summer of 2007. All of the Five Eyes (US, UK, Canada, Australia, and New Zealand), plus three of the leading developed democracies (France, Germany, and Japan) all admitted that they were suffering intrusions sponsored by Chinese threat actors. In some ways this news was several years old, as all of these countries had been under assault for several years already.

China as Victim

Thursday, September 13, 2007

China has pointed the finger back at the West, according to *China says suffers "massive" Internet spy damage*:

> China has suffered "massive" losses of state secrets through the Internet, a senior official said, as China faces reports that it has raided the computer networks of Western powers.
>
> Vice Minister of Information Industry Lou Qinjian said his country was the target of a campaign of computer infiltration and subversion...
>
> "The Internet has become the main technological channel for external espionage activities against our core, vital departments," he wrote in Chinese Cadres Tribune, a magazine.
>
> "In recent years Party, government and military organs and national defense scientific research units have had many major cases of loss, theft and leakage of secrets, and the damage to national interests has been massive and shocking..."
>
> China's computer networks were riddled with security holes that made a mockery of the ruling Communist Party's censorship and exposed valuable secrets to spies, Lou said.
>
> The United States and other "hostile" powers were exploiting those weakness [sic] and their dominance of technology to use the Internet for "political infiltration", he said.

337

"In the Internet technology products exported by the United States there are 'back doors' planted to engage in technological infiltration and theft of secrets," Lou said.

The story *Chinese Official Accuses Nations of Hacking* has more details:

> Lou said the electronic espionage against China has met with success. It therefore needs to be addressed by President Hu Jintao's government, he added, with additional investment in computer security and perhaps formation of a unified information security bureau.
>
> "In recent years, party, government and military organs and national defense scientific research units have had many major cases of loss, theft and leakage of secrets," he said, "and the damage to national interests has been massive and shocking."

Imagine the Chinese are considering a "unified information security bureau." What do we have? Check the next post for thoughts on that.

https://taosecurity.blogspot.com/2007/09/china-as-victim.html

Commentary

This is the standard Communist Party of China (CPC) response to any stories that they are conducting computer network operations against global targets: 1) denial; 2) an assertion that China follows "global norms" or similar; and 3) claims that China suffers worse attacks, perpetrated by the targets that claim China is hacking them.

China Cyberwar, or Not?

Friday, September 14, 2007

I've been writing about the Chinese threat for a while. I was glad to
see Professor Spafford chime in with *Who is Hacking Whom?*:

> It remains to be seen why so many stories are popping up
> now. It's possible that there has been a recent surge in
> activity, or perhaps some recent change has made it more
> visible to various parties involved. However, that kind of
> behavior is normally kept under wraps. That several stories
> are leaking out, with similar elements, suggests that there
> may be some kind of political positioning also going on —
> the stories are being released to create leverage in some other
> situation.
>
> Cynically, we can conclude that once some deal is concluded
> everyone will go back to quietly spying on each other and
> the stories will disappear for a while, only to surface again at
> some later time when it serves another political purpose.
> And once again, people will act surprised. If government
> and industry were really concerned, we'd see a huge surge in
> spending on defenses and research, and a big push to
> educate a cadre of cyber defenders.

You might also be wondering if the West and its allies are engaged in
a "cyberwar" with China. Some might be asking if this is
"information warfare." Here is my perspective.

DoD Joint Publication 3-13, Information Operations, differentiates
between two sorts of offensive information operations.

Computer Network Exploitation. Enabling operations and intelligence collection capabilities conducted through the use of computer networks to gather data from target or adversary automated information systems or networks. Also called CNE.

Computer Network Attack. Actions taken through the use of computer networks to disrupt, deny, degrade, or destroy information resident in computers and computer networks, or the computers and networks themselves. Also called CNA.

You can think of CNE as spycraft, and CNA as warfare. In the physical world, the former is always occurring; the latter is hopefully much rarer. I would place all of the publicly reported activity from the last few months in the CNE category.

So why the war in the media over Chinese activity? I think this is part of the answer: what else can the West or China do? Consider similar situations and their consequences.

The UK seeks the extradition of Andrei Lugovo for the murder of Alexander Litvinenko. Russia refuses, so the UK expels four Russian "diplomats." Russia responds by expelling four UK "diplomats."

Russian bombers encroach on the North Sea. The UK scrambles interceptors.

The FBI discovers Robert Hansen is a Russian spy. The US expels six Russians, and the Russians seek to match that with their own expulsions.

This is how the international relations game is played. **When the players have no way to express their concerns or make their**

**intentions known, they are left with making statements to the
media.** The question is whether anything else might happen.

https://taosecurity.blogspot.com/2007/09/china-cyberwar-or-not.ht
ml

Commentary

I concur with my judgment in this post. The CPC did not suffer any
consequences in 2007 as a result of their CNE activities. None of the
affected parties possessed the political will to inflict any cost on the
PRC. At that point in history, business interests were far too strong.
Corporate leaders saw China as a vast market waiting to buy Western
products, as well as a cheap place to manufacture those products.
Outside of the defense industrial base, most corporate leaders didn't
care if the CPC stole intellectual property or demanded technology
transfer and joint ventures as conditions for doing business in China.
This situation did not really change until 2017.

Intellectual Property: Develop or Steal

Thursday, November 20, 2008

I found the article *Internet thieves make big money stealing corporate
info* in *USA Today* to be very interesting.

> In the past year, cybercriminals have begun to infiltrate
> corporate tech systems as never before. Knowing that some
> governments and companies will pay handsomely for
> industrial secrets, data thieves are harvesting as much
> corporate data as they can, in anticipation of rising
> demand...

> Elite cybergangs can no longer make great money stealing
> and selling personal identity data. Thousands of small-time,

copycat data thieves have oversaturated the market, driving prices to commodity levels. Credit card account numbers that once fetched $100 or more, for instance, can be had for $10 or less, says Gunter Ollmann, chief security strategist at IBM ISS, IBM's tech security division.

Who buys stolen business data? Brett Kingstone, founder of Super Vision International (now Nexxus Lighting), an Orlando-based industrial lighting manufacturer, knows the answer all too well. In 2000, an intruder breached Super Vision's public-facing website and probed deep enough to snatch secrets behind the company's patented fiber-optic technology.

That intelligence made its way into the hands of a Chinese entrepreneur, Samson Wu. In his book, *The Real War Against America*, Kingstone recounts how Wu obtained Super Vision's detailed business plans, built a new Chinese factory from scratch and began mass marketing low-priced counterfeit lighting fixtures, complete with warranties referring complaints to Super Vision.

"They had an entire clone of our manufacturing facility," says Kingstone, who won a civil judgment against Wu. "What took us $10 million and 10 years to develop, they were able to do for $1.4 million in six months..."

In the past nine months, data thieves have stepped up attacks against any corporation with weak Internet defenses. The goal: harvest wide swaths of data, with no specific buyer yet in mind, according to security firm Finjan...

"Cybercriminals are focusing on data that can be easily obtained, managed and controlled in order to get the maximum profit in a minimum amount of time," says Ben-Itzhak.

Researchers at RSA, the security division of tech systems supplier EMC, have been monitoring deals on criminal message boards. One recent solicitation came from a buyer offering $50 each for e-mail addresses for top executives at U.S. corporations...

Meanwhile, corporations make it all too easy, say tech security experts and law enforcement officials.

We know amateurs study cryptography; professionals study economics, and this explains why. $1.4 million over six months vs $10 million over 10 years makes theft the more attractive proposition for those outside the law.

I'm often asked how we should think about "winning" our current cyber conflicts. I like to consider two metrics.

1. Information assurance is winning, in a broad sense, when the cost of stealing intellectual property via any means is more expensive than developing that intellectual property independently.

2. Information assurance is winning, in a narrow sense, when the cost of stealing intellectual property via digital means is more expensive than stealing that data via nontechnical means (such as human agents placed inside the organization).

Number 1 is preferred when you consider your organization as a whole. Number 2 is preferred if you only care about making IP theft the problem of your physical security organization! Obviously I prefer number 1 if possible, but achieving number 2 is more achievable in the medium to long term.

This echoes the comment I made in my March 2008 post *Ten Themes from Recent Conferences*:

> **We can not stop intruders, only raise their costs.**
> Enterprises stay dirty because we can not stop intruders, but we can make their lives more difficult. I've heard of some organizations trying to raise the $ per MB that the adversary must spend in order to exfiltrate/degrade/deny information.

https://taosecurity.blogspot.com/2008/11/intellectual-property-develop-or-steal.html

Commentary

This USA Today story on Super Vision International was one of the early mainstream media stories about the CPC's intellectual property theft. I bought the book about the case, which was out of print by the time I learned about it. The book was published in 2005 and covered a case that began in 2000. That gives a sense of the early timeframe that Chinese intruders were stealing corporate secrets.

You Down with APT?

Friday, July 10, 2009

Today I had shared a phone call with a very knowledgeable and respected security industry analyst. During the course of the conversation he made a few statements which puzzled me, so I asked him "do you know what APT means?" He might have thought I was referring to the Debian Advanced Package Tool or apt, but that's not what I meant. When I said Advanced Persistent Threat, it still didn't ring any bells with him. I decided to do some searching on the Web to see what was available regarding APT.

Helpfully, BusinessWeek just published *Under Cyberthreat: Defense Contractors* this week. The article begins like this:

> Northrop Grumman's info security chief addresses the "well-resourced, highly sophisticated" attacks against makers of high-tech weaponry...

> The defense industry faces "a near-existential threat from state-sponsored foreign intelligence services" that target sensitive IP, according to a report by the Internet Security Alliance, a nonprofit organization on whose board McKnight sits...

> [BusinessWeek asked:] Are defense contractors being singled out in highly targeted attacks?

> **[McKnight responded:] It's gotten to a point where it has a name for itself: the APT or "advanced persistent threat," meaning that they are well resourced, highly sophisticated, clearly targeting companies or information, and they're not giving up in that mission.**

Incidentally, McKnight practices NSM:

> [BusinessWeek asked:] What kind of tools do you use to keep your network secure?

> [McKnight responded:] **We've focused a lot on... capabilities where you're capturing all traffic, not just bits and pieces of it.**

Security company Mandiant devotes an entire site to APT, saying:

The Advanced Persistent Threat (APT) is a sophisticated and organized cyber attack to access and steal information from compromised computers.

The intruders responsible for the APT attacks target the Defense Industrial Base (DIB), financial industry, manufacturing industry, and research industry.

The attacks used by the APT intruders are not very different from any other intruder. **The main differentiator is the APT intruder's perseverance and resources.** They have malicious code (malware) that circumvents common safeguards such as anti-virus and they tend to generate more activity than wanton "drive by hacks" on the Internet.

The intruders also escalate their tools and techniques as a victim firm's capability to respond improves. Therefore, the APT attacks present different challenges than addressing common computer security breaches.

Combating the APT is a protracted event, requiring a sustained effort to rid your networks of the threat.

I briefly mentioned APT in my post last year *Thoughts on 2008 SANS Forensics and IR Summit.*

Aside from Northrop Grumman, Mandiant, and a few vendors (like NetWitness, one of the full capture vendors out there) mentioning APT, there's not much else available. **A Google search for "advanced persistent threat" -netwitness -mandiant -Northrop yields 34 results (prior to this blog post).**

APT is one of those subjects that is very important but not well understood outside the defense industry. Your best bet for a public introduction to APT is to watch for the next Webinar offered by

Mandiant. Ask them to do another soon; I listened to their Webinar in May and realized many participants had never heard of APT before. If you're not down with APT, you need to be.

https://taosecurity.blogspot.com/2009/07/you-down-with-apt.html

Commentary

This was a landmark post for TaoSecurity blog. Let me start by laying some groundwork.

First, here is what Mike Cloppert said in the October 2008 post I referenced:

> Mike Cloppert ruffled a few feathers (justifiably so) by stating "the advanced persistent threat has rendered the classical IR model obsolete." In other words, persistent threats make it difficult to start over when there is no end. Mike emphasized the need for "indicator management" and that "intelligence drives response." I agree; without having investigative leads, identifying intruders can be very difficult.

https://taosecurity.blogspot.com/2008/10/thoughts-on-2008-sans-forensics-and-ir.html

Second, here is the Internet Archive for the Mandiant APT site, recorded July 2009:

https://web.archive.org/web/20090710024749/http://www.mandiant.com/apt.htm

Third, this was not my first "APT" post. In an October 2007 story titled *Air Force Cyberspace Report* I included the following:

This week I attended Victory in Cyberspace, an event held at the National Press Club. It centered on the release of a report written by Dr. Rebecca Grant for the Air Force Association's Eaker Institute. The report is titled Victory in Cyberspace...

I found this one item immensely interesting, so I'll close with it:

[One] difficulty is estimating the scope of the mission. "We are well past the $5 billion per year mark, and I don't know where the top end is," commented one STRATCOM official. "The $5 billion is mostly on defense. We buy huge amounts of software and people to run that, but it's totally ineffective against Tier III" cyber [advanced persistent] threats, this official noted.

Remember that 2007 was the year that the term "APT" was invented. I had only heard it in defense industrial base discussions, usually at classified locations, so I was not comfortable about using it indiscriminately in public forums, such as a blog post in late 2007.

Fourth, I chose not to write much of anything about a very prominent 5,000 word cover story published in the April 21, 2008 issue of BusinessWeek titled *The New E-spionage Threat*. This was the cover, from a copy I used to carry with me at work:

BusinessWeek

E-SPIONAGE

A BUSINESSWEEK INVESTIGATION

The U.S. military created the Internet. Now the Web may be turning against its maker. As America fights to protect itself, we uncover startling new instances of cyber spies targeting the government and trace the path of a pernicious attack aimed at defense consultant Booz Allen.

Figure 17. BusinessWeek, Apri 21, 2008 cover

I chose not to blog about it because my then-employer was mentioned as being targeted by Chinese intruders:

> According to sources familiar with the matter, the attacks targeted sensitive information on the networks of at least seven agencies—the Defense, State, Energy, Commerce, Health & Human Services, Agriculture, and Treasury departments—and also defense contractors Boeing (BA),

Lockheed Martin, General Electric (GE), Raytheon (RTW), and General Dynamics (GD), say current and former government network security experts.

You can read the article in chunks at the Internet Archive:

https://web.archive.org/web/20080413182740/http://www.businessweek.com/magazine/content/08_16/b4080032218430.htm

I also extracted the text as a service to my readers and posted it to Pastebin:

https://pastebin.com/XF27vaqb

I did blog a link to the story but made no comment:

https://taosecurity.blogspot.com/2008/04/businessweek-on-new-e-spionage-threat.html

Finally, my last post prior to this one to mention the APT was *Northrop Grumman's Timothy McKnight on Security* in January 2009. I was still afraid at that point to write much about the term or its links to China. Here is a bit from that post:

> Ken Bradley sent me a link to *Northrop Grumman's Timothy McKnight on Security and Identity Management* by Katherine Walsh of CSO Magazine. It's an older article but I liked this part:
>
> CSO: Can you tell me about the formation of the Cyber Threat Analysis Intelligence Group and its role at Northrop Grumman?
>
> McKnight: **That team's focus is on the nation-state threat, which the DoD is now terming the "advanced**

persistent threat." These are well resourced, highly targeted attacks at corporations and governments [by groups] that are looking primarily to steal intellectual property and gain competitive advantage.

https://taosecurity.blogspot.com/2009/01/northrop-grummans-tim othy-mcknight-on.html

With that background, let's talk about this post from July 2009. The term APT had been around for two years, but it was not popular and there was no explicit linkage to China in public reporting. Note that the 2008 BusinessWeek article talks about Chinese threat actors, but doesn't use the term APT. Similarly, stories that mentioned the APT didn't mention China. Those of us working to counter the APT from 2007 to 2009 were afraid to make the association public because there was an assumption that the linkage itself was classified.

Therefore, when I wrote this cringy-titled post *You Down with APT?*, I was trying to shed some more light on the problem, yet not saying anything about China. I didn't talk about what I knew at the time, but just pointed readers to the best resources already public. Those consisted of two main sources: public statements by Northrop Grumman chief security officer Timothy McKnight, and presentations by Mandiant consultants. I also cited Michael Cloppert from Lockheed and mentioned NetWitness, but at that time neither had said that much to the public.

Looking back at what Mandiant wrote, I am disturbed to read "The Advanced Persistent Threat (APT) is a sophisticated and organized cyber attack." That is the only time I saw Mandiant improperly call the APT an "attack." Everywhere else they referred to the APT properly as a threat actor. Seriously -- it's in the *name -- advanced persistent **threat***. This oversight was perhaps an indicator of the distortions to come as the term took over the security world of the 2010s.

I don't remember the details of the conversation that prompted this blog post. In general, I remember being shocked that someone who was supposed to be providing analytical support to enterprise customers was unaware of the greatest problem facing multiple industries and organizations. I hoped this post would help people who were not fighting this threat understand a bit about the challenge.

Report on Chinese Government Sponsored Cyber Activities

Thursday, October 22, 2009

Today's Wall Street Journal features the following story:

China Expands Cyberspying in U.S., Report Says by Siobhan Gorman.

I've reprinted an excerpt below and highlighted interesting aspects. I can vouch for the quality of the Northrop Grumman team that wrote this report and for their experience in this arena.

> Congressional Advisory Panel in Washington Cites Apparent Campaign by Beijing to Steal Information From American Firms
>
> WASHINGTON -- The Chinese government is ratcheting up its cyberspying operations against the U.S., a congressional advisory panel found, citing an example of a carefully orchestrated campaign against one U.S. company that appears to have been sponsored by Beijing.
>
> **The unnamed company was just one of several successfully penetrated by a campaign of**

cyberespionage, according to the U.S.-China Economic and Security Review Commission report to be released Thursday. Chinese espionage operations are "straining the U.S. capacity to respond," the report concludes.

The bipartisan commission, formed by Congress in 2000 to investigate the security implications of growing trade with China, is made up largely of former U.S. government officials in the national security field.

The commission contracted analysts at defense giant Northrop Grumman Corp. to write the report. The analysts wouldn't name the company described in the case study, describing it only as "a firm involved in high-technology development."

The report didn't provide a damage assessment and didn't say specifically who was behind the attack against the U.S. company. But it said the company's internal analysis indicated the attack originated in or came through China.

The report concluded the attack was likely supported, if not orchestrated, by the Chinese government, because of the "professional quality" of the operation and the technical nature of the stolen information, which is not easily sold by rival companies or criminal groups. The operation also targeted specific data and processed "extremely large volumes" of stolen information, the report said.

"The case study is absolutely clearly controlled and directed with a specific purpose to get at defense technology in a related group of companies," said Larry Wortzel, vice chairman of the commission and a former U.S. Army attaché in China. "There's no doubt that that's state-controlled."

Attacks like that cited in the report hew closely to a blueprint frequently used by Chinese cyberspies, who in total steal $40 billion to $50 billion in intellectual property from U.S. organizations each year, according to U.S. intelligence agency estimates provided by a person familiar with them.

Commentary

The U.S.-China Economic and Security Review Commission (www.uscc.gov) was one of the few government entities shining a light on the digital assault perpetrated by the CPC against global targets during the 2000s. They were the first government body to which I testified, in March 2012.

Details of the hearing are here:

https://www.uscc.gov/hearings/hearing-developments-chinas-cyber-and-nuclear-capabilities

My testimony is here:

https://www.uscc.gov/sites/default/files/3.26.12bejtlich.pdf

In my testimony I say that "our team and I use the strict definition of APT as created by the Air Force in 2006, namely as an unclassified reference to intrusions sets ultimately traced back to actors in China." That was my understanding at the time. Only recently, in a private conversation with the former Air Force officer who invented the term, did I learn that he created it in 2007.

The report prepared by Northrop Grumman in the news story is still available online, courtesy of the Internet Archive:

https://web.archive.org/web/20100115130816/http://online.wsj.com/public/resources/documents/chinaspy20091022.pdf

It is titled *Capability of the People's Republic of China to Conduct Cyber Warfare and Computer Network Exploitation* and the team that wrote it included the following: Project Manager, Steve DeWeese; Principal Author, Bryan Krekel; and Subject Matter Experts George Bakos and Christopher Barnett.

This is a landmark report, from 2009, that does not get the attention it deserves.

Google v China

Tuesday, January 12, 2010

It's been a few months since I mentioned China in a blog post, but this one can't be ignored. Thanks to SW for passing me this one:

> *Google Blog: A New Approach to China*
>
> https://googleblog.blogspot.com/2010/01/new-approach-to-china.html
>
> **In mid-December, we detected a highly sophisticated and targeted attack on our corporate infrastructure originating from China that resulted in the theft of intellectual property from Google...**
>
> First, this attack was not just on Google. As part of our investigation we have discovered that **at least twenty other large companies from a wide range of**

businesses--including the Internet, finance, technology, media and chemical sectors--have been similarly targeted...

These attacks and the surveillance they have uncovered--combined with the attempts over the past year to further limit free speech on the web--have led us to conclude that we should review the feasibility of our business operations in China. We have decided we are no longer willing to continue censoring our results on Google.cn, and so over the next few weeks we will be discussing with the Chinese government the basis on which we could operate an unfiltered search engine within the law, if at all. We recognize that this may well mean having to shut down Google.cn, and potentially our offices in China.

Welcome to the party, Google. **You can use the term "advanced persistent threat" (APT) if you want to give this adversary its proper name.** See my post *Report on Chinese Government Sponsored Cyber Activities* for more details.

I have to really applaud Google for saying they might shut down operations in a country of 1.4 billion potential consumers as a result of an incident detection and response!

There were many events last year that fulfilled my prediction for 2009, *Expect at least one cloud security incident to affect something you value.* I think this one wins hands down.

Never mind the China angle for a moment. All of us should stop and consider what sort of data we are storing at Google, and in what form that data is stored. Google's *Keeping Your Data Safe* post for Enterprise customers claims

While some intellectual property on our corporate network was compromised, we believe our customer cloud-based data remains secure.

However, my experience with these sorts of incidents is that if it occurred in "mid-December," Google will be spending the next several months realizing how large the exposure really is.

https://taosecurity.blogspot.com/2010/01/google-v-china.html

Commentary

This is probably the most controversial post on TaoSecurity blog. It has less to do with the content than with what it represents. **This post was the first public document that linked the term APT to China's compromise of Google.**

As noted in the previous posts in this volume, prior to this post in January 2010, *almost* everyone publicly maintained a separation between "APT" and "China." Those of us who knew that the APT was a term referring to Chinese threat actors feared that publicizing the linkage would somehow violate our security clearances.

When Google bravely reported that it had suffered an intrusion, and that it originated with China, I felt that it was time to stop the charade. Almost three years had passed since the term "APT" was invented. Almost five years had passed since Shawn Carpenter's experience, mentioned in my post *Real Threat Reporting*, had revealed concrete evidence of CPC targeting. At least a decade had passed since incident responders had been handling Chinese intrusions. It was time to talk more openly about what was happening.

Stories which followed this post referenced the APT and China. As far as I have been able to discover, there were no stories prior to this one. There was, however, a presentation at a SANS conference which made the link between China and the APT. Please see the post *APT Presentation from July 2008*, later in this chapter, for the details!

Is this necessarily anything to warrant specific attention? Those of us who were working in the security field at the time remember the "APT avalanche" which followed. It was not a pleasant period for the security scene. Every vendor repositioned their product as the "solution" for the APT. The major security conferences became "APTCons." Whatever the case, I am glad that time has passed.

Has China Crossed a Line?

Tuesday, January 12, 2010

I'm wondering if China has crossed a line with its Google hack. It's relatively easy for the Obama administration to pretend that nothing's amiss when it's playing politics with the Chinese government. But when an American company that was just named "word of the decade" proclaims to the world that it is being exploited by Chinese intruders, can the President turn a blind eye to that? This could be the first publicity-driven incident (i.e., something that comes from public sources) that the new Cyber Czar will have to address, if not higher officials.

Oh, and expect China to issue a statement saying that it strongly denies official involvement, and that it prosecutes "hackers" to the fullest extent of its laws. That's nice.

https://taosecurity.blogspot.com/2010/01/has-china-crossed-line.html

China indeed crossed a line by compromising Google. Unfortunately, the momentum that began with this revelation in early 2010 would dissipate by mid-2013.

Why Google v China is Different

Saturday, January 16, 2010

I've been reading various comments on the Google v China issue. One caught my eye:

> *Security experts say Google cyber-attack was routine*
>
> "This wasn't in my opinion ground-breaking as an attack. We see this fairly regularly," said Mikko Hypponen, of security firm F-Secure.
>
> "Most companies just never go public," he added.

In some ways this comment is true, and in other ways I think it can mislead some readers. I believe it is true in the sense that many organizations are dealing with advanced persistent threats. However, **I believe this comment leads some readers to focus incorrectly on two rather insignificant aspects of the Google incident: vulnerabilities and malware.**

On the vulnerability front, we have a zero-day in Internet Explorer. I agree that this is completely routine, in a really disappointing way.

On the malware front, we have code submitted to Wepawet. I agree that this is also not particularly interesting, although I would like to know how it ended up being posted there!

Five issues make Google v China different for me.

1. The victim made a public statement about the intrusion. I read [citing the Wall Street Journal, below] that this was a difficult decision to make and it took strong leadership to see it through:

> Google Inc.'s startling threat to withdraw from China was an intensely personal decision, drawing its celebrated founders and other top executives into a debate over the right way to confront the issues of censorship and cyber security.
>
> Google's very public response to what it called a "highly sophisticated and targeted attack on our corporate infrastructure originating from China" was crafted over a period of weeks, with heavy involvement from Google's co-founders, Larry Page and Sergey Brin.

2. The victim is not alone. Google isn't alone in the sense that firms suffering from Conficker last month weren't alone, i.e., this isn't a case of widespread malware. Instead, we're hearing that multiple companies are affected.

3. The victim is not a national government. Don't forget all the China incidents involving national governments that I followed from summer 2007 through 2008.

4. The victim named the perpetrator. This amazes me. We need more of this to happen. By doing so a private company influenced a powerful policy maker to issue a statement of a diplomatic nature.

5. The victim could suffer further damage as a result of this statement and decision. Every CIO, CTO, CSO, and CISO magazine in the world talks about "aligning with business," blah blah. Business is supposed to rule. Instead, we have a situation where the

self-reported "theft of intellectual property from Google" plus
"accessing the Gmail accounts of Chinese human rights activists"
resulted in a business decision to alter and potentially cancel
operations. That astounds me. You can claim Baidu is beating
Google, but I don't buy it as the real reason Google is acting like this.

Bravo Google.

https://taosecurity.blogspot.com/2010/01/why-google-v-china-is-different.html

Commentary

Some of the commentary by people not involved in handling
incidents like this was laughable. I'm not going to reprint it here, but
those of you who lived through it know what I mean. This was an
early period in the "attribution wars," where anyone with a theory,
no matter how bizarre, was treated like an "expert" by the media.

What Is APT and What Does It Want?

Saturday, January 16, 2010

This has been the week to discuss the advanced persistent threat,
although some people are already telling me *Google v China* with
respect to APT is "silly," or that the attack vectors were what
everyone has been talking about for years, and were somewhat
sloppily orchestrated at that.

I think many of these critics are missing the point. As is often the
case with sensitive issues, 1) those who know often can't say and 2)
those who say often don't know. There are some exceptions worth
noting!

One company that occupies a unique position with respect to this problem is Mandiant. Keep an eye on the APT tag of their M-unition blog. Mandiant's role as a consulting firm to many APT victims helps them talk about what they see without naming any particular victim.

I also recommend following Mike Cloppert's posts. He is a deep thinker with respect to counter-APT operations. Incidentally I agree with Mike that the US Air Force invented the term "advanced persistent threat" around 2006, not Mandiant.

Reviewing my previous blogging, a few old posts stand out. 4 1/2 years ago I wrote *Real Threat Reporting*, describing the story of Shawn Carpenter as reported by Time magazine. **Back then the threat was called "Titan Rain" by Time.** (This reflects the use of a so-called **"intrusion set"** to describe an incident.) Almost a year later Air Force Maj Gen Lord noted "China has downloaded 10 to 20 terabytes of data from the NIPRNet. They're looking for your identity, so they can get into the network as you."

Now we hear of other companies beyond Google involved in this latest incident, including Yahoo, Symantec, Adobe, Northrop Grumman, Dow Chemical, Juniper Networks, and "human rights groups as well as Washington-based think tanks."

Let me put on the flight cap of a formally trained Air Force intelligence officer and try to briefly explain my understanding of APT in a few bullets.

Advanced means the adversary can operate in the full spectrum of computer intrusion. They can use the most pedestrian publicly available exploit against a well-known vulnerability, or they can elevate their game to research new vulnerabilities and develop custom exploits, depending on the target's posture.

Persistent means the adversary is formally tasked to accomplish a mission. They are not opportunistic intruders. Like an intelligence unit they receive directives and work to satisfy their masters. Persistent does not necessarily mean they need to constantly execute malicious code on victim computers. Rather, they maintain the level of interaction needed to execute their objectives.

Threat means the adversary is not a piece of mindless code. This point is crucial. Some people throw around the term "threat" with reference to malware. If malware had no human attached to it (someone to control the victim, read the stolen data, etc.), then most malware would be of little worry (as long as it didn't degrade or deny data). Rather, the adversary here is a threat because it is organized and funded and motivated. Some people speak of multiple "groups" consisting of dedicated "crews" with various missions.

Looking at the target list, we can perceive several potential objectives. Most likely, the APT supports:

Political objectives that include continuing to suppress its own population in the name of "stability."

Economic objectives that rely on stealing intellectual property from victims. Such IP can be cloned and sold, studied and underbid in competitive dealings, or fused with local research to produce new products and services more cheaply than the victims.

Technical objectives that further their ability to accomplish their mission. These include gaining access to source code for further exploit development, or learning how defenses work in order to better evade or disrupt them. Most worryingly is the thought that intruders could make changes to improve their position and weaken the victim.

Military objectives that include identifying weaknesses that allow inferior military forces to defeat superior military forces. The Report on Chinese Government Sponsored Cyber Activities addresses issues like these.

Notice "stealing money" is not listed here. Although threats exist that target cash, those groups are not considered "APT".

Footnote: my Google query for advanced persistent threat that omits a few organization names (including this blog) now yields 169 non-duplicative hits as of this writing, up from 34 in July 2009.

https://taosecurity.blogspot.com/2010/01/what-is-apt-and-what-does-it-want.html

Commentary

I was very busy in January trying to explain the APT to readers. One element that continues to be misunderstood, to this day, is the "A," for "advanced." Critics think the A means that if an intrusion doesn't use the newest, coolest, triple-backflip zero-day exploit, then a threat actor is not "advanced." They don't understand that "advanced" never meant what these critics believed. Instead, as I noted in this post:

> Advanced means the adversary can operate in the full spectrum of computer intrusion. They can use the most pedestrian publicly available exploit against a well-known vulnerability, or they can elevate their game to research new vulnerabilities and develop custom exploits, depending on the target's posture.

Advanced means being wise enough to match the operative level to the need of the mission.

Advanced means knowing that the purpose of a campaign is to accomplish a goal that was provided by management, not showing off.

Advanced means developing and exercising the capability to move the dial from pedestrian to wizard, as need be.

Advanced means not caring what anti-virus company researchers say in the press.

Perhaps it would have been more useful to call these Chinese actors the Disciplined Persistent Threat, or the Profesional Persistent Threat? (The latter would never have worked -- PPT, ugh!)

Incidentally, if you'd like to read the Time article from September 5, 2005 on Titan Rain, it's online:

https://web.archive.org/web/20190728003622/https://courses.cs.washington.edu/courses/csep590/05au/readings/titan.rain.htm

Is APT After You?

Wednesday, January 20, 2010

Jeremiah Grossman made the following request via Twitter today:

> @taosecurity blog post request. Signs that an individual or organization is or may be an APT target. + other threat naming conventions

Tough but great questions. I better answer, or Jeremiah will find me and apply Brazilian Jiu Jitsu until I do. Let me take the second question first.

As I mentioned in *Real Threat Reporting* in 2005, "Titan Rain" became the popular term for one "intrusion set" involving certain actors. DoD applies various codewords to intrusion sets, and Titan Rain became popular with the publication of the Time article I referenced. If you read the Time article again you'll see at least one other reference, but I won't cite that here. [Note: The version online doesn't appear to feature any other intrusion set names. Either I wrote in error here, or Time removed them after I first read the story.]

Some of you may remember "Solar Sunrise" from 1998 and "Moonlight Maze" from 1998-1999. Open reporting links the former to Russia and the latter to an Israeli named Ehud Tenenbaum. These are other examples of "intrusion sets," but they are not related to the current threat.

As far as other names for APT, they exist but are not shared with the public. Just as you might maintain code names for various intrusion sets or campaigns within your CIRT, various agencies track the same using their own terms. This can cause some confusion when different CIRTs try to compare notes, since none of us speak of the private names unless in an appropriate facility. **The Air Force invented "APT" as an unclassified term that could be used to quickly keep various parties on the same page when speaking with defense partners.**

Regarding who may be an APT target, I liked Steven Adair's Shadowserver post. **The way most organizations learn that they have a problem is by receiving an external notification. The FBI and certain military units have been fairly active in this respect for the previous three years.** This marks quite a change in the relationship between the US government and private sector, and it's not limited to American companies. A little searching will reveal reports of other governments warning their companies of similar problems.

If your organization has not been contacted by an external agency, you might want to look at the potential objectives that I posted in *What is APT and What Does It Want?* Does your organization possess data that falls into one of the political, economic, technical, or military categories that could interest this sort of threat? Overall, my assessment of APT progress can be summarized this way:

Phase 1, late 1990s: mainly .mil

Phase 2, 2000-2004: .gov added to target list

Phase 3, 2005-2009: cleared defense contractors, research institutes, political and infrastructure added to target list (significant expansion)

Phase 4, 2010- ? : expansion only limited by resources?

Probably the next best way to determine if you are a target is to join whatever industry groups you can find and network with your peers. Develop relationships such that your peers feel comfortable sharing threat information with you. Do the same with government actors, especially the FBI. Many times these agencies are just sitting on data trying to figure out the right contacts.

I would beware of organizations that claim any product they sell will "stop APT" or "manage APT" or act as another silver bullet. We're already seeing some vendors jump on the counter-APT bandwagon with little clue what is happening. There's a couple consultancies with deep knowledge on this topic. I'm not going to name them here but if you review the *Incident Detection Summit 2009* agenda you can find them.

The degree of counter-APT experience on the speaker list varies considerably, but you can try using that list to validate if Company X has any relationship whatsoever to this problem. That doesn't mean companies or organizations not listed as speakers are "clueless;" a lot of counter-APT activity is simply "good IT." However, you shouldn't expect a random consultant to be able to sit down and explain the specifics of this problem to your CIO or CEO. Incidentally this is NOT a commercial for my company; I run an internal CIRT that only protects our assets.

https://taosecurity.blogspot.com/2010/01/is-apt-after-you.html

Commentary

In 2010, Chinese threat actors were not targeting *everyone*, although they were certainly widely active. I failed to mention in this post that anyone with an Internet-connected server was a possible target, however. Even if your system had nothing of value to the APT, the fact that it was a legitimate system meant it could make a helpful "hop point" for APT infrastructure. By compromising and then routing activity through these systems, the APT (and other threat actors, such as Russian criminal or intelligence groups) would make attribution difficult (although not impossible).

Steven Adair's ShadowServer post is archived here:

https://web.archive.org/web/20180303025750/http://www.shadow server.org/wiki/pmwiki.php/Calendar/20100119

Mandiant M-Trends on APT

Saturday, January 30, 2010

If you want to read a concise yet informative and clue-backed report on advanced persistent threat, I recommend completing this form to receive the first *Mandiant M-Trends* report.

Mandiant occupies a unique position with respect to this problem because they are one of only two security service companies with substantial counter-APT consulting experience.

You may read blog posts and commentary from other security service providers who either 1) suddenly claim counter-APT expertise or 2) deride "APT" as just a marketing term, or FUD [fear, uncertainty, or doubt], or some other term to hide their inexperience with this problem. The fact remains that, when organizations meet in closed forums to do real work on this problem, the names and faces are fairly constant. They don't include those trying to make an APT "splash" or those pretending APT is not a real problem.

Mandiant finishes its report with the following statement:

> [T]his is a war of attrition against an enemy with extensive resources. It is a long fight, one that never ends. You will never declare victory.

I can already hear the skeptics saying "It never ends, so you can keep paying Mandiant consulting fees!" or "It never ends, so you can keep upgrading security products!" You're wrong, but nothing I say will convince some of you.

The fact of the matter is that **until the threat is addressed at the nation-state to nation-state level, victim organizations will continue to remain victims. This is not a problem that is going to be solved by victims better defending themselves.** The cost is simply too great to take a vulnerability-centric approach.

We need a threat-centric approach, where those with the authority to apply pressure on the threat are allowed to do so, using a variety of instruments of national power. This is the unfortunate reality of the conflict in which we are now engaged.

Commentary

The Mandiant M-Trends report, first published in 2010, was one of the best resources available to the general public in early 2010. Only a few weeks after the Google announcement, I was already growing tired of butting heads with others on the security scene who were not dealing with this issue. The fact of the matter was that if you were not detecting and responding to these sorts of intrusions at this time, you were likely not going to believe they were happening. The government, military, intelligence community, and law enforcement agencies were basically or totally silent on the issue, fearful of jeopardizing their sources and methods, or at least their individual clearances. It was a rough time, especially for those of us trying to counter these intrusions with little to no government support.

Two Dimensional Thinking and APT

Saturday, January 30, 2010

I expect many readers will remember the final space battle in *Star Trek II: The Wrath of Khan*. During this battle, Kirk and Spock realize Khan's tactics are limited. Khan is treating the battle like it is occurring on the open seas, not in space. Spock says:

> He is intelligent, but not experienced. His pattern indicates two-dimensional thinking.

I thought this quote could describe many of the advanced persistent threat critics, particularly those who claim "it's just espionage" or "there's nothing new about this." Consider this one last argument to change your mind. (Ha, like that will happen. For everyone else, this is how I arrive at my conclusions.)

I think the problem is APT critics are thinking in one or two dimensions at most, when really this issue has at least five. When you only consider one or two dimensions, of course the problem looks like nothing new. When you take a more complete look, it's new.

Offender. We know who the attacker is, and like many of you, I know this is not their first activity against foreign targets. I visited the country as an active duty Air Force intelligence officer in 1999. I got all the briefings, etc. etc. This is not the first time I've seen network activity from them. Wonderful.

Defender. We know the offender has targeted national governments and militaries, like any nation-state might. **What's different about APT is the breadth of their target base.** Some criticize the Mandiant report for saying:

> The APT isn't just a government problem; it isn't just a defense contractor problem. The APT is everyone's problem. No target is too small, or too obscure, or too well-defended. No organization is too large, two well-known, or too vulnerable. It's not spy-versus-spy espionage. It's spy-versus-everyone.

The phrasing here may be misleading (i.e., APT is not attacking my dry cleaner) but the point is valid. Looking over the APT target list, the victims cover a broad sweep of organizations. This is certainly new.

Means. Let's talk about espionage for a moment. Not everyone has the means to be a spy. You probably heard how effective the idiots who tried bugging Senator Landrieu's office were. With computer network exploitation (at the very least), those with sufficient knowledge and connectivity can operate at nearly the same level as a professional spy. You don't have to spend nearly as much time teaching tradecraft for CNE, compared to spycraft. You can often hire someone with private experience as a red teamer/pen tester and then just introduce them to your SOPs [standard operating procedures]. Try hiring someone who has privately learned national-level spycraft.

Motive. Besides "offender," this is the second of the two dimensions that APT critics tend to fixate upon. Yes, bad people have tried to spy on other people for thousands of years. However, in some respects even this is new, because the offender has his hands in so many aspects of the victim's centers of power. APT doesn't only want military secrets; it wants diplomatic, AND economic, AND cultural, AND...

Opportunity. Connectivity creates opportunity in the digital realm. Again, contrast the digital world with the analog world of espionage. It takes a decent amount of work to prepare, insert, handle, and remove human spies. The digital equivalent is unfortunately still trivial in comparison.

To summarize, I think **a lot of APT critics are focused on offender and motive, and ignore defender, means, and opportunity.** When you expand beyond two-dimensional thinking, you'll see that APT is indeed new, without even considering technical aspects.

https://taosecurity.blogspot.com/2010/01/two-dimensional-thinking-and-apt.html

Commentary

I was so naive, spending time trying to change minds. At least I documented what I thought.

Answering APT Misconceptions

Thursday, February 04, 2010

There's finally some good reporting on the advanced persistent threat appearing in various news sources. A new Christian Science Monitor story, one by Federal Computer Week, and one by Wired are making progress in raising awareness. Unfortunately, there's plenty of Tweeting and blogging by people who refuse to understand what is happening or are not capable of understanding what is happening. From now on, rather than repeat myself trying to answer these misconceptions, I decided to consolidate them here.

Myth 1. APT is a "new term," invented by Mandiant. Reality: Mandiant did not invent the term. The Air Force did in 2006. More info: *What Is APT and What Does It Want?*

Myth 2. APT is "not new." Reality: APT is only new to people who have not been involved with the problem. If you look solely at the offender and motive, and exclude defender, means, and opportunity, you're likely to think APT is not new; you'd be wrong. Just performing an *Attribution Using 20 Characteristics* exercise helps demonstrate that APT is not like organized crime or other structured attackers. More info: *Two-Dimensional Thinking and APT*

Myth 3. APT is "marketing hype." Some companies with little to no experience with APT are clearly jumping on the counter-APT bandwagon, even registering domain names related to APT. That is sad but not unexpected. However, companies like Mandiant are not suddenly releasing reports because of *Google v China*. Mandiant offered a public Webcast (which I attended) in March 2009 called *State of the Hack - Addressing the Advanced Persistent Threat.* **They and certain other companies have been public about APT for a**

while, but a lot of people were ignoring them. More info: *You Down With APT?*

Myth 4. APT is a "class of attacker." Reality: Most of the counter-APT community uses APT to refer to specific threats or "threat agents" if you prefer that term. Those threats are associated with a certain country. In some cases, certain counter-APT community members prefer to include other countries with similar capabilities. If required to differentiate during discussions, I prefer to prefix APT with the named country.

Myth 5. APT is "FUD." Reality: Fear can be healthy if it helps reallocate resources away from wasteful and ineffective compliance regimes like FISMA. No one I know who fights the APT sleeps very well. Regarding uncertainty and doubt, what more do you need to know? Read my post *Is APT After You?* to get a better sense if you should worry. It's better to prepare your defenses now than to start once a Federal agent comes knocking. More info: *DNI Blair Leads with APT as a "Wake-Up Call"*

I may add more myths as they appear, but for now those five seem sufficient.

By the way, I appreciate the private communication and public comments from people genuinely interested in learning about this issue. It helps focus my attention away from the critics who refuse to align with reality. It's also clear that many of you understand why I use certain phrases or address this subject in the manner that I do. I am glad those of us with similar backgrounds can at least share in that sense of solidarity. Thank you.

https://taosecurity.blogspot.com/2010/02/answering-apt-misconce ptions.html

Sometimes you just have to repeat the same message in a different format to get your point across.

APT Presentation from July 2008

Saturday, February 06, 2010

Some of you may remember me mentioning the *2008 SANS WhatWorks in Incident Response and Forensic Solutions Summit* organized by Rob Lee. I provided the keynote and really enjoyed listening to the presentations, which Rob has graciously made available here:

https://web.archive.org/web/20100716222513/http://files.sans.org/summit/forensics08/

One of the presentations, by Mandiant consultant Wendi Rafferty and then-Mandiant consultant (now GE-CIRT incident handler) Ken Bradley, was titled *Slaying the Red Dragon.*

This presentation explicitly addressed the advanced persistent threat. I didn't mention it originally because it discusses a specific attack vector. However, it's been over 18 months since the presentation was made. Therefore, to show that APT is "not a new term" but also to share some technical insights, I thought it acceptable to advertise this presentation.

I'm sure we will discuss this topic at the 2010 Incident Response Summit and the 2010 Incident Detection Summit.

https://taosecurity.blogspot.com/2010/02/apt-presentation-from-july-2008.html

Commentary

This is the post that I previously mentioned in *Google v China*. Check out the second and third slides from the October 14, 2008 presentation by my former Mandiant colleague Wendi Rafferty and former GE colleague Ken Bradley.

In the first slide, they show that the subtitle for their talk is "Remediating the China Cyber Threat."

Figure 18. First Slide from Remediating the China Cyber Threat, October 14, 2008

In the second slide, they explicitly mention the Advanced Persistent Threat.

Overview

- Who is Mandiant?
- VPN Subversion Case Study
- How to Win the Fight Against the Advanced Persistent Threat (APT)

> Even though we're talking about the APT today, these same strategies will work with tomorrow's threat.

Figure 19. Third Slide from Remediating the China Cyber Threat, October 14, 2008

Therefore, according to my research, this presentation is the first public, unclassified linking of the country China with the term Advanced Persistent Threat. You can read their whole presentation here:

https://web.archive.org/web/20100716223138/http://files.sans.org/summit/forensics08/PDFs/Wendi%20Rafferty%20-%20Ken%20Bradley%20-%20Slaying_the_Red_Dragon_FINAL.pdf

I have not seen anything else before this presentation, nor in the period leading up to my January 12, 2010 blog post *Google v China*.

If anyone can find other sources, with dates, to fill in the story, please contact me!

Response to Dan Geer Article on APT

Thursday, April 15, 2010

A few people sent me a link to Dan Geer's article *Advanced Persistent Threat*. Dan is one of my *Three Wise Men*, along with Ross Anderson and Gene Spafford. I'll reproduce a few excerpts and respond.

> Let us define the term for the purpose of this article as follows: A targeted effort to obtain or change information by means that are difficult to discover, difficult to remove, and difficult to attribute.

That describes APT's methodology, but APT is not an effort -- it's a proper noun, i.e., a specific party.

> Given that the offense has the advantage of no legacy drag, the offense's ability to insert innovation into its product mix is unconstrained. By contrast, the CIO who does the least that can be gotten away with only increases the frequency of having to do something, not the net total work deficit pending.

In other words, the offense expends work whenever innovation is needed; the defense expends work each day and never catches up.

> This "least expensive defense" is not insane, just ineffective because the offense is a sentient being with a strategic advantage.

I love the characterization of offense as having "no legacy drag," and "defense expends work each day and never catches up." That perfectly describes the advantage of offense over defense.

Even if you don't think the advanced persistent threat is all that advanced, realize that if this is so, it is only because it doesn't have to be when your defenses don't require it to be. Even more central, do not think that the supplier of defensive weapons will ever have weapons to thwart (the deployment of) offensive weapons that are sufficiently well targeted to hit only some people, some computers, some data.

Dan nicely counters the argument that some make, namely "APT doesn't sound so 'advanced.'"

The advanced persistent threat, which is to say the offense that enjoys a permanent advantage and is already funding its R&D out of revenue, will win as long as you try to block what he does. You have to change the rules. You have to block his success from even being possible, not exchange volleys of ever better tools designed in response to his. **You have to concentrate on outcomes, you have to pre-empt, you have to be your own intelligence agency, you have to instrument your enterprise, you have to instrument your data.**

In one paragraph Dan reminds us to change the plane, be field-assessed, not control-compliant (outcomes over inputs), and build intelligence and instrumentation.

With data, not networks or infrastructure, as the unit of surveillance and action, an adaptable approach to data security is possible. Not another shield for every arrow, but a comprehensive fortress of information control and risk management -- a unifying framework that can best be described as Enterprise Information Protection (EIP).

EIP unifies data-leak prevention, network access control, encryption policy and enforcement, audit and forensics, and all the other wayward data protection technologies from their present state of functional silos into an extensible platform supported by policy and operational practices.

Dan's conclusion seems too short, which is probably the result of the constraints imposed by writing for NetworkWorld. I don't think an enterprise that adopts his approach will beat the APT. **Stopping this threat requires direct and indirect pressure in a threat-centric approach, not a vulnerability-centric approach.**

https://taosecurity.blogspot.com/2010/04/response-to-dan-geer-article-on-apt.html

Commentary

What can I say? Dr. Dan Geer consistently delivers the highest value-to-word ratio in the security world. I am embarrassed to try to comment on his wisdom. *Fin.*

My Article on Advanced Persistent Threat Posted

Tuesday, July 13, 2010

My article *Understanding the Advanced Persistent Threat* provides an overview of APT. It's the cover story in the *July 2010 Information Security Magazine*. From the article:

> The term advanced persistent threat, or APT, joined the common vocabulary of the information security profession in mid-January, when Google announced its intellectual property had been the victim of a targeted attack originating from China. Google wasn't alone; more than 30 other

technology firms, defense contractors and large enterprises had been penetrated by hackers using an array of social engineering, targeted malware and monitoring technologies to quietly access reams of sensitive corporate data.

Google's public admission put a high-profile face on targeted attacks and the lengths attackers would go to gain access to proprietary corporate and military information. It also kicked off a spate of vendor marketing that promised counter-APT products and services that have only served to cloud the issue for security managers and operations people.

In this article, we'll define APT, dispel some myths and explain what you can do about this adversary.

https://taosecurity.blogspot.com/2010/07/my-article-on-advanced-persistent.html

Commentary

The following is the remainder of the text of that article, retrieved from my original draft.

What is the Advanced Persistent Threat?

The United States Air Force coined the phrase "advanced persistent threat" in 2006 because teams working within the service needed a way to communicate with counterparts in the unclassified public world. [Note that I know now the date was 2007.] Department of Defense and Intelligence Community members typically assign classified names to specific threat actors, and use the term "intrusion set" to describe activities by those threat actors. If the USAF wanted to talk about a certain intrusion set with uncleared personnel, they could not use the classified threat actor name. Therefore, the USAF developed the term APT as an unclassified moniker.

It is crucial to this discussion to recognize that APT is a "proper noun." APT refers to specific threat actors; APT does not refer to vaguely unknown and shadowy Internet forces. The term is most frequently applied to distinct groups operating from the Asia-Pacific region. [Apparently when drafting this story, I was still a bit wary of saying "China" outright!] Those knowledgeable about APT activities can conduct an honest debate as to whether the term should be used to ONLY refer to certain Asia-Pacific actors, or if it can be expanded as a general "classifier." In other words, if adversaries in Eastern Europe operate using the same tools, tactics, and procedures (TTP) as traditional "APT," should these actors also bear the APT label?

The answer to this question depends on the person asking it. A digital security practitioner in a private organization will typically not care if the threat actors attacking her enterprise originate in the Asia-Pacific or Eastern European regions. The reason is that the practitioner will likely take the same defensive actions regardless of the location or nationality of the adversary. However, someone with the legal and/or national security authority to apply diplomatic, intelligence, military, or economic (DIME) pressure would certainly want to identify the origin of an attack. For the purposes of this article, aimed at digital security practitioners, it is not necessary to answer the "who" question definitively. However, those who do have elements of DIME power should take attribution statements by Google and other victims seriously.

Most of those actively countering APT activity describe the adversary in the following manner:

- Advanced means the adversary can operate in the full spectrum of computer intrusion. They can use the most pedestrian publicly available exploit against a well-known vulnerability, or they can elevate their game to research new vulnerabilities and develop custom exploits, depending on the target's posture.

- Persistent means the adversary is formally tasked to accomplish a mission. They are not opportunistic intruders. Like an intelligence unit they receive directives and work to satisfy their masters. Persistent does not necessarily mean they need to constantly execute malicious code on victim computers. Rather, they maintain the level of interaction needed to execute their objectives.

- Threat means the adversary is not a piece of mindless code. The opposition is a threat because it is organized and funded and motivated. Some people speak of multiple "groups" consisting of dedicated "crews" with various missions.

Analysts currently assess APT activities as supporting four main goals. These include:

- Political objectives, such as maintaining internal stability.

- Economic objectives that rely on stealing intellectual property from victims. Such IP can be cloned and sold, studied and underbid in competitive dealings, or fused with local research to produce new products and services more cheaply than the victims.

- Technical objectives that further their ability to accomplish their mission. These include gaining access to source code for further exploit development, or learning how defenses work in order to better evade or disrupt them. Most worryingly is the thought that intruders could make changes to improve their position and weaken the victim.

- Military objectives that include identifying weaknesses that allow inferior military forces to defeat superior military forces.

In brief, APT is an adversary who conducts offensive digital operations (called computer network operations or perhaps computer network exploitation) to support various state-related objectives. APT is characterized by devotion to maintaining some degree of control of a target's computer infrastructure, acting persistently to preserve or regain control and access. Unclassified briefings by counter-intelligence and military analysts use the term "aggressive" to emphasize the degree to which APT pursues these objectives against a variety of government, military, and private targets.

Why Is the Advanced Persistent Threat Misunderstood?

Beginning in January 2010 and peaking in February and March, many elements of the digital security community focused their attention on APT issues. Unfortunately, some of those speaking about the problem quickly found themselves echoing statements and questionable "research" offered by parties who were not familiar with APT. Several factors contributed to an overall sense of confusion, with some of the more trustworthy voices competing with parties who would have been better advised to stay in the background. Several factors caused this phenomenon:

1. Besides Google's public statement, and subsequent second-hand reporting about allegedly affected peer companies, very little original data was available. Without details to discuss, the security community turned to almost anyone willing to talk about the incident. In too many cases the speakers turned out to be vendors who saw APT as a "marketing angle" to rejuvenate slumping security spending. The RSA 2010 show featured many companies selling "counter-APT" products, hoping to capitalize on the "new hot topic" of 2010.

2. McAfee reported it was analyzing malware that it claimed to be associated with the Google incident, independently assigning the

name "Aurora" to the affair thanks to a path found in the malware. In late March 2010 McAfee blamed "the fog of war" for mistakenly confusing a Vietnamese-targeted botnet with Google incident malware.
(http://www.darkreading.com/database_security/security/attacks/sh owArticle.jhtml?articleID=224200972) Unfortunately, by associating this false lead with the Google incident, McAfee prompted a variety of security researchers to direct their efforts on code that likely had nothing to do with the Google incident.

3. Many analysts too narrowly focused on the elements of the incident that they could best understand, regardless of the real nature of the event. For example, companies specializing in botnet research assumed botnets were involved, and talked about the Google incident in those terms. Others who focus on identifying vulnerabilities and developing exploits concentrated on a flaw in Internet Explorer (patched by MS10-002) presumably leveraged by intruders to gain access to Google resources.
(http://www.microsoft.com/technet/security/bulletin/ms10-002.ms px) Unfortunately, as this article will explain, botnets have nothing to do with APT, and vulnerabilities, exploits, and malware are only elements of APT incidents -- not the core feature of them.

Is APT "New"?

When the Google incident entered the public arena, many people wondered if APT was something "new." The answer to this question depends on one's perspective, plus understanding some history. As mentioned earlier, the term "APT" is approximately four years old. It only entered the common lexicon in early 2010 with the publicity garnered by Google's bold proclamation. However, consulting companies, particularly Mandiant have been conducting public Webcasts and presentations discussing APT, by name, since 2008.

Prior to the 2006 invention of the "APT" term, news stories of Chinese intruders attacking military and government organizations bore the label "Titan Rain." For example, a 2005 Time magazine article by Nathan Thornburgh titled "The Invasion of the Chinese Cyberspies" described battles fought by Shawn Carpenter, then defending Sandia National Laboratories. That story mentioned Carpenter's experience with similar intruders dating back to late 2003. Even in 1998, while serving as a captain in the Air Force Computer Emergency Response Team, we encountered adversaries that many would now label "APT."

Some would even argue that nothing about APT is new. To the extent that espionage is as old as warfare itself, some claim APT activity is just spying another form -- and not even a new medium, given the history of computer espionage dating from Cliff Stoll's work in the 1980s.

I argue that APT is new if those asking the question move beyond two-dimensional thinking. Considering APT activity in terms of offender, defender, means, motive, and opportunity, APT is clearly new. Points for the "old" camp include the identity of the offender (nation-states) and the motive (espionage). Points for the "new" camp make a stronger argument:

Defender: I break APT targets into four phases: 1) late 1990s - military victims; 2) 2000-2004 - non-military government victims; 3) 2005-2009 - defense industrial base; 4) 2009-present - intellectual property-rich targets and software companies. (Unfortunately there are clear examples of earlier victims, but these dates roughly cover most known cases.) The assault conducted during phases 3 and 4 is unprecedented, meaning entirely new classes of defenders must protect themselves from attackers previously a concern for the military.

Means: Too many critics focus on malware, ignoring (or being unaware) of the impressive management and administration applied to repeatedly attempting to access, or preserving access, to target organizations. APT incidents are not hit-and-run, smash-and-grab affairs.

Opportunity: The explosion of Internet connectivity in the last decade and the extreme distribution of sensitive data to end points provides cheap, low-risk, remote access options for intruders, unlike anything available to human spies.

On balance, I argue APT is new, at least when considered from the perspective of non-military targets, and remembering that phase 3 APT activity began in 2003 and became a significant problem in 2005.

What Should Defenders Do to Counter APT?

I've focused the majority of this article on describing the APT and its history, because battling this adversary does not require a technical solution. The most effective counter-APT weapon is a trained and knowledgeable digital security analyst. Many security vendors have adopted APT in their marketing literature. Some offer to find APT on a potential victim's network. Others have even registered APT-themed domain names! Tools are always helpful, but the best advice I can provide is to educate business leaders about the threat so that they support organizational security programs conducted by competent and informed staff.

A second question one is likely to ask follows: how do I know if I am an APT target? I strongly recommend contacting your local Federal Bureau of Investigation office. One of the biggest game-changers in counter-APT awareness developed during the last several years, taking the form of visits by FBI and military or counter-intelligence specialists to potential victims. It's difficult to deny a security breach when representatives from a national security agency reveal paperwork and ask "does this data belong to you?" If you have not already engaged your organization's leaders in a counter-APT conversation, requesting a threat briefing from the local FBI office is an excellent way to promote managerial attention.

On a technical level, "building visibility in" to one's organization will provide the situational awareness to have a chance to discover and hopefully frustrate APT activities. Without information from the network, hosts, logs, and other sources, even the most skilled analyst is helpless. Thankfully, obtaining such information is not a new challenge, and most security shops should be pursuing such programs already. The goal of counter-APT operations should be to make it as difficult as possible for the adversary to steal intellectual property; "increasing the cost per megabyte," to quote the NSA's Tony Sager, is the goal!

Why Russia and China Think We're Fighting Cyberwar Now

Thursday, September 30, 2010

Thanks to the Team Cymru news feed for pointing me to *Emerging Cyberthreats and Russian Views on Information Warfare and Information Operations* by Roland Heickerö of the Swedish Defence Research Agency. I found this content in pages 23-24, "Differences and similarities between Russian, US and Chinese views on IW," to be really interesting:

> In order to understand the Russian view in a wider context, a comparison has been made with Russia's most important competitors – the USA and China – and their approach to information operations...

All three countries agree on the important role information has in today's conflicts. Over time its importance will grow. The USA has influenced the mindsets of the others, especially regarding ideas about information superiority and information dominance, as well as command and control warfare. Information adds a new dimension to warfare and IW weapons could be used offensively and defensively to protect a country's own information resources and systems.

Russia and China take a broader view of the essence of information warfare than the USA in the sense that in their approach covers both peacetime and wartime situations, while the US definition is more narrow and related to times of crisis or conflict.

The Chinese view is based on four parameters: pre-emptive strike capability, asymmetric warfare (inferior versus superior), high-tech local war and people's war. In some documents the term 'unlimited warfare' has been mentioned as being a core part of a Chinese view of IW, but the term is disputed by several analysts.

The Chinese concept originates from Sun Tzu's 36 stratagems, described in his Art of War from 500 BC. One of the most important key factors in the Chinese concept is deception.

The [Chinese] IW perspective covers a long period of time and is not limited to a specific moment, period or conflict. Chinese experts criticize the US doctrine for being much too technology-driven and for not considering the strategic dimension sufficiently.

Moreover it [American doctrine] is too focused on the information and information system of the opponent and does not consider the softer, psychological factors. In the Chinese conceptual framework, cognitive elements are added, such as the opponent's will and capability to fight. It has a clear political dimension. According to Sun Tzu:

'To win the war without the fight is the greatest victory'.

In the Chinese approach IO is a component of IW, contrary to the US view. For American experts IO is a way to fight while the Chinese think that IW is the fight itself and is ongoing on many different levels and dimensions over the years.

The Russian view is more closely related to the Chinese where the information-psychological impact of IW is concerned, as well as in the idea that IW is conducted in both peacetime, in the prelude to a conflict, and in wartime and more or less constantly; and on the strategic level as well as the operational and tactical.

I couldn't agree more with this. Here's the Cliff Notes summary:

US cyberwar doctrine is too narrow, focused on technology and on information itself, ignoring the will of the population, and confined to "crisis or conflict" over short periods of time. Americans also think cyberwar is a "way to fight."

Russian and especially Chinese cyberwar doctrine is more expansive, including the will of the population, and is constant and enduring, happening during what others call "peacetime." The Chinese especially think cyberwar is "the fight itself."

This is why I believe the US is fighting a cyberwar now. The Russians and Chinese would agree with me, but other Americans probably don't.

https://taosecurity.blogspot.com/2010/09/why-russia-and-china-think-were.html

Commentary

I used arguments such as these when I debated my friend and former PhD advisor Dr. Thomas Rid on the Economist web site in July-August 2013:

https://web.archive.org/web/20130801212850/http://economist.com/debate/days/view/997

While that debate tended to center on definitions, it's certainly important to recognize how parties view a problem from different perspectives. The following post emphasizes that point.

China's View Is More Important Than Yours

Friday, June 03, 2011

In my post *Review of Dragon Bytes Posted* I wrote the following to summarize analysis of Chinese thoughts on cyberwar, as translated from original Chinese publications:

> **The Chinese military sees Western culture, particularly American culture, as an assault on China,** saying "the West uses a system of values (democracy, freedom, human rights, etc.) in a long-term attack on socialist countries...

Marxist theory opposes peaceful evolution, which... is the basic Western tactic for subverting socialist countries" (pp 102-3). **They believe the US is conducting psychological warfare operations against socialism and consider culture as a "frontier" that has extended beyond American shores into the Chinese mainland.**

The Chinese therefore consider control of information to be paramount, since they do not trust their population to "correctly" interpret American messaging (hence the "Great Firewall of China"). In this sense, **China may consider the US as the aggressor in an ongoing cyberwar.**

Today's Reuters article *China PLA officers call Internet key battleground* elaborated on these ideas:

> The essay by two PLA scholars, Senior Colonel Ye Zheng and his colleague Zhao Baoxian, in the China Youth Daily nonetheless stressed that Beijing is focused on honing its cyber-warfare skills, and sees an unfettered Internet as a threat to its Communist Party-run state.

> **"Just as nuclear warfare was the strategic war of the industrial era, cyber-warfare has become the strategic war of the information era,** and this has become a form of battle that is massively destructive and concerns the life and death of nations," they wrote in the Party-run paper...

> **"Cyberware [sic] is an entirely new mode of battle that is invisible and silent, and it is active not only in wars and conflicts, but also flares in the everyday political, economic, military, cultural and scientific activities."**

The first highlight makes me think the Chinese see the current cyberwar as being similar to the Cold War. During the Cold War, nuclear warfare (or avoiding it) was the strategic form of war. During the current "Electronic War" (my term, not sure I like it), cyberwar is the strategic form of war.

The second highlight shows that **the Chinese see cyberwar as being active right now, and "not only in wars and conflicts." By "wars and conflicts" they mean physical combat.**

The AP article *China Calls US Culprit in Global 'Internet War'* contained a few more choice quotes:

> Writing in the Communist Party-controlled China Youth Daily newspaper, the scholars did not mention Google's claims, but said recent computer attacks and incidents employing the Internet to promote regime change in Arab nations appeared to have originated with the U.S. government.

> "Of late, an Internet tornado has swept across the world ... massively impacting and shocking the globe. Behind all this lies the shadow of America," said the article, signed by Ye Zheng and Zhao Baoxian, identified as scholars with the Academy of Military Sciences.

> "Faced with this warmup for an Internet war, every nation and military can't be passive but is making preparations to fight the Internet war," it said...

> China needs to "express to the world its principled stance of maintaining an 'Internet border' and protecting its 'Internet sovereignty,' unite all advanced forces to dive into the raging torrent of the age of peaceful use of the Internet, and return

to the Internet world a healthy, orderly environment," the article said.

As you can see, **the Chinese think an information war is already being waged. The US started it, and the US continues it (in the Chinese view) as demonstrated by turbulence in the Middle East.**

China's view is more important than yours, because China is acting on its view while too many in the West and the US in particular argue about whether or not a cyberwar is happening. The Chinese believe cyberwar is ongoing, and that the US started it. From what I can tell, the Chinese intend to win it.

https://taosecurity.blogspot.com/2011/06/chinas-view-is-more-important-than.html

Commentary

This post was my attempt to counter a common reaction to the reality of the conflict with the CPC. Too often I heard others say "I don't think we're in a cyberwar with China, so it doesn't affect me." That's why I wrote "China's view is more important than yours, because China is acting on its view while too many in the West and the US in particular argue about whether or not a cyberwar is happening." Critics can bury their heads in the sand, but the world still falls apart around them.

Inside a Commission Hearing on the Chinese Threat

Monday, March 26, 2012

This morning I testified at the U.S.-China Economic and Security Review Commission at a hearing on Developments in China's

Cyber and Nuclear Capabilities, along with Nart Villeneuve and Jason Healey.

As stated on their Web site, the U.S. Congress created the U.S.-China Economic and Security Review Commission in October 2000 with the legislative mandate to monitor, investigate, and submit to Congress an annual report on the national security implications of the bilateral trade and economic relationship between the United States and the People's Republic of China, and to provide recommendations, where appropriate, to Congress for legislative and administrative action. The Commission holds hearings to solicit testimony from subject matter experts and builds on those hearings to produce an excellent annual report.

You can access the 2011 report on the Commission Web site, and even request a printed copy if you'd prefer to read paper.

A few weeks ago the Commission staff requested that I answer a set of questions, and I provided a draft response last Monday. When I testified, each of us had seven minutes to make a statement, after which the Commissioners asked questions. The testimony posted online is the "extended" version of my remarks. I used an abridged version when speaking today, but I didn't read it verbatim.

After we each made a seven minute statement, the Commissioners asked a round of questions. Each received about five minutes. We tried to keep to the rotation, which as you might expect was tough. Several questions were fairly complicated (like discussing the costs and benefits of "the cloud") so it was difficult to be anything near complete when responding. A few Commissioners were interested in supply chain questions and the problems posed by Chinese made telecommunications equipment.

I expect an audio recording of the event to be available at the Commission Web site within the next few weeks. Once that is posted I'll review it and share a few more thoughts on the Mandiant Blog.

In addition to my wife, thanks also to the members of the local computer network defense and intelligence communities who attended the briefing and said hello!

https://taosecurity.blogspot.com/2012/03/inside-commission-hearing-on-chinese.html

Commentary

As I mentioned earlier, the USCC was one of the few bright spots in the government during the early days of countering the CPC threat. I was pleased to contribute what I could to the hearing. At that time I was chief security officer at Mandiant, and I relied heavily on the wonderful work done by our consultants and intelligence team.

Mandiant APT1 Report: 25 Best Commentaries of the Last 12 Days

Saturday, March 02, 2013

Two weeks ago today our team at Mandiant was feverishly preparing the release of our APT1 report.

In the twelve days that followed publication on the evening of Monday the 18th, I've been very pleased by the amount of constructive commentary and related research published online.

In this post I'd like to list those contributions that I believe merit attention, in the event you missed them the first time around.

These sorts of posts are examples of what the security community can do to advance our collective capability to counter digital threats.

Please note I avoided mass media accounts, interviews with Mandiant team members, and most general commentary.

They are listed in no particular order.

Seth Hall (Bro): *Watching for the APT1 Intelligence*
Jason Wood (SecureIdeas): *Reading the Mandiant APT1 Report*
Chris Sanders: *Making the Mandiant APT1 Report Actionable*
Symantec: *APT1: Q&A on Attacks by the Comment Crew*
Tekdefense (NoVA Infosec): *MASTIFF Analysis of APT1*
Chort Row (@chort0): *Analyzing APT1 with Cuckoobox, Volatility, and Yara*
Ron Gula (Tenable): *We have Microsoft Tuesday, so how long until we have Indicator Wednesday?*
OpenDNS Umbrella Labs: *An intimate look at APT1, China's Cyber-Espionage Threat*
Chris Lew (Mandiant): *Chinese Advanced Persistent Threats: Corporate Cyber Espionage Processes and Organizations* (BSidesSF, slides not online yet)
Adam Segal: *Hacking back, signaling, and state-society relations*
Snorby Labs: *APT Intelligence Update*
Wendy Nather: *Exercises left to the reader*
Brad Shoop (Mandiant): *Mandiant's APT1 Domain/MD5 Intel and Security Onion for Splunk*
Brad Shoop (Mandiant): *Mandiant's APT1 Domain/MD5 Intel and Security Onion with ELSA*
Kevin Wilcox: *NSM With Bro-IDS Part 5: In-house Modules to Leverage Outside Threat Intelligence*
Cyb3rsleuth: *Chinese Threat Actor Part 5*
David Bianco: *The Pyramid of Pain*
Wesley McGrew: *Mapping of Mandiant APT1 malware names to available samples*

Russ McRee: *Toolsmith: Redline, APT1, and you – we're all owned*
Jaime Blasco (AlienVault Labs): *Yara rules for APT1/Comment Crew malware arsenal*
Brandon Dixon: *Mandiant APT2 Report Lure*
Seculert: *Spear-Phishing with Mandiant APT Report*
PhishMe: *How PhishMe addresses the top attack method cited in Mandiant's APT1 report*
Rich Mogull (Securosis): *Why China's Hacking is Different*
China Digital Times: *Netizens Gather Further Evidence of PLA Hacking*
M-Unition (Mandiant): *Netizen Research Bolsters APT1 Attribution*

I'd also like to cite Verizon for their comments and mention of IOCExtractor and Symantec for publishing their indicators via Pastebin after I asked about it.

Thank you to those who took the time to share what you found when analyzing related APT1 data, or when showing how to use APT1 indicators to do detection and response.

https://taosecurity.blogspot.com/2013/03/mandiant-apt1-report-25-best.html

Commentary

The APT1 report, titled *APT1: Exposing One of China's Cyber Espionage Units,* was one of the first modern threat intelligence reports produced by a private security company. Other notable reports prior to the APT1 report included the following:

- *Tracking GhostNet: Investigating a Cyber Espionage Network* by Information Warfare Monitor (The Citizen Lab), March 28, 2009
- *W32.Stuxnet Dossier* by Symantec (Nicolas Falliere, Liam O Murchu, and Eric Chien), November 2010

- *Global Energy Cyberattacks: "Night Dragon,"* by McAfee (Dmitri Alperovitch), February 10, 2011

The APT1 report started with the following:

> Since 2004, Mandiant has investigated computer security breaches at hundreds of organizations around the world. The majority of these security breaches are attributed to advanced threat actors referred to as the "Advanced Persistent Threat" (APT). We first published details about the APT in our January 2010 M-Trends report. As we stated in the report, our position was that "The Chinese government may authorize this activity, but there's no way to determine the extent of its involvement."
>
> **Now, three years later, we have the evidence required to change our assessment. The details we have analyzed during hundreds of investigations convince us that the groups conducting these activities are based primarily in China and that the Chinese Government is aware of them.**
>
> Mandiant continues to track dozens of APT groups around the world; however, this report is focused on the most prolific of these groups. We refer to this group as "APT1" and it is one of more than 20 APT groups with origins in China. APT1 is a single organization of operators that has conducted a cyber espionage campaign against a broad range of victims since at least 2006. From our observations, it is one of the most prolific cyber espionage groups in terms of the sheer quantity of information stolen. The scale and impact of APT1's operations compelled us to write this report.

The activity we have directly observed likely represents only a small fraction of the cyber espionage that APT1 has conducted. Though our visibility of APT1's activities is incomplete, **we have analyzed the group's intrusions against nearly 150 victims over seven years.** From our unique vantage point responding to victims, we tracked APT1 back to four large networks in Shanghai, two of which are allocated directly to the Pudong New Area.

We uncovered a substantial amount of APT1's attack infrastructure, command and control, and modus operandi (tools, tactics, and procedures). In an effort to underscore there are actual individuals behind the keyboard, **Mandiant is revealing three personas we have attributed to APT1.** These operators, like soldiers, may merely be following orders given to them by others.

Our analysis has led us to conclude that **APT1 is likely government-sponsored and one of the most persistent of China's cyber threat actors.** We believe that APT1 is able to wage such a long-running and extensive cyber espionage campaign in large part because it receives direct government support. In seeking to identify the organization behind this activity, **our research found that People's Liberation Army (PLA's) Unit 61398 is similar to APT1 in its mission, capabilities, and resources. PLA Unit 61398 is also located in precisely the same area from which APT1 activity appears to originate.**

In addition to publishing our own report online, we collaborated with reporters from the New York Times, who wrote a front-page story based on our findings. I took the following picture of a copy of that paper on February 19, 2013, as I walked from the Virginia Railway Express station to my Mandiant office.

Figure 20. The New York Times, February 19, 2013, in Alexandria, VA

I found this picture via my Tweet:

https://twitter.com/taosecurity/status/303823824229650433

This was the only blog post I wrote about the APT1 report around the time of its release. February and March 2013 were hectic months. We expected the APT1 report to be of interest to the information security world. We did not think it would make a splash outside of that world.

If you would like to read the APT1 report, you can access it here:

https://web.archive.org/web/20200815135309/https://www.fireeye.com/content/dam/fireeye-www/services/pdfs/mandiant-apt1-report.pdf

Incentives for Breaking Operational Security?

Thursday, January 08, 2015

Thanks Adam Segal for posting a link to a fascinating Wall Street Journal piece titled *Sony Hackers May Have Left Deliberate Clues, Expert Says*. From the story by Jeyup S. Kwaak:

> **Apparent slip-ups by the hackers of Sony Pictures that have helped convince U.S. investigators the hackers are North Koreans have a precedent, and may even have been deliberate to win domestic kudos, according to a top cybersecurity expert and former senior North Korean official.**
>
> The head of a group of hacking experts that have analyzed previous suspected North Korean cyberattacks on South Korea said a record of a North Korean Internet address was also left in a 2013 attack on Seoul because a detour through Chinese servers was briefly suspended, exposing the origin of the incursion...
>
> Choi Sang-myung, who is also an adviser to Seoul's cyberwarfare command, said... [w]hile it was impossible to prove whether the hackers left evidence by mistake or on purpose, that they didn't fully cover their tracks could mean North Koreans wanted to be known...
>
> That theory is supported by Jang Jin-sung, a former official in North Korea's propaganda unit, who says North Korean hackers likely have an incentive to leave some evidence because officials often secure promotions after a successful attack against enemies.

"People fiercely compete to prove their loyalty" after an order is given, he said. "They must leave proof that they did it."

These are fascinating comments, from people who understand the DPRK hacking scene better than critics of the FBI attribution statements.

This theory shows DPRK intruders may have incentives for breaking operational security ("OPSEC" or "opsec"), and that they were not just "sloppy" as mentioned by FBI Director Comey yesterday.

In the 2013 Mandiant APT1 report I suggested the following language be used:

> These actors have made poor operational choices, facilitating our research and allowing us to track their activities.

In the case of Chinese PLA Unit 61398, I think the OPSEC failures were unintentional. Others theorized differently, but the Chinese have fewer incentives to reveal themselves. They want information, above any other consideration. They would rather not have victims know who is stealing their trade secrets, commercial data, and sensitive information.

Intrusions into critical infrastructure, confirmed in an open hearing in November 2014 by NSA Director Mike Rogers, might be a different case. If a nation state is trying to signal power to an adversary, it will want the adversary to know the perpetrator.

In this case of DPRK intrusions, North and South Korean sources explain that DPRK hackers have tangible incentives to reveal their identities. Apparently hacking for the government

is one ticket to a marginally better life in North Korea, as reported by Newsweek.

All of this demonstrates that technical indicators are but one element of attribution. Personal, not just national, incentives, facing the individual intrusion operators, should be part of the attribution equation too.

Remember to read *Attributing Cyber Attacks* by my KCL professor Thomas Rid, and fellow PhD student Ben Buchanan, for the best modern report available on attribution issues.

Update: Thanks to Steven Andres for pointing out a link mistake.

https://taosecurity.blogspot.com/2015/01/incentives-for-breaking-operational.html

Commentary

One frequently encounters theories that say intruders want to be identified, as a means to signal larger geopolitical messages to the victims and their associated national policymakers. I have never been a big fan of this thesis. This article showed, however, that North Korean intruders have a different set of incentives to reveal their activities, and that they may act to fulfill them. By being recognized, DPRK operators may receive individual credit, and subsequently opportunities for a better life from their government sponsors.

An Irrelevant Thesis

Saturday, May 23, 2015

This week The Diplomat published an article by Dr Greg Austin titled *What the US Gets Wrong About Chinese Cyberespionage*. The subtitle teases the thesis: "Is it government policy in China to pass on

commercial secrets obtained via cyberespionage to civil sector firms?"
As you might expect (because it prompted me to write this post), the
author's answer is "no."

The following contains the argument:

> "Chinese actors may be particularly adept in certain stages of
> economic espionage, but it is almost certainly not Chinese
> government policy to allow the transfer of trade secrets
> collected by highly classified intelligence sources to its civil
> sector firms for non-military technologies on a wide-spread
> basis.
>
> A U.S. influencing strategy toward China premised on the
> claim that this is China's policy would appear to be
> ill-advised based on the evidence introduced so far by the
> United States in the public domain."

I find it interesting that the author concedes theft by Chinese
government actors, which the Chinese government refuses to
acknowledge. However, **the author seeks to excuse this activity
out of concern for the effect it has on US-China ties.**

One aspect of the relationship between China and the US worries
the author most:

> "There are many ways to characterize the negative impact on
> potential bilateral cooperation on cyberspace issues of the
> 'lawfare' being practised by the United States to discipline
> China for its massive cyber intrusions into the commercial
> secrets of U.S. firms. One downside is in my view more
> important than others. This is the belief being fostered by
> U.S. officials among elites in the United States and in other
> countries that China as a nation is a 'cheater" country..."

Then, in a manner similar to the way Chinese spokespeople respond to any Western accusations of wrongdoing, the author turns the often-heard "Chinese espionage as the largest transfer of wealth in history" argument against the US:

> "In the absence of any Administration taxonomy of the economic impacts of cyber espionage, alleged by some to represent the largest illicit transfer of wealth in human history, one way of evaluating it is to understand that for more than three decades it has been U.S. policy, like that of its principal allies, to undertake the largest lawful transfer of wealth in human history through trade with, investment in and technology transfer to China."

(I'm not sure I understand the cited benefits the US has accrued due to this "largest lawful transfer of wealth in human history," given the hollowing out of the American manufacturing sector and the trade imbalance with China, which totaled over $82 billion in 1Q15 alone. It's possible I am not appreciating what the author means though.)

Let's accept, for argument's sake, that it is not "official" Chinese government policy for its intelligence and military forces to steal commercial data from private and non-governmental Western organizations. How does accepting that proposition improve the situation? Would China excuse the US government if a "rogue" element of the American intelligence community or military pursued a multi-decade campaign against Chinese targets?

Even if the US government accepted this "Chinese data theft by rogue government actor" theory, it would not change the American position: stop this activity, by whatever means necessary. Given the power amassed by President Xi during his anti-corruption crackdown, I would expect he would be able to achieve at least some success in limiting his so-called "rogue actors" during the 2+ years since Mandiant released the APT1 report. As Nicole Perlroth reported this month, Chinese hacking continues unabated. In fact, China has introduced new capabilities, such as the so-called Great Cannon, used to degrade GitHub and others.

Similar to the argument I made in my post *What Does "Responsibility" Mean for Attribution?*, "responsibility" is the key issue. Based on my experience and research, I submit that **Chinese computer network exploitation of private and non-governmental Western organizations is "state-integrated" and "state-executed." Greg Austin believes the activity is, at worst, "state-rogue-conducted."** Stepping down one rung on the state spectrum of responsibility ladder is far from enough to change US government policy towards China.

Note: In addition to the article in The Diplomat, the author wrote a longer paper titled *China's Cyberespionage: The National Security Distinction and U.S. Diplomacy*.

I also plan to read Dr Austin's new book, Cyber Policy in China, which looks great! Who knows, we might even be able to collaborate, given his work with the War Studies department at KCL.

https://taosecurity.blogspot.com/2015/05/an-irrelevant-thesis.html

Commentary

My post references several terms that I extracted from one of my favorite works by Jason Healey. It appears in his February 22, 2012 report for the Atlantic Council titled *Beyond Attribution: Seeking National Responsibility for Cyber Attacks*. His "Spectrum of State Responsibility" assigns categories to various levels of state involvement in digital attacks.

1. State-prohibited. The national government will help stop the third-party attack.

2. State-prohibited-but-inadequate. The national government is cooperative but unable to stop the third-party attack.

3. State-ignored. The national government knows about the third-party attacks but is unwilling to take any official action.

4. State-encouraged. Third parties control and conduct the attack, but the national government encourages them as a matter of policy.

5. State-shaped. Third parties control and conduct the attack, but the state provides some support.

6. State-coordinated. The national government coordinates third-party attackers such as by "suggesting" operational details.

7. State-ordered. The national government directs third-party proxies to conduct the attack on its behalf.

8. State-rogue-conducted. Out-of-control elements of cyber forces of the national government conduct the attack.

9. State-executed. The national government conducts the attack using cyber forces under their direct control.

10. State-integrated. The national government attacks using integrated third-party proxies and government cyber forces.

The report is online:

https://web.archive.org/web/20200411175357/https://www.atlanticcouncil.org/wp-content/uploads/2012/02/022212_ACUS_NatlResponsibilityCyber.PDF

For the PLA, Cyber War is the Battle of Triangle Hill

Monday, October 05, 2015

In June 2011 I wrote a blog post with the ever polite title *China's View Is More Important Than Yours*. I was frustrated with the Western-centric, inward-focused view of many commentators, which put themselves at the center of debates over digital conflict, neglecting the possibility that other parties could perceive the situation differently. I remain concerned that while Western thinkers debate war using Western, especially Clausewitzian, models, Eastern adversaries, including hybrid Eastern-Western cultures, perceive war in their own terms.

I wrote in June 2011:

> The Chinese military sees Western culture, particularly American culture, as an assault on China, saying "the West uses a system of values (democracy, freedom, human rights, etc.) in a long-term attack on socialist countries...
>
> Marxist theory opposes peaceful evolution, which... is the basic Western tactic for subverting socialist countries" (pp 102-3). They believe the US is conducting psychological warfare operations against socialism and consider culture as a "frontier" that has extended beyond American shores into the Chinese mainland.
>
> The Chinese therefore consider control of information to be paramount, since they do not trust their population to "correctly" interpret American messaging (hence the "Great Firewall of China"). In this sense, China may consider the US as the aggressor in an ongoing cyberwar.

Today, thanks to a Tweet by Jennifer McArdle, I noticed a May 2015 story featuring a translation of a People's Daily article. The English translation is posted as *Cybersovereignty Symbolizes National Sovereignty.*

I recommend reading the whole article, but the following captures the spirit of the message:

> Western hostile forces and a small number of "ideological traitors" in our country use the network, and relying on

computers, mobile phones and other such information terminals, maliciously attack our Party, blacken the leaders who founded the New China, vilify our heroes, and arouse mistaken thinking trends of historical nihilism, with the ultimate goal of using "universal values" to mislead us, using "constitutional democracy" to throw us into turmoil, use "colour revolutions" to overthrow us, use negative public opinion and rumours to oppose us, and use "de-partification and depoliticization of the military" to upset us.

This article demonstrates that, four years after my first post, there are still elements, at least in the PLA, who believe that China is fighting a cyber war, and that the US started it.

I thought the last line from the PLA Daily article was especially revealing:

> Only if we act as we did at the time of the Battle of Triangle Hill, are riveted to the most forward position of the battlefield and the fight in this ideological struggle, are online "seed machines and propaganda teams", and arouse hundreds and thousands in the "Red Army", will we be able to be good shock troops and fresh troops in the construction of the "Online Great Wall", and will we be able to endure and vanquish in this protracted, smokeless war.

The Battle of Triangle Hill was an engagement during the Korean War, with Chinese forces fighting American, South Korean, Ethiopian, and Colombian forces. Both sides suffered heavy losses over a protracted engagement, although the Chinese appear to have lost more and viewed their attrition strategy as worthwhile. It's ominous this PLA editorial writer decided to cite a battle between US and Chinese forces to communicate his point about online conflict, but it should make it easier for American readers to grasp the seriousness of the issue in Chinese minds.

https://taosecurity.blogspot.com/2015/10/for-pla-cyber-war-is-battl e-of-triangle.html

Commentary

If you want to better understand your adversary, why not read what he writes? Projecting your own hopes, dreams, and values onto his situation is delusional and likely to result in bad policy..

Five Reasons I Want China Running Its Own Software

Thursday, March 23, 2017

Periodically I read about efforts by China, or Russia, or North Korea, or other countries to replace American software with indigenous or semi-indigenous alternatives. I then reply via Twitter that **I love the idea,** with a short reason why. This post will list the top five reasons why I want China and other likely targets of American foreign intelligence collection to run their own software.

1. Many (most?) non-US software companies write lousy code. The US is by no means perfect, but our developers and processes generally appear to be superior to foreign indigenous efforts. Cisco vs Huawei is a good example. Cisco has plenty of problems, but it has processes in place to manage them, plus secure code development practices. Lousy indigenous code means it is easier for American intelligence agencies to penetrate foreign targets. (An example of a foreign country that excels in writing code is Israel, but thankfully it is not the same sort of priority target like China, Russia, or North Korea.)

411

2. Many (most?) non-US enterprises are 5-10 years behind US security practices. Even if a foreign target runs decent native code, the IT processes maintaining that code are lagging compared to American counterparts. Again, the US has not solved this problem by any stretch of the imagination. However, relatively speaking, American inventory management, patch management, and security operations have the edge over foreign intelligence targets. Because non-US enterprises running indigenous code will not necessarily be able to benefit from American expertise (as they might if they were running American code), these deficiencies will make them easier targets for foreign exploitation.

3. Foreign targets running foreign code is win-win for American intel and enterprises. The current vulnerability equities process (VEP) puts American intelligence agencies in a quandary. The IC develops a zero-day exploit for a vulnerability, say for use against Cisco routers. American and Chinese organizations use Cisco routers. Should the IC sit on the vulnerability in order to maintain access to foreign targets, or should it release the vulnerability to Cisco to enable patching and thereby protect American and foreign systems?

This dilemma disappears in a world where foreign targets run indigenous software. If the IC identifies a vulnerability in Cisco software, and the majority of its targets run non-Cisco software, then the IC is more likely (or should be pushed to be more likely) to assist with patching the vulnerable software. Meanwhile, the IC continues to exploit Huawei or other products at its leisure.

4. Writing and running indigenous code is the fastest way to improve. When foreign countries essentially outsource their IT to vendors, they become program managers. They lose or never develop any ability to write and run quality software. Writing and running your own code will enroll foreign organizations in the security school of hard knocks. American intel will have a field day for 3-5 years against these targets, as they flail around in a perpetual state of compromise. However, if they devote the proper native resources and attention, they will learn from their mistakes. They will write and run better software. Now, this means they will become harder targets for American intel, but American intel will retain the advantage of point 3.

5. Trustworthy indigenous code will promote international stability. Countries like China feel especially vulnerable to American exploitation. They have every reason to be scared. They run code written by other organizations. They don't patch it or manage it well. Their security operations stink. The American intel community could initiate a complete moratorium on hacking China, and the Chinese would still be ravaged by other countries or criminal hackers, all the while likely blaming American intel. They would not be able to assess the situation. This makes for a very unstable situation.

Therefore, countries like China and others are going down the indigenous software path. They understand that **software, not oil as Daniel Yergen once wrote, is now the "commanding heights" of the economy.** Pursuing this course will subject these countries to many years of pain. However, in the end I believe it will yield a more stable situation. These countries should begin to perceive that they are less vulnerable. They will experience their own vulnerability equity process. They will be more aware and less paranoid.

In this respect, **indigenous software is a win for global politics.** The losers, of course, are global software companies. Foreign countries will continue to make short-term deals to suck intellectual property and expertise from American software companies, before discarding them on the side of Al Gore's information highway.

One final point -- a way foreign companies could jump-start their indigenous efforts would be to leverage open source software. I doubt they would necessarily honor licenses which require sharing improvements with the open source community. However, open source would give foreign organizations the visibility they need and access to expertise that they lack. Microsoft's shared source and similar programs were a step in this direction, but I suggest foreign organizations adopt open source instead.

Now, widespread open source adoption by foreign intelligence targets would erode the advantages for American intel that I explained in point 3. I'm betting that foreign leaders are likely similar to Americans in that they tend to not trust open source, and prefer to roll their own and hold vendors accountable. Therefore I'm not that worried, from an American intel perspective, about point 3 being vastly eroded by widespread foreign open source adoption.

https://taosecurity.blogspot.com/2017/03/five-reasons-i-want-china-running-its.html

Commentary

This is one of my favorite TaoSecurity blog posts of all time. I like it because it's one of the few, and perhaps the only, topics where the issue at hand benefits both the interests of the United States (my home) and the nations with which it competes, like China and Russia.

I firmly believe that reducing the reliance on American software will contribute to global stability. Countries like Russia and especially China feel vulnerable running American code and hardware. Similarly, we Americans feel the same way about Chinese hardware (e.g., Huawei) and software (e.g., TikTok). The main reason that we do not have more indigineous hardware and software is resistance from global vendors, primarily those in the United States. These companies still cling to the idea that they can sell their products into markets like China and that the benefits outweigh the costs. That calculation has changed over the last few years, and I only see the indigenous movement growing stronger.

Remembering When APT Became Public

Sunday, January 14, 2018

Last week I Tweeted the following on the 8th anniversary of Google's blog post about its compromise by Chinese threat actors:

> This intrusion made the term APT mainstream. I was the first to associate it with Aurora, in this post
>
> https://taosecurity.blogspot.com/2010/01/google-v-china.html

My first APT post was a careful reference in 2007, when we all feared being accused of "leaking classified" re China:

https://taosecurity.blogspot.com/2007/10/air-force-cyberspace-report.html

I should have added the term "publicly" to my original Tweet. There were consultants with years of APT experience involved in the Google incident response, and they recognized the work of APT17 at that company and others. Those consultants honored their NDAs and have stayed quiet.

I wrote my original Tweet as a reminder that "APT" was not a popular, recognized term until the Google announcement on January 12, 2010. In my *Google v China* blog post I wrote:

Welcome to the party, Google. You can use the term "advanced persistent threat" (APT) if you want to give this adversary its proper name.

I also Tweeted a similar statement on the same day:

> This is horrifying: http://bit.ly/7x7vVW Google admits intellectual property theft from China; it's called Advanced Persistent Threat, GOOG

I made the explicit link of China and APT because no one had done that publicly.

This slide from a 2011 briefing I did in Hawaii captures a few historical points:

Figure 21. 2011 Briefing Slide

The Google incident was a watershed, for reasons I blogged on January 16, 2010. I remember the SANS DFIR 2008 event as effectively "APTCon," but beyond Mandiant, Northrop Grumman, and NetWitness, no one was really talking publicly about the APT until after Google.

As I noted in the July 2009 blog post, *You Down With APT?* (ugh):

> Aside from Northrop Grumman, Mandiant, and a few
> vendors (like NetWitness, one of the full capture vendors
> out there) mentioning APT, there's not much else available.
> A Google search for "advanced persistent threat" -netwitness
> -mandiant -Northrop yields 34 results (prior to this blog
> post).

Today that search yields 244,000 results.

I would argue we're "past APT." APT was the buzzword for RSA
and other vendor-centric events from, say, 2011-2015, with 2013
being the peak following Mandiant's APT1 report.

The threat hasn't disappeared, but it has changed. I wrote my Tweet
to mark a milestone and to note that I played a small part in it.

All my APT posts here are reachable by this APT tag. Also see my
2010 article for Information Security Magazine titled *What APT Is,
and What It Isn't.*

https://taosecurity.blogspot.com/2018/01/remembering-when-apt-became-public.html

Commentary

I'm very glad that we're in a "post-APT" mania world. The term has
been diluted to the point that it's a synonym for "nation state," and
no longer refers only to China, as originally intended.

Bejtlich on the APT1 Report: No Hack Back

Monday, June 25, 2018

Before reading the rest of this post, I suggest reading
Mandiant/FireEye's statement *Doing Our Part -- Without Hacking
Back*.

I would like to add my own color to this situation.

**First, at no time when I worked for Mandiant or FireEye, or
afterwards, was there ever a notion that we would hack into
adversary systems.** During my six year tenure, we were publicly and
privately a "no hack back" company. I never heard anyone talk about
hack back operations. No one ever intimated we had imagery of
APT1 actors taken with their own laptop cameras. No one even said
that would be a good idea.

**Second, I would never have testified or written, repeatedly,
about our company's stance on not hacking back if I knew we
secretly did otherwise.** I have quit jobs because I had fundamental
disagreements with company policy or practice. I worked for
Mandiant from 2011 through the end of 2013, when FireEye
acquired Mandiant, and stayed until last year (2017). I never
considered quitting Mandiant or FireEye due to a disconnect
between public statements and private conduct.

**Third, I was personally involved with briefings to the press, in
public and in private, concerning the APT1 report.** I provided
the voiceover for a 5 minute YouTube video called APT1: Exposing
One of China's Cyber Espionage Units. That video was one of the
most sensitive, if not the most sensitive, aspects of releasing the
report. We showed the world how we could intercept adversary
communications and reconstruct it. There was internal debate about

whether we should do that. We decided to cover the practice in the report, as Christopher Glyer Tweeted:

> Take a look at the description in the Infrastructure section (page 39) of the original APT1 report that discusses "hop points".

> "They access hop points using a variety of techniques, the most popular being Remote Desktop and FTP."

In none of these briefings to the press did we show pictures or video from adversary laptops. We did show the video that we published to YouTube.

Fourth, I privately contacted former Mandiant personnel with whom I worked during the time of the APT1 report creation and distribution. Their reaction to Mr Sanger's allegations ranged from "I've never heard of that" to "completely false." I asked former Mandiant colleagues, like myself, in the event that current Mandiant or FireEye employees were told not to talk to outsiders about the case.

What do I think happened here? I agree with the theory that Mr Sanger misinterpreted the reconstructed RDP sessions for some sort of "camera access." I have no idea about the "bros" or "leather jackets" comments!

In the spirit of full disclosure, prior to publication, Mr Sanger tried to reach me to discuss his book via email. I was sick and told him I had to pass. Ellen Nakashima also contacted me; I believe she was doing research for the book. She asked a few questions about the origin of the term APT, which I answered. I do not have the book so I do not know if I am cited, or if my message was included.

The bottom line is that Mandiant and FireEye did not conduct any hack back for the APT1 report.

Update: Some of you wondered about Ellen's role. I confirmed last night that she was working on her own project.

https://taosecurity.blogspot.com/2018/06/bejtlich-on-apt1-report-no-hack-back.html

Commentary

Mandiant's blog post on this topic included the following:

> In his new book, *The Perfect Weapon: War, Sabotage, and Fear in the Cyber Age,* author David E. Sanger chronicles numerous examples of the impact of cyber activities on geopolitical conditions. One such example involves the scale and scope of the Chinese Army's economic and industrial espionage targeting organizations for commercial gain, which was uncovered by Mandiant after a multi-year investigation and disclosed in our APT1 report, published in February 2013.

> In our APT1 report, we provided attribution for cyber espionage conducted by the Chinese PLA Unit 61398. As part of the APT1 report's initial release, we coordinated with Mr. Sanger, giving him access to the methods we used to gather evidence of the attribution of APT1 to PLA unit 61398. Mr. Sanger's reporting on APT1 played a critical role in exposing the world to the cyber threat that private organizations were facing from Chinese nation-state backed attackers, and *The Perfect Weapon* continues to help drive a productive dialogue on the real-world implications of a changing threat landscape.

Mr. Sanger's description of how Mandiant obtained some of the evidence underlying APT1 has resulted in a serious mischaracterization of our investigative efforts. Specifically, Mr. Sanger suggests our "...investigators reached back through the network to activate the cameras on the hackers' own laptops." We did not do this, nor have we ever done this. **To state this unequivocally, Mandiant did not employ "hack back" techniques as part of our investigation of APT1, does not "hack back" in our incident response practice, and does not endorse the practice of "hacking back."**

The conclusion that we hacked back, while incorrect, is understandable. Included in the evidence we reviewed with Mr. Sanger at the time were videos of APT1 operators interacting with malware command and control servers (a.k.a. "hop points"), including the operators' "personal" web browsing (e.g. checking social media...etc.) on those systems. More information on APT1 "hop points" is available in the "Infrastructure" section starting on page 39 of the original APT1 report and demonstrated in this video, released at the same time as the report:

https://www.youtube.com/watch?v=6p7FqSav6Ho

To someone observing this video "over the shoulder" of one of our investigators, it could appear as live system monitoring. Nevertheless, Mandiant did not create these videos through "hacking back" or any hacking activity. **All of these videos were made through information obtained via consensual security monitoring on behalf of victim companies that were compromised.**

As a standard practice, in an effort to protect companies from unauthorized intrusions, we implement consensual network monitoring agreements with many victim organizations for the purposes of helping better secure those organizations. **The videos Mr. Sanger viewed were from Windows Remote Desktop Protocol (RDP) network packet captures (PCAP) of Internet traffic at these victim organizations.** Mandiant has never turned on the webcam of an attacker or victim system.

In short, we do not fight hackers by hacking, but by diligently and legally pursuing attribution with a rigor and discipline that the cause requires. The anonymity of the Internet is routinely used to mask the identities of perpetrators who violate our privacy and our laws, and it is our goal to relentlessly protect our customers and make the Internet a fair and safe place to operate. APT1 was the result of Mandiant doing our part to expose risks and share information to help organizations better protect themselves, and we will continue to do our part – without hacking back. (emphasis added)

https://www.fireeye.com/blog/executive-perspective/2018/06/doing-our-part-without-hacking-back.html

This was one of the more bizarre aspects of the APT1 story. It appeared five years after the report's release. To this day, I do not have a satisfactory explanation for the claims made by Mr. Sanger in his book.

In contrast to Mandiant's "no hacking" policy, consider the alternative, demonstrated by "Malware.lu CERT, the first private Computer Security IncidentResponse Team (CSIRT) located in Luxembourg and itrust consulting S.A.R.L, a Luxembourg based company specialising in formation system security."

This group published a report on March 27, 2013, based on their exploitation of Poison Ivy software running on computers they discovered in six Hong Kong netblocks. The screenshots and other information published in their report was indeed the result of "hacking back. You can read the report here:

https://web.archive.org/web/20140809022633/http://www.malware.lu/Pro/RAP002_APT1_Technical_backstage.1.0.pdf

Conclusion

This chapter presented only part of the odyssey of encountering and countering CPC hackers during the 2000s and 2010s. The problem has not disappeared, and with tensions rising in 2020, it appears to be an "advanced persistent conflict." The only durable way to deal with the problem, as I mentioned in testimony to Congress, is to foster better relations with China. That may require waiting until the Chinese people remove the CPC from power.

Afterword

I'll keep this short, as this book is already 10,000 words (or roughly 40 pages) longer than the last installment. My goal with these volumes is to collect concepts, research, and suggestions that I've documented in TaoSecurity Blog since 2003. While I include some material for historical or reference purposes, I believe the majority remains relevant today, in 2020, as I write this afterword.

Digital security is rooted in conflict, and humans have engaged in conflict for millenia. The digital realm is only the latest arena for that conflict. While I agree that elements of cyber security are new, other aspects remain tied to the roots of human conflict. By at least being familiar with how people wrestled with these problems in the past, I hope readers can accelerate their own countermeasures in the present and future.

Books by This Author

The Tao of Network Security Monitoring: Beyond Intrusion Detection

https://amzn.to/2XfBeCH

Extrusion Detection: Security Monitoring for Internal Intrusions

https://amzn.to/2RNX1eK

Real Digital Forensics: Computer Security and Incident Response

https://amzn.to/2Nnh1pW

The Practice of Network Security Monitoring: Understanding Incident Detection and Response

https://amzn.to/2RLM5hn

Reach Your Goal: Stretching & Mobility Exercises for Fitness, Personal Training, & Martial Arts

https://amzn.to/2LpNhpL

The Best of TaoSecurity Blog, Volume 1: Milestones, Philosophy and Strategy, Risk, and Advice

https://amzn.to/3lBm1UM

About the Author

Richard Bejtlich is an author and Principal Security Strategist at Corelight. He was previously Chief Security Strategist at FireEye, and Mandiant's Chief Security Officer when FireEye acquired Mandiant in 2013. At General Electric, as Director of Incident Response, he built and led the 40-member GE Computer Incident Response Team (GE-CIRT). Richard began his digital security career as a military intelligence officer in 1997 at the Air Force Computer Emergency Response Team (AFCERT), Air Force Information Warfare Center (AFIWC), and Air Intelligence Agency (AIA). Richard is a graduate of Harvard University and the United States Air Force Academy. He has authored, co-authored, and contributed to over a dozen books (listed at www.taosecurity.com). He also writes for his blog (taosecurity.blogspot.com) and Twitter (@taosecurity).

Richard took his first martial arts classes in judo, karate, boxing, and combatives as a cadet at the US Air Force Academy in 1990, and continued practicing several styles until 2001. He resumed training in 2016 by practicing within the Krav Maga Global system, earning Graduate 1 rank. Richard now studies Brazilian Jiu-Jitsu with Team Pedro Sauer and is the founder of Martial History Team and Martial Vitality.

Richard lives with his wife Amy, their two children, two cats, and other wildlife in northern Virginia.

Made in the USA
Middletown, DE
02 February 2021